The Essential
Keto Diet
Cookbook
for Beginners

. . . .

1900+

Days Easy, Low Carb & Yummy Keto Recipes Book - Help
Lose Extra Body Fat | 30-Day Meal Plan for Better Eating
Habits

Jacqueline C. Estrada

Warning-Disclaimer

The purpose of this book is to educate and entertain. The author or publisher does not guarantee that anyone following the techniques, suggestions, tips, ideas, or strategies will become successful. The author and publisher shall have neither liability or responsibility to anyone with respect to any loss or damage caused, or alleged to be caused, directly or indirectly by the information contained in this book.

Table of Contents

Chapter 9 Desserts 80

Chapter 10 Stews and Soups 89

Appendix 1: Measurement Conversion Chart 97

Appendix 2: The Dirty Dozen and Clean Fifteen 98

INTRODUCTION

Are you ready to spice up your kitchen with some delicious and healthy recipes? Look no further than the Keto Diet Cookbook! This cookbook is filled with mouth-watering meals that will keep you feeling satisfied and energized throughout the day. Say goodbye to boring salads and hello to flavorful dishes! Whether you're a seasoned keto dieter or just starting out, this cookbook has something for everyone. So grab your apron and get ready to cook up a storm with the Keto Diet Cookbook!

Growing up, my mother was always passionate about health and wellness. She taught me the importance of eating a balanced diet and staying active. However, as I got older, I found myself struggling to maintain a healthy weight and feeling sluggish throughout the day.

That's when my mother introduced me to the ketogenic diet. She explained how it worked and the potential benefits it could have on my overall health. Skeptical at first, I decided to give it a try.

To my surprise, I quickly fell in love with the keto lifestyle. Not only did I start to shed excess weight, but I also felt more energized and focused than ever before. I began experimenting with different recipes and ingredients, and soon realized that there was a lack of variety in the current keto cookbooks on the market.

That's when I decided to write my own cookbook one that would not only provide delicious and satisfying meals, but also offer a wide range of options for those following the keto diet. I consulted with my mother, who is a health expert, to ensure that each recipe was nutritionally balanced and packed with wholesome ingredients.

Now, I'm proud to share my Keto Diet Cookbook with others who are looking to improve their health and enjoy delicious meals at the same time. I hope that my book will inspire others to embrace the keto lifestyle and discover all of its amazing benefits.

Overview of the Ketogenic Diet

The ketogenic diet, also known as the keto diet, is a high-fat, low-carbohydrate diet that has gained popularity in recent years for its potential health benefits. The goal of the diet is to put the body into a state of ketosis, where it burns fat for energy instead of carbohydrates.

When following the keto diet, individuals typically consume 70-80% of their daily calories from fat, 20-25% from protein, and only 5-10% from carbohydrates. This means that foods such as meat, fish, eggs, nuts, seeds, and oils are encouraged, while starchy vegetables, grains, and sugary foods are limited.

Research has suggested that the keto diet may help with weight loss, improve blood sugar control, reduce inflammation, and even potentially benefit those with neurological disorders such as epilepsy and Alzheimer's disease.

However, it is important to note that the keto diet is not suitable for everyone, and it should be approached with caution. It can be difficult to maintain and may cause side effects such as fatigue, headaches, and constipation.

Before starting the keto diet, it is recommended to consult with a healthcare professional to determine if it is appropriate for your individual needs and goals. Additionally, it is important to ensure that you are getting enough nutrients and staying hydrated while on the diet.

Benefits and Potential Risks

Benefits of following the keto diet:

1. Weight loss: One of the most significant benefits of the keto diet is weight loss. By reducing carbohydrate intake and increasing fat intake, the body enters a state of ketosis where it burns fat for energy instead of glucose. This can lead to a reduction in body fat and weight loss.

2. Improved blood sugar control: The keto diet has been shown to improve insulin sensitivity and blood sugar control, making it a potential option for those with type 2 diabetes. By reducing carbohydrate intake, the body produces less insulin, which can help regulate blood sugar levels.

3. Reduced inflammation: The high-fat content in the keto diet may reduce inflammation in the body, which is associated with many chronic diseases such as heart disease, cancer, and Alzheimer's disease.

4. Potential benefits for neurological disorders: The keto diet has been shown to potentially benefit those with epilepsy and Alzheimer's disease. In some cases, it may also improve symptoms of Parkinson's disease and multiple sclerosis.

5. Increased energy levels: Some people report feeling more energized and focused on the keto diet. This may be due to the fact that the body is burning fat for energy instead of glucose, which can lead to more stable energy levels throughout the day.

Potential risks of following the keto diet:

1. Nutrient deficiencies: The keto diet restricts many food groups such as fruits, grains, and legumes, which can lead to nutrient deficiencies if not carefully planned. It is important to ensure that you are getting enough vitamins and minerals through other sources such as leafy greens, nuts, and seeds.

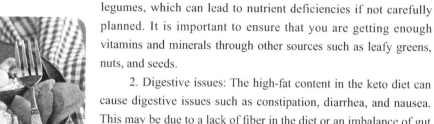

2. Digestive issues: The high-fat content in the keto diet can cause digestive issues such as constipation, diarrhea, and nausea. This may be due to a lack of fiber in the diet or an imbalance of gut bacteria.

3. Keto flu: Some people experience flu-like symptoms when first starting the keto diet, including fatigue, headaches, and irritability. This is often referred to as the "keto flu" and may be due to the body adjusting to a new way of eating.

4. Difficulty maintaining the diet: The keto diet can be difficult to maintain long-term, and may require significant lifestyle changes. It can also be challenging to eat out or travel while on the diet.

5. Increased risk of heart disease: The high-fat content in the keto diet may increase the risk of heart disease if unhealthy fats are consumed. It is important to focus on healthy sources of fat such as avocado, olive oil, and nuts.

Who is Recommended to Keto Diet

The keto diet may be beneficial for several groups of people, including:

1. People with obesity: The keto diet can help promote weight loss by reducing hunger and increasing satiety.

2. People with type 2 diabetes: The keto diet can help improve blood sugar control and reduce insulin resistance, which are important factors in managing type 2 diabetes.

3. People with neurological disorders: The keto diet has been shown to have therapeutic benefits for certain neurological disorders, such as epilepsy and Alzheimer's disease.

4. People with polycystic ovary syndrome (PCOS): The keto diet may help improve hormonal imbalances associated with PCOS, such as insulin resistance and high levels of androgens.

5. Athletes: The keto diet may be beneficial for endurance athletes, as it can help improve fat utilization and reduce the reliance on carbohydrates for fuel.

However, it's important to note that the keto diet is not appropriate for everyone, and it may have potential side effects and risks. It's always recommended to speak with a healthcare professional before starting any new diet or lifestyle change.

Who is Not Recommended to the Keto Diet

While the keto diet may be beneficial for some people, it may not be appropriate for everyone. Here are some groups of people who should be cautious or avoid the keto diet altogether:

1. **People with certain medical conditions:** The keto diet may not be appropriate for people with liver or pancreatic disease, gallbladder disease, or a history of pancreatitis.

2. **Pregnant or breastfeeding women:** The keto diet may not provide adequate nutrients for fetal development and may also affect milk production.

3. **People with a history of eating disorders:** The strict dietary restrictions of the keto diet may trigger disordered eating patterns in some individuals.

4. **People with a history of kidney stones:** The high fat intake on the keto diet may increase the risk of kidney stone formation in some people.

5. **Children:** The keto diet may not be appropriate for children, as their bodies require more carbohydrates for growth and development.

It's important to speak with a healthcare professional before starting any new diet or lifestyle change, especially if you have any underlying medical conditions or concerns.

Tips for Getting Started with the Diet

Getting started with the keto diet can be challenging, but there are several tips that can help make the transition easier:

1. **Research and plan:** Before starting the keto diet, it is important to do your research and plan out your meals. This will ensure that you are getting enough nutrients and staying within the recommended macronutrient ratios.

2. **Gradually reduce carbohydrate intake:** Instead of cutting out all carbohydrates at once, gradually reduce your intake over a period of a few weeks. This will help minimize the side effects of the "keto flu" and make the transition smoother.

3. **Focus on healthy fats:** While the keto diet is high in fat, it is important to focus on healthy sources such as avocado, olive oil, nuts, and seeds.

4. **Stay hydrated:** Drinking plenty of water is important on the keto diet, as it can help prevent dehydration and constipation.

5. **Monitor your ketone levels:** You can monitor your ketone levels using urine strips or blood tests. This can help ensure that you are in a state of ketosis and staying within the recommended range.

6. **Be prepared for social situations:** Eating out or attending social events can be challenging on the keto diet. Plan ahead by researching restaurant menus or bringing your own snacks.

7. **Consider working with a healthcare professional:** A healthcare professional can help determine if the keto diet is appropriate for your individual needs and provide guidance on how to safely follow the diet.

Remember, the keto diet may not be suitable for everyone and should be approached with caution. It is important to consult with a healthcare professional before starting the diet and to ensure that you are getting enough nutrients and staying hydrated while on the diet.

Chapter 1 Essential Guidelines for the Ketogenic Diet

Macronutrient Ratios and Daily Calorie Intake

The macronutrient ratios and daily calorie intake of the keto diet can vary depending on individual needs and goals. However, the general recommended macronutrient ratios for the keto diet are:

70-80% of daily calories from fat

20-25% of daily calories from protein

5-10% of daily calories from carbohydrates

This means that individuals following the keto diet should focus on consuming healthy sources of fat such as avocado, olive oil, nuts, and seeds, while limiting their intake of carbohydrates to less than 50 grams per day.

In terms of daily calorie intake, this will also depend on individual factors such as age, gender, weight, and activity level. However, a general guideline for calculating daily calorie intake on the keto diet is:

1. Determine your basal metabolic rate (BMR) using an online calculator or by consulting with a healthcare professional.

2. Multiply your BMR by your activity level (sedentary, lightly active, moderately active, very active) to determine your total daily energy expenditure (TDEE).

3. Subtract 500-1000 calories from your TDEE to create a calorie deficit for weight loss.

For example, a sedentary woman with a BMR of 1500 calories and a TDEE of 1800 calories may aim for a daily calorie intake of 1300-1500 calories on the keto diet.

It is important to note that calorie intake and macronutrient ratios should be tailored to individual needs and goals. It is recommended to consult with a healthcare professional or registered dietitian before starting the keto diet to determine the appropriate macronutrient ratios and daily calorie intake for your individual needs.

Food Choices and Restrictions

The keto diet restricts many food groups that are high in carbohydrates and sugar, while encouraging foods that are high in healthy fats and moderate in protein. Here are some examples of foods that are allowed and restricted on the keto diet:

Foods to eat on the keto diet:

Meat: beef, pork, chicken, turkey, lamb, etc.

Fish and seafood: salmon, tuna, trout, shrimp, crab, etc.

Eggs: preferably pastured or omega-3 enriched

High-fat dairy: cheese, butter, cream, full-fat yogurt, etc.

Nuts and seeds: almonds, macadamia nuts, walnuts, pumpkin seeds, etc.

Healthy oils: olive oil, coconut oil, avocado oil, etc.

Low-carb vegetables: leafy greens, broccoli, cauliflower, zucchini, etc.

Berries: strawberries, raspberries, blackberries, etc.

Foods to avoid on the keto diet:

Grains: wheat, rice, oats, corn, etc.

Sugary foods: candy, soda, juice, desserts, etc.

Starchy vegetables: potatoes, sweet potatoes, carrots, etc.

Legumes: beans, lentils, chickpeas, etc.

Fruits: bananas, apples, oranges, etc.

Processed foods: packaged snacks, chips, crackers, etc.

It is important to note that not all foods within these categories are created equal. For example, some low-carb vegetables such as onions and tomatoes may be consumed in moderation, while others like peas and corn should be avoided. Additionally, it is important to focus on healthy sources of fat and protein, and to limit processed and unhealthy foods even if they are technically "allowed" on the keto diet.

Meal Planning and Portion Control

When it comes to meal planning and portion control on the keto diet, there are a few key principles to keep in mind:

1. Focus on whole, nutrient-dense foods: The foundation of any healthy diet is whole, nutrient-dense foods like vegetables, fruits, nuts, seeds, and high-quality proteins. On the keto diet, this means focusing on low-carb vegetables like leafy greens, broccoli, cauliflower, and zucchini, as well as healthy fats like avocado, olive oil, and coconut oil.

2. Keep track of your macros: To stay in ketosis, it's important to keep track of your macronutrient intake. This means monitoring your intake of carbohydrates, protein, and fat to ensure you're getting the right balance for your body. A typical keto diet may involve consuming around 5-10% of calories from carbs, 20-25% from protein, and 70-75% from fat.

3. Plan your meals ahead of time: Planning your meals ahead of time can help you stay on track with your keto diet. This might involve preparing meals in advance or simply making a list of keto-friendly foods and recipes to choose from throughout the week.

4. Practice portion control: While the keto diet is focused on healthy fats and protein, it's still important to practice portion control to avoid overeating. Using measuring cups or a food scale can help you accurately portion out your meals and snacks.

By following these principles, you can successfully plan and portion your meals on the keto diet and achieve your health and wellness goals.

Importance of Hydration and Electrolyte Balance

Hydration and electrolyte balance are both important considerations when following a keto diet. Here's why:

1. Dehydration: The keto diet can cause increased water loss due to lower insulin levels and reduced glycogen stores in the body. This can lead to dehydration if you don't drink enough water. Dehydration can cause symptoms such as headaches, fatigue, and constipation.

2. Electrolyte imbalance: When you reduce your carbohydrate intake on the keto diet, your body produces less insulin, which can cause your kidneys to excrete more sodium. This can lead to an electrolyte imbalance, particularly low levels of sodium, potassium, and magnesium. Symptoms of an electrolyte imbalance can include muscle cramps, weakness, and fatigue.

To avoid these issues, it's important to prioritize hydration and electrolyte balance when following a keto diet. Here are some tips:

1. Drink plenty of water: Aim to drink at least 8-10 glasses of water per day, or more if you're physically active or live in a hot climate.

2. Stick to protein and veggies: Choose dishes that are centered around protein and vegetables, like grilled chicken or fish with a side of steamed broccoli or salad. Avoid dishes that are high in carbs, like pasta, rice, and bread.

3. Ask for modifications: Don't be afraid to ask for modifications to dishes to make them more keto-friendly. For example, you could ask for a burger without the bun, or for a salad without croutons.

4. Be cautious of sauces and dressings: Many sauces and dressings contain hidden sugars and carbs, so ask for them on the side and use them sparingly.

5. Avoid sugary drinks: Stick to water, unsweetened tea, or coffee. Avoid sugary drinks like soda, juice, and sweetened cocktails.

6. Don't be afraid to bring your own snacks: If you're worried about not being able to find keto-friendly options, bring along some nuts, seeds, or jerky to snack on.

7. Practice portion control: Restaurant portions are often much larger than what you would eat at home, so consider splitting a dish with a friend or taking leftovers home.

By following these tips, you can enjoy dining out while still sticking to your keto diet.

2. Consume electrolyte-rich foods: Include foods like leafy greens, avocado, nuts, and seeds in your diet, which are rich in potassium and magnesium.

3. Consider using an electrolyte supplement: If you're struggling to get enough electrolytes from your diet alone, consider using an electrolyte supplement that contains sodium, potassium, and magnesium.

By prioritizing hydration and electrolyte balance, you can support your overall health and wellness while following a keto diet.

Tips for Dining Out While on Keto

Dining out while on keto can be a challenge, but it's definitely doable with some planning and preparation. Here are some tips for dining out while on keto:

1. Research the restaurant beforehand: Look up the menu online and see if they have any keto-friendly options. You can also call ahead and ask if they can accommodate your dietary needs.

Chapter 2 Get Started

Maintaining a healthy lifestyle can be challenging, but it's important to remember that the benefits are well worth the effort. Here are some words of encouragement and motivation to help you stay on track:

1. Remember your "why": Why did you start on this journey in the first place? Whether it's to improve your health, feel more confident, or have more energy, remind yourself of your goals and keep them at the forefront of your mind.

2. Take it one day at a time: Making lasting changes takes time, so focus on making small, sustainable changes each day. Celebrate your successes, no matter how small, and don't get discouraged by setbacks.

3. Find a support system: Surround yourself with people who support and encourage your healthy lifestyle choices. This could be friends, family members, or even an online community.

4. Practice self-care: Taking care of yourself is essential for maintaining a healthy lifestyle. Make time for activities that bring you joy and relaxation, such as reading, yoga, or spending time outdoors.

5. Keep things interesting: Mix up your routine and try new things to keep your healthy lifestyle exciting and engaging. This could be trying a new healthy recipe, taking a different workout class, or exploring a new hiking trail.

Remember, maintaining a healthy lifestyle is a journey, not a destination. It's okay to make mistakes and have setbacks - what matters is that you keep moving forward and stay committed to your goals.

30-Day Meal Plan

DAYS	BREAKFAST	LUNCH	DINNER	SNACK/DESSERT
1	Perfect Scrambled Eggs 17	Tandoori Chicken 24	Korean Ground Beef Bowl 44	Tapenade 55
2	Morning Buzz Iced Coffee 13	Easy Chicken Chili 24	Homemade Classic Beef Burgers 42	Cheddar Cauliflower Rice 57
3	Tuscan "Quiche" Bites 12	Chicken Nuggets 25	Pepper Steak Stir-Fry 37	Buttered Cabbage 59
4	Jalapeño Popper Stuffed Omelet 12	Grilled Paprika Chicken with Steamed Broccoli 25	Lemon Pork Chops with Buttered Brussels Sprouts 40	Chicken-Pecan Salad Cucumber Bites 55
5	Sausage and Greens Hash Bowl 12	Bacon-Wrapped Stuffed Chicken Breasts 31	Filipino Pork Loin 37	Savory Mackerel & Goat'S Cheese "Paradox" Balls 55
6	Indian Masala Omelet 13	Sesame Chicken with Broccoli 32	Eggplant Pork Lasagna 37	Buttered Cabbage 59
7	Sausage Egg Cup 16	Chicken and Bacon Rolls 25	Beef Burgers with Kale and Cheese 41	Brussels Sprouts with Aioli Sauce 57
8	Smoked Ham and Egg Muffins 16	Instant Pot Crack Chicken 31	Coconut Milk Ginger Marinated Pork Tenderloin 35	Low-Carb Zucchini Fritters 58
9	Greek Yogurt Parfait 14	Chicken Pesto Parmigiana 24	Ground Beef Stroganoff 35	Classy Crudités and Dip 56
10	Thanksgiving Balls 15	Thanksgiving Turkey Breast 26	Pepperoni Pizza Casserole 35	Keto Asian Dumplings 56
11	Quick Low-Carb Avocado Toasts 13	Zucchini Rolls 36	Parmesan Mackerel with Coriander 45	Goat Cheese–Mackerel Pâté 56
12	Buffalo Chicken Breakfast Muffins 17	Cardamom Pork Ribs 34	Salmon with Cauliflower 48	Strawberry Shortcake Coconut Ice 55
13	Breakfast Sammies 16	Cheese Shell Tacos 34	Sole Asiago 47	Chipped Artichokes 56
14	Quick Keto Blender Muffins 15	Pork Casserole 34	Firecracker Shrimp 46	Grandma's Meringues 57
15	Cauliflower and Cheese Quiche 14	Easy Zucchini Beef Lasagna 35	Italian Tuna Roast 47	Lemon Pepper Wings 58
16	Classic Coffee Cake 17	Garlic Pork Chops with Mint Pesto 44	Coconut Curry Mussels 52	Strawberry Panna Cotta 80
17	Parmesan Baked Eggs 21	Beef Big Mac Salad 36	Lemon Mahi-Mahi 48	Pecan Butter Cookies 80
18	Breakfast Cobbler 14	Sausage-Stuffed Peppers 36	Simple Fish Curry 48	Traditional Cheesecake 80

DAYS	BREAKFAST	LUNCH	DINNER	SNACK/DESSERT
19	Sticky Wrapped Eggs 14	Five-Spice Pork Belly 39	Tuna Avocado Bites 45	County Fair Cinnamon Donuts 81
20	Cheese & Aioli Eggs 15	Pork Meatballs 39	Stuffed Trout 45	Lemon Drops 81
21	Kielbasa and Roquefort Waffles 15	Foil-Packet Salmon 48	Chicken Cauliflower Bake 26	Lemon-Poppyseed Cookies 81
22	Chocoholic Granola 19	Tuna with Herbs 50	Simple Shredded Chicken 26	Coconut Muffins 84
23	Spinach and Chicken Casserole 18	Baked Coconut Haddock 51	Chicken Skewers with Celery Fries 26	Halle Berries-and-Cream Cobbler 82
24	Nutty "Oatmeal" 19	Salmon & Kale 46	Chipotle Chicken Fajita Bowl 33	Coconut Cupcakes 82
25	Chocolate Chip Waffle 18	Steamed Halibut with Lemon 48	Buttery Garlic Chicken 31	Espresso Cream 84
26	Radish Hash Browns 20	Sushi 47	Bacon Lovers' Stuffed Chicken 27	Mint–Chocolate Chip Ice Cream 84
27	Bacon, Cheese, and Avocado Melt 23	Creamy Shrimp and Bacon Skillet 46	Baked Pecorino Toscano Chicken 27	Hazelnut Butter Cookies 87
28	Sawdust Oatmeal 16	Apple Cider Mussels 51	Chicken Piccata with Mushrooms 28	Cream Cheese Shortbread Cookies 81
29	Bell Peppers Stuffed with Eggs 17	Coconut Milk-Braised Squid 47	Homemade Chicken Pizza Calzone 28	Berry-Pecan Mascarpone Bowl 85
30	Broccoli & Colby Cheese Frittata 23	Noodles & Glazed Salmon 54	Nashville Hot Chicken 28	Iced Tea Lemonade Gummies 84

Sausage and Greens Hash Bowl

Prep time: 25 minutes | Cook time: 25 minutes | Serves 2

Hash:
- ⅔ cup (100 g) peeled and ½-inch-cubed rutabaga
- 2 tablespoons lard
- 2 precooked sausages (about

For The Bowls:
- 2 cups (140 g) fresh spinach
- ½ large Hass avocado, sliced
- 2 strips bacon, cooked and

- 4 ounces/115 g), cut into ½-inch cubes
- ¼ cup (20 g) chopped green onions, green parts only

- cut into bite-sized pieces
- 1 teaspoon finely chopped fresh parsley

1. Steam the rutabaga for 8 to 10 minutes, until fork-tender. 2. Melt the lard in a medium-sized frying pan over medium heat. Add the steamed rutabaga and cook for 7 to 10 minutes, until the rutabaga begins to brown. 3. Add the sausages and green onions and cook for 3 to 5 minutes, until the sausages begin to brown. 4. Meanwhile, assemble the bowls: Divide the spinach equally between 2 5. medium-sized serving bowls. When the hash is ready, divide it equally between 6. the bowls, laying it on top of the bed of spinach. Place equal amounts of the sliced avocado, bacon pieces, and parsley on top.

Per Serving:
calories: 560 | fat: 50g | protein: 17g | carbs: 12g | net carbs: 6g | fiber: 6g

Jalapeño Popper Stuffed Omelet

Prep time: 10 minutes | Cook time: 10 minutes | Serves 1

- 1 ounce (28 g) cream cheese, softened at room temperature
- 4 tablespoons (1 ounce / 28 g) shredded Cheddar cheese, divided into 2 tablespoons and 2 tablespoons
- 2 tablespoons cooked bacon bits
- 1½ teaspoons thinly sliced

- green onions
- 1½ teaspoons finely diced seeded jalapeño pepper (about ⅛ medium)
- 2 large eggs
- 2 tablespoons heavy cream
- ¼ teaspoon sea salt
- ⅛ teaspoon black pepper
- 1 tablespoon butter

1. In a medium bowl, mash together the cream cheese, 2 tablespoons of the Cheddar, and the bacon bits. Stir in the green onions and jalapeño. Set the cream cheese mixture aside. 2. In another medium bowl, whisk together the eggs, heavy cream, sea salt, and black pepper. 3. In a medium skillet, melt the butter over medium heat. Pour in the egg mixture. Cover and cook for 1 to 2 minutes, until mostly cooked through. You can lift with a spatula to get more of the egg underneath if needed, but don't stir or scramble. 4. Drop dollops of the cream cheese mixture onto half of the omelet, distributing as evenly as possible. Use a spatula to fold the omelet over. Sprinkle the remaining 2 tablespoons Cheddar cheese on top. 5. Reduce the heat to medium-low. Cover and cook for a couple of minutes, until the cheese melts on top and inside.

Per Serving:
calories: 416 | fat: 35g | protein: 22g | carbs: 3g | net carbs: 3g | fiber: 0g

Tuscan "Quiche" Bites

Prep time: 15 minutes | Cook time: 45 minutes | serves 4

- 2 tablespoons cold-pressed olive oil
- ½ cup sliced cremini mushrooms
- ⅓ cup chopped onion
- ¼ cup sliced cherry tomatoes
- 1 teaspoon garlic powder
- 1 cup coarsely chopped fresh spinach
- ¼ cup sliced black olives
- 1 (14-ounce) block organic firm sprouted tofu, drained

- ¼ cup water
- 2 tablespoons tahini
- 2 tablespoons nutritional yeast
- 1 teaspoon dried basil
- 1 teaspoon dried oregano
- ¼ teaspoon ground cumin
- ⅛ teaspoon turmeric powder
- ½ teaspoon kala namak salt (optional)
- Nonstick cooking spray

1. Preheat the oven to 350°F. 2. Heat the olive oil in a large skillet over medium heat. Add the mushrooms, onion, tomatoes, and garlic powder, and sauté for about 5 minutes. Once the mushrooms start to sweat and the tomatoes start to blister, turn off the heat. 3. Stir in the spinach and olives and set aside. 4. In a blender, combine the tofu with the water, tahini, nutritional yeast, basil, oregano, cumin, turmeric, and salt (if using). Blend until a fluffy, egglike consistency is obtained, adding a little more water if needed. 5. Transfer the mixture to a large mixing bowl and fold in the sautéed vegetables. 6. Coat a six-cup muffin pan with cooking spray. Divide the batter equally among the muffin cups. 7. Bake in the preheated oven for 45 minutes until a toothpick inserted into the center of a quiche comes out clean. 8. Allow the quiches to cool for 10 minutes before serving, because the centers will be very hot.

Per Serving:
calories: 241 | fat: 18g | protein: 14g | carbs: 7g | net carbs: 4g | fiber: 3g

Indian Masala Omelet

Prep time: 8 minutes | Cook time: 25 minutes | Makes 1 large omelet

- ◁ 3 tablespoons avocado oil, coconut oil, or ghee
- ◁ ¼ cup (20 g) sliced green onions
- ◁ 1 clove garlic, minced
- ◁ 1 small tomato, diced
- ◁ 1 green chili pepper, seeded

- and finely diced
- ◁ 1½ teaspoons curry powder
- ◁ ½ teaspoon garam masala
- ◁ 6 large eggs, beaten
- ◁ ¼ cup (15 g) chopped fresh cilantro leaves and stems

1. Heat the oil in a large frying pan over medium heat until it shimmers. When the oil is shimmering, add the green onions, garlic, tomato, and chili pepper. Cook for 10 minutes, or until the liquid from the tomatoes has evaporated. 2. Reduce the heat to low and sprinkle the tomato mixture with the curry powder and garam masala. Stir to incorporate, then drizzle the beaten eggs over the top. 3. Cover and cook for 5 minutes, or until the edges are cooked through. 4. Sprinkle with the cilantro, fold one side over the other, cover, and cook for another 10 minutes. 5. Remove from the heat, cut in half, and serve.

Per Serving:

calories: 438 | fat: 36g | protein: 20g | carbs: 8g | net carbs: 6g | fiber: 2g

Quick Low-Carb Avocado Toasts

Prep time: 10 minutes | Cook time: 10 minutes | Makes 4 toasts

Quick Bread Base:
- ◁ ¼ cup (28 g/1 ounce) flax meal
- ◁ 2 tablespoons (16 g/0.6 ounce) coconut flour
- ◁ 2 teaspoons (2 g) psyllium powder
- ◁ ⅛ teaspoon baking soda
- ◁ Optional: ½ teaspoon dried herbs, ¼ teaspoon paprika or ground turmeric

Avocado Topping:
- ◁ 1 large ripe avocado
- ◁ ¼ small red onion or 1 spring onion, minced
- ◁ 1 tablespoon extra-virgin olive oil
- ◁ 1 tablespoon fresh lemon juice
- ◁ Salt, black pepper, and/or

- ◁ Salt and black pepper, to taste
- ◁ ¼ teaspoon apple cider vinegar
- ◁ 1 teaspoon extra-virgin olive oil or ghee, plus more for greasing
- ◁ 1 large egg
- ◁ 2 tablespoons water

chile flakes, to taste
- ◁ 2 teaspoons chopped fresh herbs, such as parsley or chives
- ◁ Optional: 2 ounces (57 g) smoked salmon and/or poached egg

Make The Bread Base: 1. Combine all the dry ingredients in a bowl. Add the wet ingredients. Combine and set aside for 5 minutes. 2.Divide the mixture between two wide ramekins lightly greased with the olive oil and microwave on high for about 2 minutes, checking every 30 to 60 seconds to avoid overcooking. (If the bread ends up too dry, you can "rehydrate" it: Pour 1 tablespoon [15 ml] of water evenly over it, then return it to the microwave for 30 seconds.) 3.Let it cool slightly, then cut widthwise. Place on a dry nonstick pan and toast for 1 to 2 minutes per side. Set aside. Make The Topping: 4. In a bowl, mash the avocado with the onion, oil, lemon juice, salt, pepper, and chile flakes. To serve, spread the avocado mixture on top of the sliced bread and add fresh herbs. Optionally, top with smoked salmon. 5.Store the bread separately from the topping at room temperature in a sealed container for 1 day, in the fridge for up to 5 days, or freeze for up to 3 months. 6.Refrigerate the topping in a sealed jar for up to 3 days.

Per Serving:

calories: 188 | fat: 17g | protein: 4g | carbs: 8g | net carbs: 3g | fiber: 5g

Heart-Healthy Hazelnut-Collagen Shake

Prep time: 5 minutes | Cook time: 0 minutes | Serves 1

- ◁ 1½ cups unsweetened almond milk
- ◁ 2 tablespoons hazelnut butter
- ◁ 2 tablespoons grass-fed collagen powder
- ◁ ½–1 teaspoon cinnamon

- ◁ ⅛ teaspoon LoSalt or pink Himalayan salt
- ◁ ⅛ teaspoon sugar-free almond extract
- ◁ 1 tablespoon macadamia oil or hazelnut oil

1. Place all of the ingredients in a blender and pulse until smooth and frothy. Serve immediately.

Per Serving:

calories: 345 | fat: 32g | protein: 13g | carbs: 8g | net carbs: 3g | fiber: 5g

Morning Buzz Iced Coffee

Prep time: 10 minutes | Cook time: 0 minutes | Serves 1

- ◁ 1 cup freshly brewed strong black coffee, cooled slightly
- ◁ 1 tablespoon extra-virgin olive oil
- ◁ 1 tablespoon half-and-half or heavy cream (optional)

- ◁ 1 teaspoon MCT oil (optional)
- ◁ ⅛ teaspoon almond extract
- ◁ ⅛ teaspoon ground cinnamon

1. Pour the slightly cooled coffee into a blender or large glass (if using an immersion blender). 2. Add the olive oil, half-and-half (if using), MCT oil (if using), almond extract, and cinnamon. 3. Blend well until smooth and creamy. Drink warm and enjoy.

Per Serving:

calories: 51 | fat: 5g | protein: 0g | carbs: 1g | net carbs: 1g | fiber: 0g

Sticky Wrapped Eggs

Prep time: 10 minutes | Cook time: 30 minutes | Makes 12 wrapped eggs

- ¼ cup (60 ml) coconut aminos
- 2 tablespoons hot sauce
- 12 hard-boiled eggs
- 12 strips bacon (about 12 ounces/340 g)
- 6 cups (100 g) arugula

1. Preheat the oven to 400°F (205°C). Line a standard-size 12-well muffin pan with muffin liners, or use a silicone muffin pan, which won't require liners. 2. Place the coconut aminos and hot sauce in a small bowl and whisk to combine. Set the bowl close to the muffin pan. 3. Peel the hard-boiled eggs. One at a time, wrap each egg in a strip of bacon, then dunk it in the hot sauce mixture and place it in a well of the muffin pan. 4. Bake for 30 minutes, flipping the eggs over halfway through. 5. Divide the arugula evenly among 6 small serving plates. Top each with 2 sticky eggs and the sauce from their muffin liners.

Per Serving:

calories: 438 | fat: 33g | protein: 33g | carbs: 4g | net carbs: 4g | fiber: 0g

Breakfast Cobbler

Prep time: 20 minutes | Cook time: 30 minutes | Serves 4

Filling:
- 10 ounces (283 g) bulk pork sausage, crumbled
- ¼ cup minced onions
- 2 cloves garlic, minced
- ½ teaspoon fine sea salt
- ½ teaspoon ground black pepper

Biscuits:
- 3 large egg whites
- ¾ cup blanched almond flour
- 1 teaspoon baking powder
- ¼ teaspoon fine sea salt
- 1 (8 ounces / 227 g) package cream cheese (or Kite Hill brand cream cheese style spread for dairy-free), softened
- ¾ cup beef or chicken broth
- 2½ tablespoons very cold unsalted butter, cut into ¼-inch pieces
- Fresh thyme leaves, for garnish

1. Preheat the air fryer to 400°F (204°C). 2. Place the sausage, onions, and garlic in a pie pan. Using your hands, break up the sausage into small pieces and spread it evenly throughout the pie pan. Season with the salt and pepper. Place the pan in the air fryer and bake for 5 minutes. 3. While the sausage cooks, place the cream cheese and broth in a food processor or blender and purée until smooth. 4. Remove the pork from the air fryer and use a fork or metal spatula to crumble it more. Pour the cream cheese mixture into the sausage and stir to combine. Set aside. 5. Make the biscuits: Place the egg whites in a medium-sized mixing bowl or the bowl of a stand mixer and whip with a hand mixer or stand mixer until stiff peaks form. 6. In a separate medium-sized bowl, whisk together the almond flour, baking powder, and salt, then cut in the butter. When

you are done, the mixture should still have chunks of butter. Gently fold the flour mixture into the egg whites with a rubber spatula. 7. Use a large spoon or ice cream scoop to scoop the dough into 4 equal-sized biscuits, making sure the butter is evenly distributed. Place the biscuits on top of the sausage and cook in the air fryer for 5 minutes, then turn the heat down to 325°F (163°C) and bake for another 17 to 20 minutes, until the biscuits are golden brown. Serve garnished with fresh thyme leaves. 8. Store leftovers in an airtight container in the refrigerator for up to 3 days. Reheat in a preheated 350°F (177°C) air fryer for 5 minutes, or until warmed through.

Per Serving:

calories: 586 | fat: 53g | protein: 20g | carbs: 8g | net carbs: 6g | fiber: 2g

Greek Yogurt Parfait

Prep time: 5 minutes | Cook time: 0 minutes | Serves 1

- ½ cup plain whole-milk Greek yogurt
- 2 tablespoons heavy whipping cream
- ¼ cup frozen berries, thawed with juices
- ½ teaspoon vanilla or
- almond extract (optional)
- ¼ teaspoon ground cinnamon (optional)
- 1 tablespoon ground flaxseed
- 2 tablespoons chopped nuts (walnuts or pecans)

1. In a small bowl or glass, combine the yogurt, heavy whipping cream, thawed berries in their juice, vanilla or almond extract (if using), cinnamon (if using), and flaxseed and stir well until smooth. Top with chopped nuts and enjoy.

Per Serving:

calories: 401 | fat: 32g | protein: 15g | carbs: 16g | net carbs: 11g | fiber: 5g

Cauliflower and Cheese Quiche

Prep time: 10 minutes | Cook time: 10 minutes | Serves 2

- 1 cup chopped cauliflower
- ¼ cup shredded Cheddar cheese
- 5 eggs, beaten
- 1 teaspoon butter
- 1 teaspoon dried oregano
- 1 cup water

1. Grease the instant pot baking pan with butter from inside. 2. Pour water in the instant pot. 3. Sprinkle the cauliflower with dried oregano and put it in the prepared baking pan. Flatten the vegetables gently. 4. After this, add eggs and stir the vegetables. 5. Top the quiche with shredded cheese and transfer it in the instant pot. Close and seal the lid. Cook the quiche on Manual mode (High Pressure) for 10 minutes. Make a quick pressure release.

Per Serving:

calories: 246 | fat: 18g | protein: 18g | carbs: 4g | net carbs: 2g | fiber: 2g

Thanksgiving Balls

Prep time: 20 minutes | Cook time: 35 minutes | Serves 14

- ¼ cup (52 g) duck fat
- 4½ ounces (125 g) chicken sausages, chopped
- ½ cup (85 g) chopped celery
- 3 white mushrooms (about 2¼ ounces/65 g), chopped
- 2 small cloves garlic, minced
- 2 teaspoons dried thyme leaves
- ½ teaspoon dried ground sage
- ½ teaspoon finely ground gray sea salt
- ¼ teaspoon ground black pepper
- ¾ cup (85 g) raw walnut pieces, soaked for 12 hours, then drained and rinsed
- ¼ packed cup (16 g) fresh parsley leaves, finely chopped

1. Preheat the oven to 350°F (177°C) and line a rimmed baking sheet with parchment paper or a silicone baking mat. 2. Place the duck fat, sausages, celery, mushrooms, and garlic in a frying pan over medium heat. Cook for 7 to 10 minutes, until the celery is fork-tender and the sausages reach an internal temperature of 165°F (74°C). 3. Add the thyme, sage, salt, and pepper and continue to cook for 1 to 2 minutes, until fragrant. Remove from the heat and transfer the contents of the pan to a blender or food processor. 4. Add the walnuts and pulse until the ingredients are broken down but still have some texture. 5. Transfer 3 tablespoons of the mixture to a bowl, then blend the rest until smooth. 6. Transfer the blended-smooth ingredients to the bowl and stir in the parsley. 7. Scoop up a heaping tablespoon of the mixture, roll it into a ball, and place it on the prepared baking sheet. Repeat with the remaining mixture. 8. Bake the meatballs for 22 to 25 minutes, until browned and lightly cracked on the tops. Allow to cool on the baking sheet for 30 minutes before serving.

Per Serving:

calories: 82 | fat: 8g | protein: 2g | carbs: 1g | net carbs: 1g | fiber: 1g

Quick Keto Blender Muffins

Prep time: 5 minutes | Cook time: 25 minutes | Makes 12 muffins

- Butter, ghee, or coconut oil for greasing the pan
- 6 eggs
- 8 ounces (227 g) cream cheese, at room temperature
- 2 scoops flavored collagen powder
- 1 teaspoon ground cinnamon
- 1 teaspoon baking powder
- Few drops or dash sweetener (optional)

1. Preheat the oven to 350ºF (180ºC). Grease a 12-cup muffin pan very well with butter, ghee, or coconut oil. Alternatively, you can use silicone cups or paper muffin liners. 2. In a blender, combine the eggs, cream cheese, collagen powder, cinnamon, baking powder, and sweetener (if using). Blend until well combined and pour the mixture into the muffin cups, dividing equally. 3. Bake for 22 to 25 minutes until the muffins are golden brown on top and firm. 4. Let

cool then store in a glass container or plastic bag in the refrigerator for up to 2 weeks or in the freezer for up to 3 months. 5. To serve refrigerated muffins, heat in the microwave for 30 seconds. To serve from frozen, thaw in the refrigerator overnight and then microwave for 30 seconds, or microwave straight from the freezer for 45 to 60 seconds or until heated through.

Per Serving:

1 muffin: calories: 120 | fat: 10g | protein: 6g | carbs: 1g | net carbs: 1g | fiber: 0g

Cheese & Aioli Eggs

Prep time: 15 minutes | Cook time: 0 minutes | Serves 8

- 8 eggs, hard-boiled, chopped
- 28 ounces tuna in brine, drained
- ½ cup lettuces, torn into pieces

For Aioli:
- 1cup mayonnaise
- 2cloves garlic, minced
- 1 tablespoon lemon juice
- ½ cup green onions, finely chopped
- ½ cup feta cheese, crumbled
- ⅓ cup sour cream
- ½ tablespoon mustard
- Salt and black pepper, to taste

1. Set the eggs in a serving bowl. Place in tuna, onion, mustard, cheese, lettuce, and sour cream. 2. To prepare aioli, mix in a bowl mayonnaise, lemon juice, and garlic. Add in black pepper and salt. Stir in the prepared aioli to the bowl to incorporate everything. Serve with pickles.

Per Serving:

calories: 471 | fat: 32g | protein: 40g | carbs: 5g | net carbs: 5g | fiber: 1g

Kielbasa and Roquefort Waffles

Prep time: 10 minutes | Cook time: 10 minutes | Serves 2

- 2 tablespoons butter, melted
- Salt and black pepper, to taste
- ½ teaspoon parsley flakes
- ½ teaspoon chili pepper flakes
- 4 eggs
- ½ cup Roquefort cheese, crumbled
- 4 slices kielbasa, chopped
- 2 tablespoons fresh chives, chopped

1. In a mixing bowl, combine all ingredients except fresh chives. Preheat waffle iron and spray with a cooking spray. Pour in the batter and close the lid. 2. Cook for 5 minutes or until golden-brown, do the same with the rest of the batter. Decorate with fresh chives and serve while warm.

Per Serving:

calories: 655 | fat: 57g | protein: 28g | carbs: 4g | net carbs: 4g | fiber: 0g

Sausage Egg Cup

Prep time: 10 minutes | Cook time: 15 minutes | Serves 6

◁ 12 ounces (340 g) ground pork breakfast sausage
◁ 6 large eggs
◁ ½ teaspoon salt
◁ ¼ teaspoon ground black pepper
◁ ½ teaspoon crushed red pepper flakes

1. Place sausage in six 4-inch ramekins (about 2 ounces / 57 g per ramekin) greased with cooking oil. Press sausage down to cover bottom and about ½-inch up the sides of ramekins. Crack one egg into each ramekin and sprinkle evenly with salt, black pepper, and red pepper flakes. 2. Place ramekins into air fryer basket. Adjust the temperature to 350ºF (177ºC) and set the timer for 15 minutes. Egg cups will be done when sausage is fully cooked to at least 145ºF (63ºC) and the egg is firm. Serve warm.

Per Serving:

calories: 268 | fat: 23g | protein: 14g | carbs: 1g | net carbs: 1g | fiber: 0g

Breakfast Sammies

Prep time: 15 minutes | Cook time: 20 minutes | Serves 5

Biscuits:
◁ 6 large egg whites
◁ 2 cups blanched almond flour, plus more if needed
◁ 1½ teaspoons baking powder
◁ ½ teaspoon fine sea salt

◁ ¼ cup (½ stick) very cold unsalted butter (or lard for dairy-free), cut into ¼-inch pieces

Eggs:
◁ 5 large eggs
◁ ½ teaspoon fine sea salt
◁ ¼ teaspoon ground black pepper

◁ 5 (1 ounce / 28 g) slices Cheddar cheese (omit for dairy-free)
◁ 10 thin slices ham

1. Spray the air fryer basket with avocado oil. Preheat the air fryer to 350ºF (177ºC). Grease two pie pans or two baking pans that will fit inside your air fryer. 2. Make the biscuits: In a medium-sized bowl, whip the egg whites with a hand mixer until very stiff. Set aside. 3. In a separate medium-sized bowl, stir together the almond flour, baking powder, and salt until well combined. Cut in the butter. Gently fold the flour mixture into the egg whites with a rubber spatula. If the dough is too wet to form into mounds, add a few tablespoons of almond flour until the dough holds together well. 4. Using a large spoon, divide the dough into 5 equal portions and drop them about 1 inch apart on one of the greased pie pans. (If you're using a smaller air fryer, work in batches if necessary.) Place the pan in the air fryer and bake for 11 to 14 minutes, until the biscuits are golden brown. Remove from the air fryer and set aside to cool. 5. Make the eggs: Set the air fryer to 375ºF (191ºC). Crack the eggs into the remaining greased pie pan and sprinkle with the salt and pepper. Place the eggs in the air fryer to bake for 5 minutes, or until they are cooked to your liking. 6. Open the air fryer and top each egg yolk with a slice of cheese (if using). Bake for another minute, or until the cheese is melted. 7. Once the biscuits are cool, slice them in half lengthwise. Place 1 cooked egg topped with cheese and 2 slices of ham in each biscuit. 8. Store leftover biscuits, eggs, and ham in separate airtight containers in the fridge for up to 3 days. Reheat the biscuits and eggs on a baking sheet in a preheated 350ºF (177ºC) air fryer for 5 minutes, or until warmed through.

Per Serving:

calories: 454 | fat: 35g | protein: 27g | carbs: 8g | net carbs: 4g | fiber: 4g

Sawdust Oatmeal

Prep time: 5 minutes | Cook time: 0 minutes | Serves 1

◁ ⅓ cup boiling water
◁ 2 tablespoons chia seeds
◁ 2 tablespoons flaxseed meal
◁ 2 tablespoons heavy
whipping cream
◁ 1 (1-gram) packet 0g net carb sweetener

1. Add all ingredients to a small glass or porcelain bowl. Stir to mix. Be careful as water is very hot. 2. Stir every couple of minutes as it cools to ensure even cooling. The chia seeds soften and expand as they absorb liquid. 3. When it's cool, it's ready to eat.

Per Serving:

calories: 189 | fat: 22g | protein: 8g | carbs: 15g | net carbs: 4g | fiber: 11g

Smoked Ham and Egg Muffins

Prep time: 5 minutes | Cook time: 25 minutes | Serves 9

◁ 2 cups chopped smoked ham
◁ ⅓ cup grated Parmesan cheese
◁ ¼ cup almond flour
◁ 9 eggs
◁ ⅓ cup mayonnaise, sugar-free
◁ ¼ teaspoon garlic powder
◁ ¼ cup chopped onion
◁ Sea salt to taste

1. Preheat your oven to 370ºF. 2. Lightly grease nine muffin pans with cooking spray and set aside. Place the onion, ham, garlic powder, and salt, in a food processor, and pulse until ground. Stir in the mayonnaise, almond flour, and Parmesan cheese. Press this mixture into the muffin cups. 3. Make sure it goes all the way up the muffin sides so that there will be room for the egg. Bake for 5 minutes. Crack an egg into each muffin cup. Return to the oven and bake for 20 more minutes or until the tops are firm to the touch and eggs are cooked. Leave to cool slightly before serving.

Per Serving:

calories: 165 | fat: 11g | protein: 14g | carbs: 2g | net carbs: 1g | fiber: 1g

Buffalo Chicken Breakfast Muffins

Prep time: 7 minutes | Cook time: 13 to 16 minutes | Serves 10

- 6 ounces (170 g) shredded cooked chicken
- 3 ounces (85 g) blue cheese, crumbled
- 2 tablespoons unsalted butter, melted
- ⅓ cup Buffalo hot sauce,
- such as Frank's RedHot
- 1 teaspoon minced garlic
- 6 large eggs
- Sea salt and freshly ground black pepper, to taste
- Avocado oil spray

1. In a large bowl, stir together the chicken, blue cheese, melted butter, hot sauce, and garlic. 2. In a medium bowl or large liquid measuring cup, beat the eggs. Season with salt and pepper. 3. Spray 10 silicone muffin cups with oil. Divide the chicken mixture among the cups, and pour the egg mixture over top. 4. Place the cups in the air fryer and set to 300°F (149°C). Bake for 13 to 16 minutes, until the muffins are set and cooked through. (Depending on the size of your air fryer, you may need to cook the muffins in batches.)

Per Serving:

calories: 129 | fat: 9g | protein: 10g | carbs: 1g | net carbs: 1g | fiber: 0g

Classic Coffee Cake

Prep time: 5 minutes | Cook time: 40 minutes | Serves 5 to 6

Base:
- 2 eggs
- 2 tablespoons salted grass-fed butter, softened
- 1 cup blanched almond flour
- 1 cup chopped pecans
- ¼ cup sour cream, at room temperature

Topping:
- 1 cup sugar-free chocolate chips
- 1 cup chopped pecans
- ½ cup Swerve, or more to

- ¼ cup full-fat cream cheese, softened
- ½ teaspoon salt
- ½ teaspoon ground cinnamon
- ½ teaspoon ground nutmeg
- ¼ teaspoon baking soda

taste
- ½ cup heavy whipping cream

1. Pour 1 cup of filtered water into the inner pot of the Instant Pot, then insert the trivet. Using an electric mixer, combine the eggs, butter, flour, pecans, sour cream, cream cheese, salt, cinnamon, nutmeg, and baking soda. Mix thoroughly. Transfer this mixture into a well-greased, Instant Pot-friendly pan (or dish). 2. Using a sling if desired, place the pan onto the trivet, and cover loosely with aluminum foil. Close the lid, set the pressure release to Sealing, and select Manual. Set the Instant Pot to 40 minutes on High Pressure and let cook. 3. While cooking, in a large bowl, mix the chocolate chips, pecans, Swerve, and whipping cream thoroughly. Set aside. 4. Once cooked, let the pressure naturally disperse from the Instant Pot for about 10 minutes, then carefully switch the pressure release to Venting. 5. Open the Instant Pot and remove the pan. Evenly sprinkle the topping mixture over the cake. Let cool, serve, and enjoy!

Per Serving:

calories: 267 | fat: 23g | protein: 7g | carbs: 9g | net carbs: 7g | fiber: 2g

Perfect Scrambled Eggs

Prep time: 5 minutes | Cook time: 5 minutes | Serves 2

- 4 eggs
- 1 to 2 tablespoons water
- 1 tablespoon butter
- Salt and freshly ground black pepper, to taste

- Sliced scallion, green parts only, or chopped fresh chives, for topping (optional)

1. Heat a large nonstick skillet over medium-high heat. 2. Into a medium bowl, crack the eggs, add the water, and whisk vigorously until the whites and yolks are well incorporated (you want to be able to lift your whisk from the bowl and have a smooth, continuous strand of egg—nothing lumpy). 3. Add the butter to the skillet and stir with a spatula to coat the entire surface area. Once the butter melts completely, add the eggs and give them a quick stir. Reduce the heat to medium and repeat stirring the eggs and tilting the pan around so the runny parts continue to make contact with the hot surface. 4. When the eggs are mostly cooked, 3 to 4 minutes, reduce the heat to low and continue to fold the eggs over themselves using the spatula. 5. Season with salt and pepper and serve hot when the eggs are cooked to your liking (I prefer mine completely cooked through, but some people like them a little underdone). Top with sliced scallion (if using).

Per Serving:

calories: 177 | fat: 15g | protein: 11g | carbs: 1g | net carbs: 1g | fiber: 0g

Bell Peppers Stuffed with Eggs

Prep time: 5 minutes | Cook time: 14 minutes | Serves 2

- 2 eggs, beaten
- 1 tablespoon coconut cream
- ¼ teaspoon dried oregano
- ¼ teaspoon salt

- 1 large bell pepper, cut into halves and deseeded
- 1 cup water

1. In a bowl, stir together the eggs, coconut cream, oregano and salt. 2. Pour the egg mixture in the pepper halves. 3. Pour the water and insert the trivet in the Instant Pot. Put the stuffed pepper halves on the trivet. 4. Set the lid in place. Select the Manual mode and set the cooking time for 14 minutes on High Pressure. When the timer goes off, do a quick pressure release. Carefully open the lid. 5. Serve warm.

Per Serving:

calories: 99 | fat: 6g | protein: 6g | carbs: 5g | net carbs: 4g | fiber: 1g

Chocolate Chip Waffle

Prep time: 5 minutes | Cook time: 5 minutes | Serves 1

- ◄ ⅓ cup blanched almond flour
- ◄ ½ tablespoon coconut flour
- ◄ ¼ teaspoon baking powder
- ◄ 2 large eggs
- ◄ ¼ teaspoon vanilla extract
- ◄ 4 drops liquid stevia
- ◄ 1 tablespoon stevia-sweetened chocolate chips
- ◄ For Topping (optional)
- ◄ Swerve confectioners'-style sweetener
- ◄ Sugar-free syrup
- ◄ Salted butter

1. Preheat a waffle maker to medium-high heat. 2. Place all the ingredients except the chocolate chips in a large bowl and blend until smooth. Fold in the chocolate chips. 3. Spray the hot waffle maker with nonstick cooking spray. 4. Pour the batter into the hot waffle iron and cook for 3 to 5 minutes, until light golden brown. 5 Serve dusted with Swerve confectioners'-style sweetener and topped with sugar-free syrup and butter, if desired.

Per Serving:

1 waffle: calories: 398 | fat: 31g | protein: 23g | carbs: 14g | net carbs: 6g | fiber: 8g

Spinach and Chicken Casserole

Prep time: 5 minutes | Cook time: 15 minutes | Serves 5

- ◄ 1 tablespoon avocado oil
- ◄ 1 tablespoon coconut oil
- ◄ 1 tablespoon unflavored MCT oil
- ◄ 1 avocado, mashed
- ◄ ½ cup shredded full-fat Cheddar cheese
- ◄ ½ cup chopped spinach
- ◄ ½ teaspoon dried basil
- ◄ ½ teaspoon kosher salt
- ◄ ½ teaspoon freshly ground black pepper
- ◄ ¼ cup sugar-free or low-sugar salsa
- ◄ ¼ cup heavy whipping cream
- ◄ 1 pound (454 g) ground chicken

1. Pour 1 cup of filtered water inside the inner pot of the Instant Pot, then insert the trivet. 2. In a large bowl, combine and mix the avocado oil, coconut oil, MCT oil, avocado, cheese, spinach, basil, salt, black pepper, salsa, and whipping cream. 3. In a greased Instant Pot-safe dish, add the ground chicken in an even layer. Pour the casserole mixture over the chicken and cover with aluminum foil. Using a sling, place this dish on top of the trivet. 4. Close the lid, set the pressure release to Sealing, and select Manual. Set the Instant Pot to 15 minutes on High Pressure, and let cook. 5. Once cooked, carefully switch the pressure release to Venting. Open the Instant Pot, serve, and enjoy!

Per Serving:

calories: 405 | fat: 30g | protein: 30g | carbs: 5g | net carbs: 2g | fiber: 3g

Brussels Sprouts, Bacon, and Eggs

Prep time: 5 minutes | Cook time: 20 minutes | Serves 2

- ◄ ½ pound Brussels sprouts, cleaned, trimmed, and halved
- ◄ 1 tablespoon olive oil
- ◄ Pink Himalayan salt
- ◄ Freshly ground black pepper
- ◄ Nonstick cooking spray
- ◄ 6 bacon slices, diced
- ◄ 4 large eggs
- ◄ Pinch red pepper flakes
- ◄ 2 tablespoons grated Parmesan cheese

1. Preheat the oven to 400°F. 2. In a medium bowl, toss the halved Brussels sprouts in the olive oil, and season with pink Himalayan salt and pepper. 3. Coat a 9-by-13-inch baking pan with cooking spray. 4. Put the Brussels sprouts and bacon in the pan, and roast for 12 minutes. 5. Take the pan out of the oven, and stir the Brussels sprouts and bacon. Using a spoon, create 4 wells in the mixture. 6. Carefully crack an egg into each well. 7. Season the eggs with pink Himalayan salt, black pepper, and red pepper flakes. 8. Sprinkle the Parmesan cheese over the Brussels sprouts and eggs. 9. Cook in the oven for 8 more minutes, or until the eggs are cooked to your preference, and serve.

Per Serving:

calories: 401 | fat: 29g | protein: 27g | carbs: 12g | net carbs: 7g | fiber: 5g

Mushroom & Cheese Lettuce Wraps

Prep time: 10 minutes | Cook time: 10 minutes | Serves 4

For the Wraps:
- ◄ 6 eggs
- ◄ 2 tablespoons almond milk

For the Filling:
- ◄ 1 teaspoon olive oil
- ◄ 1 cup mushrooms, chopped
- ◄ Salt and black pepper, to taste
- ◄ 1 tablespoon olive oil
- ◄ Sea salt, to taste
- ◄ ½ teaspoon cayenne pepper
- ◄ 8 fresh lettuce leaves
- ◄ 4 slices gruyere cheese
- ◄ 2 tomatoes, sliced

1. Mix all the ingredients for the wraps thoroughly. 2. Set a frying pan over medium heat. Add in ¼ of the mixture and cook for 4 minutes on both sides. Do the same thrice and set the wraps aside, they should be kept warm. 3. In a separate pan over medium heat, warm 1 teaspoon of olive oil. Cook the mushrooms for 5 minutes until soft; add cayenne pepper, black pepper, and salt. Set 1-2 lettuce leaves onto every wrap, split the mushrooms among the wraps and top with tomatoes and cheese.

Per Serving:

calories: 273 | fat: 20g | protein: 18g | carbs: 5g | net carbs: 4g | fiber: 1g

Chocoholic Granola

Prep time: 5 minutes | Cook time: 10 minutes | Makes 3½ cups

- ⅓ cup (65 g) erythritol
- 2 tablespoons water
- 1 teaspoon vanilla extract
- ⅓ cup (27 g) cocoa powder
- 1 teaspoon ground cinnamon
- ¾ teaspoon finely ground sea salt
- 3 cups (190 g) unsweetened coconut flakes

1. Cover a cutting board or baking sheet with a piece of parchment paper and set aside. 2. Place the erythritol, water, and vanilla in a large saucepan over medium-low heat. Bring to a light simmer, stirring every 30 seconds. Continue to Step 3 if using confectioners'-style erythritol; if using granulated erythritol, continue to simmer until the granules can no longer be felt on the back of the spoon. 3. Reduce the heat to low and add the cocoa powder, cinnamon, and salt; mix until fully incorporated. 4. Add the coconut flakes and continue to stir frequently, keeping the temperature low to prevent burning. Cook for 6 to 7 minutes, until the bottom of the pan gets sticky. 5. Remove from the heat and transfer the granola to the parchment paper. Allow to cool completely, about 20 minutes, before enjoying, or transfer to a 1-quart (950-ml) or larger airtight container for storage.

Per Serving:

calories: 106 | fat: 9g | protein: 1g | carbs: 5g | net carbs: 2g | fiber: 3g

Nutty "Oatmeal"

Prep time: 5 minutes | Cook time: 4 minutes | Serves 4

- 2 tablespoons coconut oil
- 1 cup full-fat coconut milk
- 1 cup heavy whipping cream
- ½ cup macadamia nuts
- ½ cup chopped pecans
- ⅓ cup Swerve, or more to taste
- ¼ cup unsweetened coconut flakes
- 2 tablespoons chopped hazelnuts
- 2 tablespoons chia seeds
- ½ teaspoon ground cinnamon

1. Before you get started, soak the chia seeds for about 5 to 10 minutes (can be up to 20, if desired) in 1 cup of filtered water. After soaking, set the Instant Pot to Sauté and add the coconut oil. Once melted, pour in the milk, whipping cream, and 1 cup of filtered water. Then add the macadamia nuts, pecans, Swerve, coconut flakes, hazelnuts, chia seeds, and cinnamon. Mix thoroughly inside the Instant Pot. 2. Close the lid, set the pressure release to Sealing, and hit Cancel to stop the current program. Select Manual, set the Instant Pot to 4 minutes on High Pressure, and let cook. 3. Once cooked, carefully switch the pressure release to Venting. 4. Open the Instant Pot, serve, and enjoy!

Per Serving:

calories: 506 | fat: 53g | protein: 6g | carbs: 11g | net carbs: 5g | fiber: 6g

Breakfast Calzone

Prep time: 15 minutes | Cook time: 15 minutes | Serves 4

- 1½ cups shredded Mozzarella cheese
- ½ cup blanched finely ground almond flour
- 1 ounce (28 g) full-fat cream cheese
- 1 large whole egg
- 4 large eggs, scrambled
- ½ pound (227 g) cooked breakfast sausage, crumbled
- 8 tablespoons shredded mild Cheddar cheese

1. In a large microwave-safe bowl, add Mozzarella, almond flour, and cream cheese. Microwave for 1 minute. Stir until the mixture is smooth and forms a ball. Add the egg and stir until dough forms. 2. Place dough between two sheets of parchment and roll out to ¼-inch thickness. Cut the dough into four rectangles. 3. Mix scrambled eggs and cooked sausage together in a large bowl. Divide the mixture evenly among each piece of dough, placing it on the lower half of the rectangle. Sprinkle each with 2 tablespoons Cheddar. 4. Fold over the rectangle to cover the egg and meat mixture. Pinch, roll, or use a wet fork to close the edges completely. 5. Cut a piece of parchment to fit your air fryer basket and place the calzones onto the parchment. Place parchment into the air fryer basket. 6. Adjust the temperature to 380ºF (193ºC) and air fry for 15 minutes. 7. Flip the calzones halfway through the cooking time. When done, calzones should be golden in color. Serve immediately.

Per Serving:

calories: 533 | fat: 42g | protein: 33g | carbs: 6g | net carbs: 5g | fiber: 1g

Southwestern Ham Egg Cups

Prep time: 5 minutes | Cook time: 12 minutes | Serves 2

- 4 (1 ounce / 28 g) slices deli ham
- 4 large eggs
- 2 tablespoons full-fat sour cream
- ¼ cup diced green bell pepper
- 2 tablespoons diced red bell pepper
- 2 tablespoons diced white onion
- ½ cup shredded medium Cheddar cheese

1. Place one slice of ham on the bottom of four baking cups. 2. In a large bowl, whisk eggs with sour cream. Stir in green pepper, red pepper, and onion. 3. Pour the egg mixture into ham-lined baking cups. Top with Cheddar. Place cups into the air fryer basket. 4. Adjust the temperature to 320ºF (160ºC) and bake for 12 minutes or until the tops are browned. 5. Serve warm.

Per Serving:

calories: 413 | fat: 31g | protein: 28g | carbs: 5g | net carbs: 4g | fiber: 1g

Rocket Fuel Hot Chocolate

Prep time: 5 minutes | Cook time: 0 minutes | Makes 2

- 2 cups (475 ml) milk (nondairy or regular), hot
- 2 tablespoons cocoa powder
- 2 tablespoons collagen peptides or protein powder
- 2 tablespoons coconut oil, MCT oil, unflavored MCT

- oil powder, or ghee
- 1 tablespoon coconut butter
- 1 tablespoon erythritol, or 4 drops liquid stevia
- Pinch of ground cinnamon (optional)

1. Place all the ingredients in a blender and blend for 10 seconds, or until the ingredients are fully incorporated. 2. Divide between 2 mugs, sprinkle with cinnamon if you'd like, and enjoy!

Per Serving:

calories: 357 | fat: 29g | protein: 13g | carbs: 11g | net carbs: 7g | fiber: 4g

Breakfast Chili

Prep time: 10 minutes | Cook time: 2 hours 15 minutes | Serves 12

- 4 slices bacon, diced
- 1 pound (454 g) 80% lean ground beef
- 1 pound (454 g) Mexican-style fresh (raw) chorizo, removed from casings
- 1 (28 ounces / 794 g) can diced tomatoes with juices
- 1 cup tomato sauce
- ¼ cup chopped onions
- 1 red bell pepper, chopped
- 2 green chiles, chopped
- ½ cup beef bone broth, homemade or store-bought
- 2 tablespoons chili powder

Toppings (per serving):
- 1 large egg, fried sunny side up (omit for egg-free)
- ¼ avocado, cut into ½-inch dice

- 2 teaspoons dried ground oregano
- 2 teaspoons minced garlic
- 1 teaspoon ground cumin
- ½ teaspoon cayenne pepper
- ½ teaspoon paprika
- ½ teaspoon fine sea salt
- ½ teaspoon freshly ground black pepper
- 2 tablespoons Swerve confectioners'-style sweetener or equivalent amount of liquid or powdered sweetener (optional)

- 2 tablespoons diced cooked bacon (about 1 strip)
- 1 teaspoon chopped fresh chives

1. In a stockpot over medium-high heat, fry the diced bacon until crisp, then remove from the pot with a slotted spoon and set aside. Crumble the ground beef and chorizo into the hot pot and cook, stirring often to break up the meat, until evenly browned, about 7 minutes. 2. Pour in the diced tomatoes and tomato sauce. Add the onions, bell pepper, chiles, cooked bacon, and beef broth and stir to combine. Season with the chili powder, oregano, garlic, cumin, cayenne, paprika, salt, black pepper, and sweetener, if using. Stir to blend, then cover and bring to a simmer over medium heat. Once at a simmer, reduce the heat to low and continue to simmer for at least 2 hours, stirring occasionally. The longer the chili simmers, the better it will taste. 3. After 2 hours, taste and add more salt, pepper, and chili powder, if desired. Remove from the heat and serve each portion with a sunny-side-up egg, diced avocado, diced cooked bacon, and chopped chives. Store extras in an airtight container in the fridge for up to 5 days, or freeze for up to 2 months.

Per Serving:

calories: 440 | fat: 34g | protein: 25g | carbs: 8g | net carbs: 5g | fiber: 3g

Traditional Eggs and Bacon Cooked in Butter

Prep time: 5 minutes | Cook time: 15 minutes | Serves 1

- 1 tablespoon grass-fed butter, divided
- 2 strips uncured bacon
- 2 eggs

- Sea salt, for seasoning
- Freshly ground black pepper, for seasoning

1. Cook the bacon. In a large skillet over medium-high heat, melt ½ tablespoon of butter. Add the bacon to the pan and fry until it is cooked through and crispy, turning once, about 10 minutes total. Transfer the bacon to paper towels to drain and wipe the skillet with more paper towels. 2. Cook the eggs. Turn the heat down to medium. Add the remaining ½ tablespoon of butter to the skillet. Carefully crack the eggs into the skillet and cook until the whites are completely set, about 3 minutes. 3. Serve. Carefully transfer the eggs and bacon to a plate and season the eggs with salt and pepper.

Per Serving:

calories: 322 | fat: 26g | protein: 19g | carbs: 3g | net carbs: 2g | fiber: 1g

Radish Hash Browns

Prep time: 10 minutes | Cook time: 40 minutes | Serves 10

- 2 pounds radishes, trimmed
- 4 tablespoons olive oil
- 1 large egg, whisked

- ⅛ teaspoon salt
- ⅛ teaspoon black pepper

1. Shred radishes using a food processor or hand grater and squeeze out extra moisture using cheesecloth or clean dish towel. 2. In a medium skillet over medium heat, heat oil. Add radishes and stir often. Sauté 20–30 minutes until golden. Remove from heat and place into a medium bowl. 3. Stir whisked egg into bowl with salt and pepper. 4. Form ten small pancakes. Add back to hot skillet. Heat 3–5 minutes on each side until solid and brown. 5. Serve warm.

Per Serving:

calories: 63 | fat: 6g | protein: 1g | carbs: 2g | net carbs: 1g | fiber: 1g

Vegetable-Beef Hash with Nested Eggs

Prep time: 5 minutes | Cook time: 35 minutes | Serves 4

◅ 2 tablespoons good-quality olive oil
◅ ½ pound grass-fed ground beef
◅ ½ red bell pepper, diced
◅ ½ zucchini, diced
◅ ¼ onion, diced
◅ 2 teaspoons minced garlic

◅ 1½ cups low-carb tomato sauce
◅ 1 tablespoon dried basil
◅ 1 teaspoon dried oregano
◅ ⅛ teaspoon sea salt
◅ ⅛ teaspoon freshly ground black pepper
◅ 4 eggs

1. Cook the beef. In a large deep skillet over medium-high heat, warm the olive oil. Add the beef and, stirring it occasionally, cook until it is completely browned, about 10 minutes. 2. Make the sauce. Add the bell pepper, zucchini, onion, and garlic to the skillet and sauté for 3 minutes. Stir in the tomato sauce, basil, oregano, salt, and pepper, bring it to a boil, and cook for about 10 minutes. 3. Cook the eggs. Make four wells in the beef mixture using the back of a spoon. Crack an egg into each well, then cover the skillet, reduce the heat to medium-low, and simmer until the eggs are cooked through, about 10 minutes. 4. Serve. Divide the mixture between four bowls, making sure to include an egg in each serving.

Per Serving:

calories: 275 | fat: 19g | protein: 18g | carbs: 8g | net carbs: 6g | fiber: 2g

Smoked Sausage and Mushroom Breakfast Skillet

Prep time: 15 minutes | Cook time: 35 minutes | serves 6

◅ 8 large eggs
◅ ¼ cup heavy whipping cream
◅ 1 cup shredded cheddar cheese
◅ Pinch of salt
◅ Pinch of ground black pepper

◅ 12 ounces smoked sausage, sliced
◅ 1 cup diced white mushrooms
◅ ¼ cup sliced green onions, plus extra for garnish if desired

1. In a medium-sized bowl, whisk together the eggs and cream, then stir in the cheese, salt, and pepper. Set aside. 2. Preheat the oven to 400°F. 3. Heat a 12-inch cast-iron skillet or other ovenproof skillet over medium heat. Cook the sausage slices until browned on both sides, 5 to 6 minutes. Add the mushrooms and green onions and continue cooking until the mushrooms are tender, about 5 minutes. Turn off the heat. 4. Pour the egg mixture evenly over the sausage and vegetables in the skillet. Bake for 25 minutes or until the eggs are set. 5. Run a knife around the edge of the skillet before slicing. Garnish with more green onions, if desired, and serve immediately.

Leftovers can be stored in the refrigerator for up to 5 days. Reheat just until warmed; be careful not to overheat or the eggs will become rubbery.

Per Serving:

calories: 281 | fat: 23g | protein: 16g | carbs: 3g | net carbs: 2g | fiber: 0g

Parmesan Baked Eggs

Prep time: 5 minutes | Cook time: 10 minutes | Serves 1

◅ 1 tablespoon butter, cut into small pieces
◅ 2 tablespoons keto-friendly low-carb Marinara sauce
◅ 3 eggs

◅ 2 tablespoons grated Parmesan cheese
◅ ¼ teaspoon Italian seasoning
◅ 1 cup water

1. Place the butter pieces on the bottom of the oven-safe bowl. Spread the marinara sauce over the butter. Crack the eggs on top of the marinara sauce and top with the cheese and Italian seasoning. 2. Cover the bowl with aluminum foil. Pour the water and insert the trivet in the Instant Pot. Put the bowl on the trivet. 3. Set the lid in place. Select the Manual mode and set the cooking time for 10 minutes on Low Pressure. When the timer goes off, do a quick pressure release. Carefully open the lid. 4. Let the eggs cool for 5 minutes before serving.

Per Serving:

calories: 375 | fat: 30g | protein: 23g | carbs: 2g | net carbs: 2g | fiber: 0g

Italian Sausage Stacks

Prep time: 10 minutes | Cook time: 10 minutes | Serves 6

◅ 6 Italian sausage patties
◅ 4 tablespoons olive oil
◅ 2 ripe avocados, pitted
◅ 2 teaspoons fresh lime juice

◅ Salt and black pepper to taste
◅ 6 fresh eggs
◅ Red pepper flakes to garnish

1. In a skillet, warm the oil over medium heat and fry the sausage patties about 8 minutes until lightly browned and firm. Remove the patties to a plate. 2. Spoon the avocado into a bowl, mash with the lime juice, and season with salt and black pepper. Spread the mash on the sausages. 3. Boil 3 cups of water in a wide pan over high heat, and reduce to simmer (don't boil). 4. Crack each egg into a small bowl and gently put the egg into the simmering water; poach for 2 to 3 minutes. Use a perforated spoon to remove from the water on a paper towel to dry. Repeat with the other 5 eggs. Top each stack with a poached egg, sprinkle with chili flakes, salt, black pepper, and chives. Serve with turnip wedges.

Per Serving:

calories: 537 | fat: 45g | protein: 22g | carbs: 12g | net carbs: 7g | fiber: 8g

Eggs & Crabmeat with Creme Fraiche Salsa

Prep time: 10 minutes | Cook time: 10 minutes | Serves 3

- 1 tablespoon olive oil
- 6 eggs, whisked
- 1 (6 ounces) can crabmeat,
For the Salsa:
- ¾ cup crème fraiche
- ½ cup scallions, chopped
- ½ teaspoon garlic powder
- Salt and black pepper to
- flaked
- Salt and black pepper to taste
- taste
- ½ teaspoon fresh dill, chopped

1. Set a sauté pan over medium heat and warm olive oil. Crack in eggs and scramble them. Stir in crabmeat and season with salt and black pepper; cook until cooked thoroughly. 2. In a mixing dish, combine all salsa ingredients. Equally, split the egg/crabmeat mixture among serving plates; serve alongside the scallions and salsa to the side.

Per Serving:

calories: 364 | fat: 26g | protein: 25g | carbs: 5g | net carbs: 5g | fiber: 0g

Lemon-Blueberry Muffins

Prep time: 5 minutes | Cook time: 20 to 25 minutes | Makes 6 muffins

- 1¼ cups almond flour
- 3 tablespoons Swerve
- 1 teaspoon baking powder
- 2 large eggs
- 3 tablespoons melted butter
- 1 tablespoon almond milk
- 1 tablespoon fresh lemon juice
- ½ cup fresh blueberries

1. Preheat the air fryer to 350ºF (177ºC). Lightly coat 6 silicone muffin cups with vegetable oil. Set aside. 2. In a large mixing bowl, combine the almond flour, Swerve, and baking soda. Set aside. 3. In a separate small bowl, whisk together the eggs, butter, milk, and lemon juice. Add the egg mixture to the flour mixture and stir until just combined. Fold in the blueberries and let the batter sit for 5 minutes. 4. Spoon the muffin batter into the muffin cups, about two-thirds full. Air fry for 20 to 25 minutes, or until a toothpick inserted into the center of a muffin comes out clean. 5. Remove the basket from the air fryer and let the muffins cool for about 5 minutes before transferring them to a wire rack to cool completely.

Per Serving:

calories: 188 | fat: 15g | protein: 6g | carbs: 7g | net carbs: 5g | fiber: 2g

Breakfast Pizza

Prep time: 5 minutes | Cook time: 8 minutes | Serves 1

- 2 large eggs
- ¼ cup unsweetened, unflavored almond milk (or unflavored hemp milk for nut-free)
- ¼ teaspoon fine sea salt
- ⅛ teaspoon ground black pepper
- ¼ cup diced onions
- ¼ cup shredded Parmesan cheese (omit for dairy-free)
- 6 pepperoni slices (omit for vegetarian)
- ¼ teaspoon dried oregano leaves
- ¼ cup pizza sauce, warmed, for serving

1. Preheat the air fryer to 350ºF (177ºC). Grease a cake pan. 2. In a small bowl, use a fork to whisk together the eggs, almond milk, salt, and pepper. Add the onions and stir to mix. Pour the mixture into the greased pan. Top with the cheese (if using), pepperoni slices (if using), and oregano. 3. Place the pan in the air fryer and bake for 8 minutes, or until the eggs are cooked to your liking. 4. Loosen the eggs from the sides of the pan with a spatula and place them on a serving plate. Drizzle the pizza sauce on top. Best served fresh.

Per Serving:

calories: 406 | fat: 31g | protein: 24g | carbs: 8g | net carbs: 6g | fiber: 2g

Blackberry Vanilla Cake

Prep time: 10 minutes | Cook time: 25 minutes | Serves 8

- 1 cup almond flour
- 2 eggs
- ½ cup erythritol
- 2 teaspoons vanilla extract
- 1 cup blackberries
- 4 tablespoons melted butter
- ¼ cup heavy cream
- ½ teaspoon baking powder
- 1 cup water

1. In large bowl, mix all ingredients except water. Pour into 7-inch round cake pan or divide into two 4-inch pans, if needed. Cover with foil. 2. Pour water into Instant Pot and place steam rack in bottom. Place pan on steam rack and click lid closed. Press the Cake button and press the Adjust button to set heat to Less. Set time for 25 minutes. 3. When timer beeps, allow a 15-minute natural release then quick-release the remaining pressure. Let cool completely.

Per Serving:

calories: 174 | fat: 15g | protein: 10g | carbs: 17g | net carbs: 15g | fiber: 2g

Bacon, Cheese, and Avocado Melt

Prep time: 5 minutes | Cook time: 3 to 5 minutes | Serves 2

◀ 1 avocado
◀ 4 slices cooked bacon, chopped
◀ 2 tablespoons salsa

◀ 1 tablespoon heavy cream
◀ ¼ cup shredded Cheddar cheese

1. Preheat the air fryer to 400°F (204°C). 2. Slice the avocado in half lengthwise and remove the stone. To ensure the avocado halves do not roll in the basket, slice a thin piece of skin off the base. 3. In a small bowl, combine the bacon, salsa, and cream. Divide the mixture between the avocado halves and top with the cheese. 4. Place the avocado halves in the air fryer basket and air fry for 3 to 5 minutes until the cheese has melted and begins to brown. Serve warm.

Per Serving:

calories: 357 | fat: 30g | protein: 14g | carbs: 11g | net carbs: 4g | fiber: 7g

Broccoli & Colby Cheese Frittata

Prep time: 15 minutes | Cook time: 20 minutes | Serves 4

◀ 3 tablespoons olive oil
◀ ½ cup onions, chopped
◀ 1 cup broccoli, chopped
◀ 8 eggs, beaten

◀ ½ teaspoon jalapeño pepper, minced
◀ Salt and red pepper, to taste
◀ ¾ cup colby cheese, grated
◀ ¼ cup fresh cilantro, to serve

1.Set an ovenproof frying pan over medium heat and warm the oil. Add onions and sauté until caramelized. Place in the broccoli and cook until tender. Add in jalapeno pepper and eggs; season with red pepper and salt. Cook until the eggs are set. 2. Scatter colby cheese over the frittata. Set oven to 370°F and cook for approximately 12 minutes, until frittata is set in the middle. Slice into wedges and decorate with fresh cilantro before serving.

Per Serving:

calories: 426 | fat: 34g | protein: 23g | carbs: 8g | net carbs: 6g | fiber: 2g

Egg Muffins in Ham Cups

Prep time: 5 minutes | Cook time: 18 minutes | Serves 6

◀ 1 tablespoon coconut oil, melted
◀ 6 slices ham (thin-sliced is better)
◀ 6 large eggs

◀ Salt and pepper, to taste
◀ 3 tablespoons shredded Cheddar cheese (optional)

1. Preheat the oven to 400°F (205°C). Brush six cups of a muffin tin with the melted coconut oil. 2. Line each cup with 1 slice of ham. Crack 1 egg into each cup. Season with salt and pepper, then sprinkle ½ tablespoon of Cheddar cheese on each egg. 3. Bake for 13 to 18 minutes depending on how you like your egg yolks set. 4. Remove from the oven and let cool for a few minutes before carefully removing the "muffins." Refrigerate in a glass or plastic container so they don't get smushed or dried out.

Per Serving:

calories: 178 | fat: 13g | protein: 14g | carbs: 1g | net carbs: 1g | fiber: 0g

Tandoori Chicken

Prep time: 30 minutes | Cook time: 15 minutes | Serves 4

◁ 1 pound (454 g) chicken tenders, halved crosswise
◁ ¼ cup plain Greek yogurt
◁ 1 tablespoon minced fresh ginger
◁ 1 tablespoon minced garlic
◁ ¼ cup chopped fresh cilantro or parsley
◁ 1 teaspoon kosher salt
◁ ½ to 1 teaspoon cayenne pepper
◁ 1 teaspoon ground turmeric
◁ 1 teaspoon garam masala
◁ 1 teaspoon sweet smoked paprika
◁ 1 tablespoon vegetable oil or melted ghee
◁ 2 teaspoons fresh lemon juice
◁ 2 tablespoons chopped fresh cilantro

1. In a large glass bowl, toss together the chicken, yogurt, ginger, garlic, cilantro, salt, cayenne, turmeric, garam masala, and paprika to coat. Marinate at room temperature for 30 minutes, or cover and refrigerate for up to 24 hours. 2. Place the chicken in a single layer in the air fryer basket. (Discard remaining marinade.) Spray the chicken with oil. Set the air fryer to 350ºF (177ºC) for 15 minutes. Halfway through the cooking time, spray the chicken with more vegetable oil spray, and toss gently to coat. Cook for 5 minutes more. 3. Transfer the chicken to a serving platter. Sprinkle with lemon juice and toss to coat. Sprinkle with the cilantro and serve.

Per Serving:

calories: 191 | fat: 9g | protein: 24g | carbs: 3g | net carbs: 2g | fiber: 1g

Easy Chicken Chili

Prep time: 10 minutes | Cook time: 25 minutes | Serves 4

◁ 4 chicken breasts, skinless, boneless, cubed
◁ 1 tablespoon butter
◁ ½ onion, chopped
◁ 2 cups chicken broth
◁ 8 ounces diced tomatoes
◁ 2 ounces tomato puree
◁ 1 tablespoon chili powder
◁ 1 tablespoon cumin
◁ ½ tablespoon garlic powder
◁ 1 serrano pepper, minced
◁ ½ cup shredded cheddar cheese
◁ Salt and black pepper to taste

1. Set a large pan over medium-high heat and add the chicken. Cover with water and bring to a boil. Cook until no longer pink, for 10 minutes. Transfer the chicken to a flat surface to shred with forks. 2. In a large pot, pour in the butter and set over medium heat. Sauté onion until transparent for 5 minutes. Stir in the chicken, tomatoes, cumin, serrano pepper, garlic powder, tomato puree, broth, and chili powder. Adjust the seasoning and let the mixture boil. Reduce heat to simmer for about 10 minutes. Divide chili among bowls and top with shredded cheese to serve.

Per Serving:

calories: 331 | fat: 12g | protein: 44g | carbs: 9g | net carbs: 7g | fiber: 2g

Chicken Pesto Parmigiana

Prep time: 10 minutes | Cook time: 23 minutes | Serves 4

◁ 2 large eggs
◁ 1 tablespoon water
◁ Fine sea salt and ground black pepper, to taste
◁ 1 cup powdered Parmesan cheese (about 3 ounces / 85 g)
◁ 2 teaspoons Italian seasoning
◁ 4 (5-ounce / 142-g) boneless, skinless chicken breasts or
thighs, pounded to ¼ inch thick
◁ 1 cup pesto
◁ 1 cup shredded Mozzarella cheese (about 4 ounces / 113 g)
◁ Finely chopped fresh basil, for garnish (optional)
◁ Grape tomatoes, halved, for serving (optional)

1. Spray the air fryer basket with avocado oil. Preheat the air fryer to 400ºF (204ºC). 2. Crack the eggs into a shallow baking dish, add the water and a pinch each of salt and pepper, and whisk to combine. In another shallow baking dish, stir together the Parmesan and Italian seasoning until well combined. 3. Season the chicken breasts well on both sides with salt and pepper. Dip one chicken breast in the eggs and let any excess drip off, then dredge both sides of the breast in the Parmesan mixture. Spray the breast with avocado oil and place it in the air fryer basket. Repeat with the remaining 3 chicken breasts. 4. Air fry the chicken in the air fryer for 20 minutes, or until the internal temperature reaches 165ºF (74ºC) and the breading is golden brown, flipping halfway through. 5. Dollop each chicken breast with ¼ cup of the pesto and top with the Mozzarella. Return the breasts to the air fryer and cook for 3 minutes, or until the cheese is melted. Garnish with basil and serve with halved grape tomatoes on the side, if desired. 6. Store leftovers in an airtight container in the refrigerator for up to 4 days. Reheat in a preheated 400ºF (204ºC) air fryer for 5 minutes, or until warmed through.

Per Serving:

calories: 725 | fat: 54g | protein: 62g | carbs: 8g | net carbs: 7g | fiber: 1g

Cheesy Chicken and Ham Roll-ups

Prep time: 5 minutes | Cook time: 40 minutes | Serves 4

- 4 boneless, skinless chicken breast halves (approximately 2½ pounds / 1.1 kg)
- 4 slices prosciutto
- 4 slices Swiss cheese
- 1 teaspoon salt, or more as needed
- 1 teaspoon black pepper, or more as needed
- 2 teaspoons dried thyme
- Avocado oil
- 1 cup shredded Gruyère cheese
- ½ cup chicken broth, preferably homemade
- 1 tablespoon Dijon mustard
- 2 tablespoons butter
- ½ cup heavy cream
- ½ cup grated Parmesan cheese

1. One at a time, place the chicken breasts between two slices of wax paper or parchment paper and use a flat meat hammer or rolling pin to pound the chicken until each piece is ½ inch (13 mm) thick. Try to pound so that the chicken ends up in a long rectangular shape instead of a circle. 2. Cut the sliced prosciutto in half lengthwise. Place ½ slice of prosciutto and 1 slice of Swiss cheese on each piece of chicken, then roll up. Secure with toothpicks. 3. Mix the salt, pepper, and thyme in a small bowl, then use the mixture to generously season the outside of each roll. 4. Heat the oil in a skillet large enough to fit the 4 rolls. Brown the rolls on all sides, starting with the side with the seam. 5. Once browned, place ½ slice of prosciutto on top of each roll and sprinkle with Gruyère. Pour in the broth, cover the pan with a tight-fitting lid, and cook over medium-low heat for 30 minutes, or until the chicken is cooked through. 6. Use tongs to remove the chicken rolls to a broiler pan or heavy rimmed baking sheet and let rest. Preheat the broiler (on low heat if adjustable). 7. Heat the liquid left over in the skillet over medium heat. Add the mustard, then the butter, then the cream, whisking constantly. Finally, add the Parmesan cheese and whisk until melted. Taste and adjust salt and pepper as needed. 8. Place the chicken under the broiler for a minute to give the cheese a nice golden-brown color. Pour the sauce over the chicken and serve immediately.

Per Serving:

calories: 507 | fat: 40g | protein: 33g | carbs: 4g | net carbs: 4g | fiber: 0g

Chicken Nuggets

Prep time: 10 minutes | Cook time: 15 minutes | Serves 4

- 1 pound (454 g) ground chicken thighs
- ½ cup shredded Mozzarella cheese
- 1 large egg, whisked
- ½ teaspoon salt
- ¼ teaspoon dried oregano
- ¼ teaspoon garlic powder

1. In a large bowl, combine all ingredients. Form mixture into twenty nugget shapes, about 2 tablespoons each. 2. Place nuggets into ungreased air fryer basket, working in batches if needed. Adjust the temperature to 375°F (191°C) and air fry for 15 minutes, turning nuggets halfway through cooking. Let cool 5 minutes before serving.

Per Serving:

calories: 214 | fat: 13g | protein: 22g | carbs: 1g | net carbs: 1g | fiber: 0g

Grilled Paprika Chicken with Steamed Broccoli

Prep time: 10 minutes | Cook time: 22 minutes | Serves 6

- 3 tablespoons smoked paprika
- Salt and black pepper to taste
- 2 teaspoons garlic powder
- 1 tablespoon olive oil
- 6 chicken breasts
- 1 head broccoli, cut into florets

1. Place broccoli florets onto the steamer basket over the boiling water; steam approximately 8 minutes or until crisp-tender. Set aside. Grease grill grate with cooking spray and preheat to 400°F. 2. Combine paprika, salt, black pepper, and garlic powder in a bowl. Brush chicken with olive oil and sprinkle spice mixture over and massage with hands. 3. Grill chicken for 7 minutes per side until well-cooked, and plate. Serve warm with steamed broccoli.

Per Serving:

calories: 388 | fat: 32g | protein: 22g | carbs: 3g | net carbs: 2g | fiber: 1g

Chicken and Bacon Rolls

Prep time: 10 minutes | Cook time: 35 minutes | Serves 4

- 1 tablespoon fresh chives, chopped
- 8 ounces blue cheese
- 2 pounds chicken breasts, skinless, boneless, halved
- 12 bacon slices
- 2 tomatoes, chopped
- Salt and ground black pepper, to taste

1. Set a pan over medium heat, place in the bacon, cook until halfway done, remove to a plate. 2. In a bowl, stir together blue cheese, chives, tomatoes, pepper and salt. 3. Use a meat tenderizer to flatten the chicken breasts, season and lay blue cheese mixture on top. 4 Roll them up, and wrap each in a bacon slice. 5 Place the wrapped chicken breasts in a greased baking dish, and roast in the oven at 370°F for 30 minutes. 6 Serve on top of wilted kale.

Per Serving:

calories: 632 | fat: 38g | protein: 67g | carbs: 6g | net carbs: 5g | fiber: 1g

Prep time: 5 minutes | Cook time: 30 minutes | Serves 4

◄ 1½ teaspoons fine sea salt
◄ 1 teaspoon ground black pepper
◄ 1 teaspoon chopped fresh rosemary leaves
◄ 1 teaspoon chopped fresh sage
◄ 1 teaspoon chopped fresh

tarragon
◄ 1 teaspoon chopped fresh thyme leaves
◄ 1 (2 pounds / 907 g) turkey breast
◄ 3 tablespoons ghee or unsalted butter, melted
◄ 3 tablespoons Dijon mustard

1. Spray the air fryer with avocado oil. Preheat the air fryer to 390°F (199°C). 2. In a small bowl, stir together the salt, pepper, and herbs until well combined. Season the turkey breast generously on all sides with the seasoning. 3. In another small bowl, stir together the ghee and Dijon. Brush the ghee mixture on all sides of the turkey breast. 4. Place the turkey breast in the air fryer basket and air fry for 30 minutes, or until the internal temperature reaches 165°F (74°C). Transfer the breast to a cutting board and allow it to rest for 10 minutes before cutting it into ½-inch-thick slices. 5. Store leftovers in an airtight container in the refrigerator for up to 4 days or in the freezer for up to a month. Reheat in a preheated 350°F (177°C) air fryer for 4 minutes, or until warmed through.

Per Serving:

calories: 351 | fat: 18g | protein: 44g | carbs: 3g | net carbs: 2g | fiber: 1g

Prep time: 10 minutes | Cook time: 45 minutes | Serves 6

◄ 3 cups cubed leftover chicken
◄ 3 cups spinach
◄ 2 cauliflower heads, cut into florets
◄ 3 cups water
◄ 3 eggs, lightly beaten
◄ 2 cups grated sharp cheddar cheese

◄ 1 cup pork rinds, crushed
◄ ½ cup unsweetened almond milk
◄ 3 tablespoons olive oil
◄ 3 cloves garlic, minced
◄ Salt and black pepper to taste
◄ Cooking spray

1. Preheat the oven to 350°F and grease a baking dish with cooking spray. Set aside. 2. Pour the cauli florets and water in a pot; bring to boil over medium heat. Cover and steam the cauli florets for 8 minutes. Drain them through a colander and set aside. 3. Also, combine the cheddar cheese and pork rinds in a large bowl and mix in the chicken. Set aside. 4. Heat the olive oil in a skillet and cook the garlic and spinach until the spinach has wilted, about 5 minutes. Season with salt and black pepper, and add the spinach mixture and cauli florets to the chicken bowl. 5. Top with the eggs and almond milk, mix and transfer everything to the baking dish. Layer the top of the ingredients and place the dish in the oven to bake for 30 minutes. 6. By this time the edges and top must have

browned nicely, then remove the chicken from the oven, let rest for 5 minutes, and serve. Garnish with steamed and seasoned green beans.

Per Serving:

calories: 395 | fat: 31g | protein: 24g | carbs: 5g | net carbs: 3g | fiber: 2g

Prep time: 5 minutes | Cook time: 6 to 8 hours | Serves 8

◄ 4 pounds (1.8 kg) boneless, skinless chicken thighs
◄ Sea salt, to taste

◄ 2 cups chicken broth, homemade or store-bought
◄ 10 cloves garlic, peeled

Make This in a Slow Cooker: 1. Season the chicken with the salt on both sides. Place the meat, broth, and garlic in a slow cooker and cook on low for 6 to 8 hours. 2. Remove the chicken from the slow cooker, reserving any liquid. Allow it to cool slightly, then shred it with 2 forks. Taste the shredded meat and spoon some of the reserved liquid over it if needed for additional flavor. Make This in an Instant Pot: 1. Season the chicken with the salt on both sides. Place it in the multicooker and add the broth and garlic. Cook on high pressure for 12 minutes. When cooking is finished, allow the cooker to depressurize on its own; don't flip the valve to release it. 2. Store in an airtight container in the refrigerator for up to 5 days.

Per Serving:

calories: 547 | fat: 34g | protein: 54g | carbs: 3g | net carbs: 3g | fiber: 0g

Prep time: 5 minutes | Cook time: 40 minutes | Serves 4

◄ 2 chicken breasts
◄ ½ teaspoon salt
◄ ¼ teaspoon ground black
For the fries
◄ 1 pound celery root
◄ 2 tablespoons olive oil
◄ ½ teaspoon salt

pepper
◄ 2 tablespoons olive oil
◄ ¼ cup chicken broth

◄ ¼ teaspoon ground black pepper

1. Set oven to 400°F. Grease and line a baking sheet. In a bowl, mix oil, spices and the chicken; set in the fridge for 10 minutes while covered. Peel and chop celery root to form fry shapes and place into a separate bowl. Apply oil to coat and add pepper and salt for seasoning. Arrange to the baking tray in an even layer and bake for 10 minutes. 2. Take the chicken from the refrigerator and thread onto the skewers. Place over the celery, pour in the chicken broth, then set in the oven for 30 minutes. Serve with lemon wedges.

Per Serving:

calories: 293 | fat: 15g | protein: 22g | carbs: 18g | net carbs: 14g | fiber: 4g

Chicken Wings with Thyme Chutney

Prep time: 10 minutes | Cook time: 25 minutes | Serves 4

- 12 chicken wings, cut in half
- 1 tablespoon turmeric
- 1 tablespoon cumin
- 3 tablespoons fresh ginger, grated
- 1 tablespoon cilantro, chopped
- 2 tablespoons paprika
- Salt and ground black pepper, to taste
- 3 tablespoons olive oil
- Juice of ½ lime
- 1 cup thyme leaves
- ¾ cup cilantro, chopped
- 1 tablespoon water
- 1 jalapeño pepper

1.In a bowl, stir together 1 tablespoon ginger, cumin, paprika, salt, 2 tablespoons olive oil, black pepper, and turmeric. Place in the chicken wings pieces, toss to coat, and refrigerate for 20 minutes. 2. Heat the grill, place in the marinated wings, cook for 25 minutes, turning from time to time, remove and set to a serving plate. 3. Using a blender, combine thyme, remaining ginger, salt, jalapeno pepper, black pepper, lime juice, cilantro, remaining olive oil, and water, and blend well. Drizzle the chicken wings with the sauce to serve.

Per Serving:

calories: 479 | fat: 27g | protein: 45g | carbs: 10g | net carbs: 6g | fiber: 3g

Parmesan Wings with Yogurt Sauce

Prep time: 5 minutes | Cook time: 20 minutes | Serves 6

For the Dipping Sauce
- 1 cup plain yogurt
- 1 teaspoon fresh lemon juice

For the Wings
- 2 pounds (907 g) chicken wings
- Salt and black pepper to taste
- Cooking spray
- Salt and black pepper to taste
- ½ cup melted butter
- ½ cup Hot sauce
- ¼ cup grated Parmesan cheese

1. Mix the yogurt, lemon juice, salt, and black pepper in a bowl. Chill while making the chicken. 2. Preheat oven to 400ºF and season wings with salt and black pepper. Line them on a baking sheet and grease lightly with cooking spray. Bake for 20 minutes until golden brown. Mix butter, hot sauce, and Parmesan cheese in a bowl. Toss chicken in the sauce to evenly coat and plate. Serve with yogurt dipping sauce and celery strips.

Per Serving:

calories: 435 | fat: 31g | protein: 33g | carbs: 6g | net carbs: 4g | fiber: 2g

Bacon Lovers' Stuffed Chicken

Prep time: 10 minutes | Cook time: 20 minutes | Serves 4

- 4 (5-ounce / 142-g) boneless, skinless chicken breasts, pounded to ¼ inch thick
- 2 (5.2-ounce / 147-g) packages Boursin cheese (or Kite Hill brand chive
- cream cheese style spread, softened, for dairy-free)
- 8 slices thin-cut bacon or beef bacon
- Sprig of fresh cilantro, for garnish (optional)

1. Spray the air fryer basket with avocado oil. Preheat the air fryer to 400ºF (204ºC). 2. Place one of the chicken breasts on a cutting board. With a sharp knife held parallel to the cutting board, make a 1-inch-wide incision at the top of the breast. Carefully cut into the breast to form a large pocket, leaving a ½-inch border along the sides and bottom. Repeat with the other 3 chicken breasts. 3. Snip the corner of a large resealable plastic bag to form a ¾-inch hole. Place the Boursin cheese in the bag and pipe the cheese into the pockets in the chicken breasts, dividing the cheese evenly among them. 4. Wrap 2 slices of bacon around each chicken breast and secure the ends with toothpicks. Place the bacon-wrapped chicken in the air fryer basket and air fry until the bacon is crisp and the chicken's internal temperature reaches 165ºF (74ºC), about 18 to 20 minutes, flipping after 10 minutes. Garnish with a sprig of cilantro before serving, if desired. 5. Store leftovers in an airtight container in the refrigerator for up to 4 days. Reheat in a preheated 400ºF (204ºC) air fryer for 5 minutes, or until warmed through.

Per Serving:

calories: 634 | fat: 49g | protein: 43g | carbs: 3g | net carbs: 3g | fiber: 0g

Baked Pecorino Toscano Chicken

Prep time: 10 minutes | Cook time: 40 minutes | Serves 4

- 3 chicken breasts, halved
- ½ cup mayonnaise
- ½ cup buttermilk
- Salt and black pepper, to taste
- ¾ cup Pecorino Toscano
- cheese, grated
- 8 mozzarella cheese slices
- 1 teaspoon garlic powder
- 1 tablespoon parsley, chopped

1. Spray a baking dish with cooking spray and add in the chicken breasts. 2. In a bowl, combine mayonnaise, buttermilk, Pecorino Toscano cheese, garlic powder, salt, and black pepper. Spread half of the mixture over the chicken, arrange the mozzarella over, and finish with a layer of the remaining mixture. Bake in the oven for 35-40 minutes at 370ºF. Sprinkle with parsley to serve.

Per Serving:

calories: 657 | fat: 45g | protein: 60g | carbs: 3g | net carbs: 3g | fiber: 0g

Chicken Piccata with Mushrooms

Prep time: 25 minutes | Cook time: 25 minutes | Serves 4

- 1 pound (454 g) thinly sliced chicken breasts
- 1½ teaspoons salt, divided
- ½ teaspoon freshly ground black pepper
- ¼ cup ground flaxseed
- 2 tablespoons almond flour
- 8 tablespoons extra-virgin olive oil, divided
- 4 tablespoons butter, divided
- 2 cups sliced mushrooms
- ½ cup dry white wine or chicken stock
- ¼ cup freshly squeezed lemon juice
- ¼ cup roughly chopped capers
- Zucchini noodles, for serving
- ¼ cup chopped fresh flat-leaf Italian parsley, for garnish

1. Season the chicken with 1 teaspoon salt and the pepper. On a plate, combine the ground flaxseed and almond flour and dredge each chicken breast in the mixture. Set aside. 2. In a large skillet, heat 4 tablespoons olive oil and 1 tablespoon butter over medium-high heat. Working in batches if necessary, brown the chicken, 3 to 4 minutes per side. Remove from the skillet and keep warm. 3. Add the remaining 4 tablespoons olive oil and 1 tablespoon butter to the skillet along with mushrooms and sauté over medium heat until just tender, 6 to 8 minutes. 4. Add the white wine, lemon juice, capers, and remaining ½ teaspoon salt to the skillet and bring to a boil, whisking to incorporate any little browned bits that have stuck to the bottom of the skillet. Reduce the heat to low and whisk in the final 2 tablespoons butter. 5. Return the browned chicken to skillet, cover, and simmer over low heat until the chicken is cooked through and the sauce has thickened, 5 to 6 more minutes. 6. Serve chicken and mushrooms warm over zucchini noodles, spooning the mushroom sauce over top and garnishing with chopped parsley.

Per Serving:

calories: 617 | fat: 49g | protein: 30g | carbs: 10g | net carbs: 6g | fiber: 4g

Homemade Chicken Pizza Calzone

Prep time: 10 minutes | Cook time: 45 minutes | Serves 4

- 2 eggs
- 1 low carb pizza crust
- ½ cup Pecorino cheese, grated
- 1 pound chicken breasts, skinless, boneless, halved
- ½ cup sugar-free marinara sauce
- 1 teaspoon Italian seasoning
- 1 teaspoon onion powder
- 1 teaspoon garlic powder
- Salt and black pepper, to taste
- ¼ cup flax seed, ground
- 6 ounces provolone cheese

1. In a bowl, combine the Italian seasoning with onion powder, salt, Pecorino cheese, pepper, garlic powder, and flax seed. In a separate bowl, combine the eggs with pepper and salt. 2. Dip the chicken pieces in eggs, and then in seasoning mixture, lay all parts on a lined baking sheet, and bake for 25 minutes in the oven at 390º F. 3. Place the pizza crust dough on a lined baking sheet and spread half of the provolone cheese on half. Remove chicken from oven, chop it, and scatter it over the provolone cheese. Spread over the marinara sauce and top with the remaining cheese. 4. Cover with the other half of the dough and shape the pizza in a calzone. Seal the edges, set in the oven and bake for 20 minutes. Allow the calzone to cool down before slicing and enjoy.

Per Serving:

calories: 476 | fat: 29g | protein: 44g | carbs: 9g | net carbs: 6g | fiber: 3g

Nashville Hot Chicken

Prep time: 20 minutes | Cook time: 24 to 28 minutes | Serves 8

- 3 pounds (1.4 kg) bone-in, skin-on chicken pieces, breasts halved crosswise
- 1 tablespoon sea salt
- 1 tablespoon freshly ground black pepper
- 1½ cups finely ground blanched almond flour
- 1½ cups grated Parmesan cheese
- 1 tablespoon baking powder
- 2 teaspoons garlic powder, divided
- ½ cup heavy (whipping) cream
- 2 large eggs, beaten
- 1 tablespoon vinegar-based hot sauce
- Avocado oil spray
- ½ cup (1 stick) unsalted butter
- ½ cup avocado oil
- 1 tablespoon cayenne pepper (more or less to taste)
- 2 tablespoons Swerve

1. Sprinkle the chicken with the salt and pepper. 2. In a large shallow bowl, whisk together the almond flour, Parmesan cheese, baking powder, and 1 teaspoon of the garlic powder. 3. In a separate bowl, whisk together the heavy cream, eggs, and hot sauce. 4. Dip the chicken pieces in the egg, then coat each with the almond flour mixture, pressing the mixture into the chicken to adhere. Allow to sit for 15 minutes to let the breading set. 5. Set the air fryer to 400ºF (204ºC). Place the chicken in a single layer in the air fryer basket, being careful not to overcrowd the pieces, working in batches if necessary. Spray the chicken with oil and roast for 13 minutes. 6. Carefully flip the chicken and spray it with more oil. Reduce the air fryer temperature to 350ºF (177ºC). Roast for another 11 to 15 minutes, until an instant-read thermometer reads 160ºF (71ºC). 7. While the chicken cooks, heat the butter, avocado oil, cayenne pepper, Swerve, and remaining 1 teaspoon of garlic powder in a saucepan over medium-low heat. Cook until the butter is melted and the sugar substitute has dissolved. 8. Remove the chicken from the air fryer. Use tongs to dip the chicken in the sauce. Place the coated chicken on a rack over a baking sheet, and allow it to rest for 5 minutes before serving.

Per Serving:

calories: 693 | fat: 54g | protein: 46g | carbs: 7g | net carbs: 5g | fiber: 2g

Chicken Wings with Piri Piri Sauce

Prep time: 30 minutes | Cook time: 30 minutes | Serves 6

- 12 chicken wings
- 1½ ounces (43 g) butter, melted
- Sauce:
- 2 ounces (57 g) piri piri peppers, stemmed and chopped
- 1 tablespoon pimiento, seeded and minced
- 1 teaspoon onion powder
- ½ teaspoon cumin powder
- 1 teaspoon garlic paste
- 1 garlic clove, chopped
- 2 tablespoons fresh lemon juice
- ⅓ teaspoon sea salt
- ½ teaspoon tarragon

1. Steam the chicken wings using a steamer basket that is placed over a saucepan with boiling water; reduce the heat. 2. Now, steam the wings for 10 minutes over a moderate heat. Toss the wings with butter, onion powder, cumin powder, and garlic paste. 3. Let the chicken wings cool to room temperature. Then, refrigerate them for 45 to 50 minutes. 4. Roast in the preheated air fryer at 330ºF (166ºC) for 25 to 30 minutes; make sure to flip them halfway through. 5. While the chicken wings are cooking, prepare the sauce by mixing all of the sauce ingredients in a food processor. Toss the wings with prepared Piri Piri Sauce and serve.

Per Serving:

calories: 473 | fat: 35g | protein: 38g | carbs: 1g | net carbs: 1g | fiber: 0g

Chili Lime Turkey Burgers

Prep time: 10 minutes | Cook time: 3 minutes | Serves 4

- Burgers:
- 2 pounds (907 g) ground turkey
- 1½ ounces (43 g) diced red onion
- 2 cloves garlic, minced
- 1½ teaspoons minced
- Dipping Sauce:
- ½ cup sour cream
- 4 teaspoons sriracha
- 1 tablespoon chopped
- cilantro
- 1½ teaspoons salt
- 1 teaspoon Mexican chili powder
- Juice and zest of 1 lime
- ½ cup water
- cilantro, plus more for garnish
- 1 teaspoon lime juice

1. Make the burgers: In a large bowl, add the turkey, onion, garlic, cilantro, salt, chili powder, and lime juice and zest. Use a wooden spoon to mix until the ingredients are well distributed. 2. Divide the meat into four 8-ounce / 227-g balls. Use a kitchen scale to measure for accuracy. Pat the meat into thick patties, about 1 inch thick. 3. Add the water and trivet to the Instant Pot. Place the turkey patties on top of the trivet, overlapping if necessary. 4. Close the lid and seal the vent. Cook on High Pressure for 3 minutes. Quick release the steam. 5. Remove the patties from the pot. 6. Make the dipping sauce: In a small bowl, whisk together the sour cream, sriracha, cilantro, and lime juice. 7. Top each patty with 2 tablespoons of the sauce and garnish with fresh cilantro.

Per Serving:

calories: 417 | fat: 25g | protein: 44g | carbs: 5g | net carbs: 4g | fiber: 1g

Biscuit-Topped Chicken Pot Pie

Prep time: 25 minutes | Cook time: 30 minutes | Serves 4

- Biscuits:
- 1 cup almond flour
- 1½ teaspoons baking powder
- ½ teaspoon salt
- 2 tablespoons cold butter, diced into small chunks
- Filling:
- 2 tablespoons extra-virgin olive oil
- ½ small yellow onion, finely chopped
- 4 ribs celery, diced small (about 1 cup diced celery)
- 4 ounces (113 g) chopped mushrooms
- ¼ cup diced carrot (about 1 small carrot)
- 1½ teaspoons dried thyme
- 1 teaspoon salt
- 2 tablespoons heavy cream
- 1 large egg
- 2 ounces (57 g) shredded Mozzarella or Cheddar cheese
- ¼ teaspoon freshly ground black pepper
- 4 cloves garlic, minced
- ¼ cup dry white wine or chicken stock
- 1 cup heavy cream, divided
- 4 ounces (113 g) cream cheese, room temperature
- 1 teaspoon Worcestershire sauce
- 2 cups (4 or 5 thighs) cooked chicken thigh meat, diced

1. Preheat the oven to 375ºF (190ºC). 2. To make the biscuits. In a large bowl, combine the almond flour, baking powder, and salt in a large bowl and mix well. Add the cubed butter and use a fork or your hands to crumble it into the flour mixture until it resembles coarse pebbles. 3. Whisk in the heavy cream, 1 tablespoon at a time. Whisk in the egg and cheese until the mixture forms a smooth dough. Set aside. 4. To make the filling. Heat the olive oil in a large skillet over medium-high heat. Add the onion, celery, mushrooms, carrot, thyme, salt, and pepper and sauté until vegetables are just tender, 5 to 6 minutes. Add the garlic and sauté for an additional 30 seconds. 5. Add the wine or stock, stirring until most of the liquid has evaporated. Whisk in ¾ cup of heavy cream, and bring to just below a simmer. Reduce heat to low and cook, stirring occasionally, for 4 to 5 minutes. 6. In a microwave-safe bowl, combine the remaining ¼ cup of heavy cream, cream cheese, and Worcestershire sauce and microwave on high for 45 to 60 seconds, or until the cream cheese is melted. Whisk until smooth. Add the cream mixture to the vegetable mixture, stirring until smooth. 7. Add the diced chicken and stir to combine. Pour the chicken-and-vegetable mixture into an 8-inch square glass baking dish or pie pan. 8. Form the biscuit dough into 8 balls (the mixture will be sticky), flatten into 8 flat biscuits, and place atop the chicken and vegetables. Bake until bubbly and biscuits are golden brown, 16 to 18 minutes.

Per Serving:

calories: 776 | fat: 68g | protein: 32g | carbs: 13g | net carbs: 9g | fiber: 4g

Broccoli and Cheese Stuffed Chicken

Prep time: 15 minutes | Cook time: 20 minutes | Serves 4

- 2 ounces (57 g) cream cheese, softened
- 1 cup chopped fresh broccoli, steamed
- ½ cup shredded sharp Cheddar cheese
- 4 (6-ounce / 170-g) boneless,
- skinless chicken breasts
- 2 tablespoons mayonnaise
- ¼ teaspoon salt
- ¼ teaspoon garlic powder
- ⅛ teaspoon ground black pepper

1. In a medium bowl, combine cream cheese, broccoli, and Cheddar. Cut a 4-inch pocket into each chicken breast. Evenly divide mixture between chicken breasts; stuff the pocket of each chicken breast with the mixture. 2. Spread ¼ tablespoon mayonnaise per side of each chicken breast, then sprinkle both sides of breasts with salt, garlic powder, and pepper. 3. Place stuffed chicken breasts into ungreased air fryer basket so that the open seams face up. Adjust the temperature to 350ºF (177ºC) and air fry for 20 minutes, turning chicken halfway through cooking. When done, chicken will be golden and have an internal temperature of at least 165ºF (74ºC). Serve warm.

Per Serving:

calories: 368 | fat: 23g | protein: 38g | carbs: 4g | net carbs: 3g | fiber: 1g

Lemon-Rosemary Spatchcock Chicken

Prep time: 20 minutes | Cook time: 45 minutes | Serves 6 to 8

- ½ cup extra-virgin olive oil, divided
- 1 (3- to 4-pound/ 1.4- to 1.8-kg) roasting chicken
- 8 garlic cloves, roughly chopped
- 2 to 4 tablespoons chopped fresh rosemary
- 2 teaspoons salt, divided
- 1 teaspoon freshly ground black pepper, divided
- 2 lemons, thinly sliced

1. Preheat the oven to 425°F(220ºC). 2. Pour 2 tablespoons olive oil in the bottom of a 9-by-13-inch baking dish or rimmed baking sheet and swirl to coat the bottom. 3. To spatchcock the bird, place the whole chicken breast-side down on a large work surface. Using a very sharp knife, cut along the backbone, starting at the tail end and working your way up to the neck. Pull apart the two sides, opening up the chicken. Flip it over, breast-side up, pressing down with your hands to flatten the bird. Transfer to the prepared baking dish. 4. Loosen the skin over the breasts and thighs by cutting a small incision and sticking one or two fingers inside to pull the skin away from the meat without removing it. 5. To prepare the filling, in a small bowl, combine ¼ cup olive oil, garlic, rosemary, 1 teaspoon salt, and ½ teaspoon pepper and whisk together. 6. Rub the garlic-

herb oil evenly under the skin of each breast and each thigh. Add the lemon slices evenly to the same areas. 7. Whisk together the remaining 2 tablespoons olive oil, 1 teaspoon salt, and ½ teaspoon pepper and rub over the outside of the chicken. 8. Place in the oven, uncovered, and roast for 45 minutes, or until cooked through and golden brown. Allow to rest 5 minutes before carving to serve.

Per Serving:

calories: 555 | fat: 444g | protein: 34g | carbs: 6g | net carbs: 4g | fiber: 2g

Chicken Gumbo

Prep time: 20 minutes | Cook time: 30 minutes | Serves 5

- 2 sausages, sliced
- 3 chicken breasts, cubed
- 1 cup celery, chopped
- 2 tablespoons dried oregano
- 2 bell peppers, seeded and chopped
- 1 onion, peeled and chopped
- 2 cups tomatoes, chopped
- 4 cups chicken broth
- 3 tablespoons dried thyme
- 2 tablespoons garlic powder
- 2 tablespoons dry mustard
- 1 teaspoon cayenne powder
- 1 tablespoon chili powder
- Salt and black pepper, to taste
- 6 tablespoons cajun seasoning
- 3 tablespoons olive oil

1.In a pot over medium heat warm olive oil. Add the sausages, chicken, pepper, onion, dry mustard, chili, tomatoes, thyme, bell peppers, salt, oregano, garlic powder, cayenne, and cajun seasoning. 2. Cook for 10 minutes. Add the remaining ingredients and bring to a boil. Reduce the heat and simmer for 20 minutes covered. Serve hot divided between bowls.

Per Serving:

calories: 376 | fat: 17g | protein: 36g | carbs: 20g | net carbs: 16g | fiber: 6g

Paprika Chicken Wings

Prep time: 10 minutes | Cook time: 13 minutes | Serves 4

- 1 pound (454 g) boneless chicken wings
- 1 teaspoon ground paprika
- 1 teaspoon avocado oil
- ¼ teaspoon minced garlic
- ¾ cup beef broth

1. Pour the avocado oil in the instant pot. 2. Rub the chicken wings with ground paprika and minced garlic and put them in the instant pot. 3. Cook the chicken on Sauté mode for 4 minutes from each side. 4. Then add beef broth and close the lid. 5. Sauté the meal for 5 minutes more.

Per Serving:

calories: 226 | fat: 9g | protein: 34g | carbs: 1g | net carbs: 1g | fiber: 0g

Bacon-Wrapped Stuffed Chicken Breasts

Prep time: 15 minutes | Cook time: 30 minutes | Serves 4

- ½ cup chopped frozen spinach, thawed and squeezed dry
- ¼ cup cream cheese, softened
- ¼ cup grated Parmesan cheese
- 1 jalapeño, seeded and chopped
- ½ teaspoon kosher salt
- 1 teaspoon black pepper
- 2 large boneless, skinless chicken breasts, butterflied and pounded to ½-inch thickness
- 4 teaspoons salt-free Cajun seasoning
- 6 slices bacon

1. In a small bowl, combine the spinach, cream cheese, Parmesan cheese, jalapeño, salt, and pepper. Stir until well combined. 2. Place the butterflied chicken breasts on a flat surface. Spread the cream cheese mixture evenly across each piece of chicken. Starting with the narrow end, roll up each chicken breast, ensuring the filling stays inside. Season chicken with the Cajun seasoning, patting it in to ensure it sticks to the meat. 3. Wrap each breast in 3 slices of bacon. Place in the air fryer basket. Set the air fryer to 350ºF (177ºC) for 30 minutes. Use a meat thermometer to ensure the chicken has reached an internal temperature of 165ºF (74ºC). 4. Let the chicken stand 5 minutes before slicing each rolled-up breast in half to serve.

Per Serving:

calories: 467 | fat: 28g | protein: 49g | carbs: 3g | net carbs: 3g | fiber: 1g

Instant Pot Crack Chicken

Prep time: 15 minutes | Cook time: 20 minutes | Serves 4

- 1 cup chicken broth
- 1 teaspoon dried dill
- 1 teaspoon dried oregano
- ½ teaspoon onion powder
- 1 pound (454 g) skinless, boneless chicken breast
- ½ teaspoon salt
- 2 tablespoons mascarpone cheese
- 2 ounces (57 g) Cheddar cheese, shredded

1. Pour the chicken broth in the instant pot. 2. Add dried ill, oregano, onion powder, chicken breast, and salt. 3. Close and seal the lid. 4. Cook the chicken breast on Manual mode (High Pressure) for 15 minutes. 5. Then make a quick pressure release and transfer the cooked chicken in the bowl. 6. Blend the chicken broth mixture with the help of the immersion blender. 7. Add mascarpone cheese and Cheddar cheese. Sauté the liquid for 2 minutes on Sauté mode. 8. Meanwhile, shred the chicken. 9. Add it in the mascarpone mixture and mix it up. Sauté the meal for 3 minutes more.

Per Serving:

calories: 212 | fat: 9g | protein: 30g | carbs: 1g | net carbs: 1g | fiber: 0g

Buttery Garlic Chicken

Prep time: 5 minutes | Cook time: 40 minutes | Serves 2

- 2 tablespoons ghee, melted
- 2 boneless skinless chicken breasts
- Pink Himalayan salt
- Freshly ground black pepper
- 1 tablespoon dried Italian seasoning
- 4 tablespoons butter
- 2 garlic cloves, minced
- ¼ cup grated Parmesan cheese

1. Preheat the oven to 375°F. Choose a baking dish that is large enough to hold both chicken breasts and coat it with the ghee. 2. Pat dry the chicken breasts and season with pink Himalayan salt, pepper, and Italian seasoning. Place the chicken in the baking dish. 3. In a medium skillet over medium heat, melt the butter. Add the minced garlic, and cook for about 5 minutes. You want the garlic very lightly browned but not burned. 4. Remove the butter-garlic mixture from the heat, and pour it over the chicken breasts. 5. Roast the chicken in the oven for 30 to 35 minutes, until cooked through. Sprinkle some of the Parmesan cheese on top of each chicken breast. Let the chicken rest in the baking dish for 5 minutes. 6. Divide the chicken between two plates, spoon the butter sauce over the chicken, and serve.

Per Serving:

calories: 642 | fat: 45g | protein: 57g | carbs: 2g | net carbs: 2g | fiber: 0g

Merry Christmas Chicken

Prep time: 10 minutes | Cook time: 23 minutes | Serves 4

- 4 (4.2-ounce) boneless, skinless chicken breasts
- 1 medium red bell pepper, seeded and chopped
- 1 medium green bell pepper, seeded and chopped
- 4 ounces full-fat cream cheese, softened
- ¼ teaspoon salt
- ¼ teaspoon black pepper
- ¼ teaspoon paprika
- ¼ teaspoon dried parsley

1. Preheat oven to 375°F. 2. Place wax paper on both sides of chicken breasts. Use a rolling pin, kitchen mallet, or cast iron skillet to pound chicken until thin (less than ¼"). 3. In a medium microwave-safe bowl, microwave bell peppers 3 minutes. 4. In a separate medium bowl, mix cream cheese and softened bell peppers. Add salt and pepper. 5. Cover a large baking sheet with foil. Coat evenly with cooking spray. Lay flattened breasts on baking sheet. 6. Place one-quarter of the cream cheese mixture into the center of each pounded chicken and roll. Secure with a wet toothpick. 7. Garnish chicken with paprika and parsley to continue Christmas theme. 8. Bake 20 minutes. Serve warm.

Per Serving:

calories: 240 | fat: 11g | protein: 28g | carbs: 5g | net carbs: 4g | fiber: 1g

Sesame Chicken with Broccoli

Prep time: 15 minutes | Cook time: 12 minutes | Serves 2

- ½ teaspoon five spices
- ½ teaspoon sesame seeds
- ½ cup chopped broccoli
- 6 ounces (170 g) chicken
- fillet, sliced
- ½ cup chicken broth
- 1 teaspoon coconut aminos
- 1 tablespoon avocado oil

1. In the mixing bowl, mix up avocado oil, coconut aminos, and sesame seeds. 2. Add five spices. 3. After this, mix up sliced chicken fillet and coconut aminos mixture. 4. Put the chicken in the instant pot. Add chicken broth and broccoli. 5. Close and seal the lid. 6. Cook the meal on Manual mode (High Pressure) for 12 minutes. Make a quick pressure release.

Per Serving:

calories: 195 | fat: 8g | protein: 27g | carbs: 3g | net carbs: 2g | fiber: 1g

Basil Turkey Meatballs

Prep time: 5 minutes | Cook time: 10 minutes | Serves 4

- 1 pound ground turkey
- 2 tablespoons chopped sun-dried tomatoes
- 2 tablespoons chopped basil
- ½ teaspoon garlic powder
- 1 egg
- ½ teaspoon salt
- ¼ cup almond flour
- 2 tablespoons olive oil
- ½ cup shredded mozzarella cheese
- ¼ teaspoon pepper

1. Place everything, except the oil in a bowl. Mix with your hands until combined. Form into 16 balls. Heat the olive oil in a skillet over medium heat. Cook the meatballs for 4-5 minutes per each side. Serve.

Per Serving:

calories: 343 | fat: 22g | protein: 28g | carbs: 7g | net carbs: 5g | fiber: 2g

Garlic Parmesan Drumsticks

Prep time: 5 minutes | Cook time: 25 minutes | Serves 4

- 8 (4-ounce / 113-g) chicken drumsticks
- ½ teaspoon salt
- ⅛ teaspoon ground black pepper
- ½ teaspoon garlic powder
- 2 tablespoons salted butter, melted
- ½ cup grated Parmesan cheese
- 1 tablespoon dried parsley

1. Sprinkle drumsticks with salt, pepper, and garlic powder.

Place drumsticks into ungreased air fryer basket. 2. Adjust the temperature to 400ºF (204ºC) and air fry for 25 minutes, turning drumsticks halfway through cooking. Drumsticks will be golden and have an internal temperature of at least 165ºF (74ºC) when done. 3. Transfer drumsticks to a large serving dish. Pour butter over drumsticks, and sprinkle with Parmesan and parsley. Serve warm.

Per Serving:

calories: 452 | fat: 28g | protein: 45g | carbs: 2g | net carbs: 2g | fiber: 0g

Indian Chicken Breast

Prep time: 5 minutes | Cook time: 4 minutes | Serves 2

- ¼ teaspoon cumin seeds
- ½ teaspoon turmeric
- 1 teaspoon ground paprika
- ¾ teaspoon chili paste
- ½ teaspoon ground coriander
- ½ cup coconut milk
- 14 ounces (397 g) chicken breast, skinless, boneless
- 1 tablespoon coconut oil

1. Blend together the cumin seeds, turmeric, ground paprika, chili paste, coriander, coconut milk, and coconut oil. 2. When the mixture is smooth, pour it in the instant pot bowl. 3. Chop the chicken breast roughly and transfer it in the spice mixture. Stir gently with the help of the spatula. 4. Lock the lid and seal it. 5. Set the Manual mode for 4 minutes (High Pressure). 6. After this, make quick-release pressure. Enjoy!

Per Serving:

calories: 435 | fat: 17g | protein: 44g | carbs: 5g | net carbs: 3g | fiber: 2g

Lemon Thyme Roasted Chicken

Prep time: 10 minutes | Cook time: 60 minutes | Serves 6

- 1 (4-pound / 1.8-kg) chicken
- 2 teaspoons dried thyme
- 1 teaspoon garlic powder
- ½ teaspoon onion powder
- 2 teaspoons dried parsley
- 1 teaspoon baking powder
- 1 medium lemon
- 2 tablespoons salted butter, melted

1. Rub chicken with thyme, garlic powder, onion powder, parsley, and baking powder. 2. Slice lemon and place four slices on top of chicken, breast side up, and secure with toothpicks. Place remaining slices inside of the chicken. 3. Place entire chicken into the air fryer basket, breast side down. 4. Adjust the temperature to 350ºF (177ºC) and air fry for 60 minutes. 5. After 30 minutes, flip chicken so breast side is up. 6. When done, internal temperature should be 165ºF (74ºC) and the skin golden and crispy. To serve, pour melted butter over entire chicken.

Per Serving:

calories: 495 | fat: 32g | protein: 43g | carbs: 2g | net carbs: 2g | fiber: 1g

Chicken and Mixed Greens Salad

Prep time: 5 minutes | Cook time: 20 minutes | Serves 4

Chicken:
- 2 tablespoons avocado oil
- 1 pound (454 g) chicken breast, cubed
- ½ cup filtered water
- ½ teaspoon ground turmeric

Salad:
- 1 avocado, mashed
- 1 cup chopped arugula
- 1 cup chopped Swiss chard

- ½ teaspoon dried parsley
- ½ teaspoon dried basil
- ½ teaspoon kosher salt
- ½ teaspoon freshly ground black pepper

- 1 cup chopped kale
- ½ cup chopped spinach
- 2 tablespoons pine nuts, toasted

1. Combine all the chicken ingredients in the Instant Pot. 2. Secure the lid. Select the Manual mode and set the cooking time for 20 minutes at High Pressure. 3. Meanwhile, toss all the salad ingredients in a large salad bowl. 4. Once cooking is complete, do a quick pressure release. Carefully open the lid. 5. Remove the chicken to the salad bowl and serve.

Per Serving:

calories: 378 | fat: 23g | protein: 35g | carbs: 8g | net carbs: 4g | fiber: 4g

Chipotle Chicken Fajita Bowl

Prep time: 10 minutes | Cook time: 30 minutes | Serves 4

- 3 tablespoons unsalted butter
- 1½ pounds boneless, skinless chicken thighs, cut into thin strips
- ¼ teaspoon salt
- 1 small yellow onion, peeled and diced
- 1 large green bell pepper, seeded and diced
- 2 tablespoons taco seasoning

- 6 cups chopped romaine lettuce
- 1 cup shredded Mexican cheese
- ½ cup full-fat sour cream
- 2 large avocados, peeled, pitted, and diced
- 1 small tomato, chopped
- 4 tablespoons finely chopped cilantro

1. In a large skillet over medium heat, add butter and fry chicken for 5 minutes while stirring just to brown. Season chicken with salt. Sauté 10–15 minutes, stirring regularly. 2. Add onion, bell pepper, and taco seasoning. Reduce heat to low and cook 7–10 minutes. Stir often until vegetables have softened. 3. Distribute lettuce evenly to serving bowls, then add cooked chicken and vegetables. Top with cheese, sour cream, diced avocados, tomato, and cilantro.

Per Serving:

calories: 732 | fat: 57g | protein: 38g | carbs: 20g | net carbs: 10g | fiber: 10g

Chapter 5 Beef, Pork, and Lamb

Cardamom Pork Ribs

Prep time: 15 minutes | Cook time: 25 minutes | Serves 3

◁ ¼ teaspoon ground cardamom
◁ ½ teaspoon minced ginger
◁ 4 tablespoons apple cider vinegar
◁ ¼ teaspoon sesame seeds
◁ 10 ounces (283 g) pork ribs, chopped
◁ ¼ teaspoon chili flakes
◁ 1 tablespoon avocado oil

1. In the mixing bowl, mix up ground cardamom. Minced ginger, apple cider vinegar, sesame seeds, chili flakes, and avocado oil. 2. Then brush the pork ribs with the cardamom mixture and leave for 10 minutes to marinate. 3. After this, heat up the instant pot on Sauté mode for 2 minutes. 4. Add the marinated pork ribs and all remaining marinade. 5. Cook the pork ribs on Sauté mode for 25 minutes. Flip the ribs on another side every 5 minutes.

Per Serving:
calories: 271 | fat: 17g | protein: 1g | carbs: 1g | net carbs: 1g | fiber: 0g

Cheese Shell Tacos

Prep time: 5 minutes | Cook time: 20 minutes | Serves 6

◁ Cheese Shells
◁ (makes 6 large shells)
◁ 2 cups shredded cheddar cheese
◁ Taco Filling
◁ ½ pound ground beef
◁ 1 tablespoon sugar-free taco seasoning, homemade or store-bought
◁ ¼ cup water
◁ Topping Suggestions
◁ 2 cups shredded lettuce
◁ 1 medium tomato, diced
◁ 1 avocado, sliced
◁ ¾ cup sour cream
◁ ⅓ cup chopped yellow onions
◁ Fresh cilantro, for garnish (optional)

1. Preheat the oven to 375°F. Line 2 baking sheets with parchment paper. 2. Arrange the shredded cheese into 6 piles on the parchment-lined baking sheet, leaving several inches between piles so the shells don't run together. Bake for 7 to 10 minutes, until the edges start to brown and the cheese is no longer runny. 3. Meanwhile, prop up a wooden spoon or two kabob skewers, spaced 1 inch apart, with two cups or cans. 4. Remove the melted cheese rounds from the oven and, while the cheese is still flexible, use a spatula to transfer the cheese and drape over a wooden spoon handle or skewers. Prop up the wooden spoon or skewers with 2 cups or cans. The shell will harden as it cools. Repeat this process with the remaining shells. 5. In a medium-sized skillet, brown the ground beef, then drain the fat. Add the taco seasoning and water. Stir well, bring to a simmer, and allow to reduce for 3 to 5 minutes. Remove from the heat. 6. Fill each cheese shell with meat and the toppings of your choice. 7. Garnish with cilantro, if desired.

Per Serving:
calories: 389 | fat: 30g | protein: 28g | carbs: 3g | net carbs: 3g | fiber: 0g

Pork Casserole

Prep time: 15 minutes | Cook time: 30 minutes | Serves 4

◁ 1 pound (454 g) ground pork
◁ 1 large yellow squash, thinly sliced
◁ Salt and black pepper to taste
◁ 1 clove garlic, minced
◁ 4 green onions, chopped
◁ 1 cup chopped cremini mushrooms
◁ 1 (15 -ounce / 425-g) can diced tomatoes
◁ ½ cup pork rinds, crushed
◁ ¼ cup chopped parsley
◁ 1 cup cottage cheese
◁ 1 cup Mexican cheese blend
◁ 3 tablespoons olive oil
◁ ⅓ cup water

1. Preheat the oven to 370ºF. 2. Heat the olive oil in a skillet over medium heat, add the pork, season it with salt and black pepper, and cook for 3 minutes or until no longer pink. Stir occasionally while breaking any lumps apart. 3. Add the garlic, half of the green onions, mushrooms, and 2 tablespoons of pork rinds. Cook for 3 minutes. Stir in the tomatoes, half of the parsley, and water. Cook further for 3 minutes, and then turn the heat off. 4. Mix the remaining parsley, cottage cheese, and Mexican cheese blend. Set aside. Sprinkle the bottom of a baking dish with 3 tablespoons of pork rinds; top with half of the squash and a season of salt, 2/3 of the pork mixture, and the cheese mixture. Repeat the layering process a second time to exhaust the ingredients. 5. Cover the baking dish with foil and bake for 20 minutes. After, remove the foil and brown the top of the casserole with the broiler side of the oven for 2 minutes. Remove the dish when ready and serve warm.

Per Serving:
calories: 717 | fat: 58g | protein: 36g | carbs: 14g | net carbs: 9g | fiber: 5g

Ground Beef Stroganoff

Prep time: 10 minutes | Cook time: 20 minutes | serves 6

◄ 1½ pounds ground beef
◄ ½ cup finely chopped onions
◄ 2 cloves garlic, minced
◄ 4 ounces white mushrooms, sliced
◄ 4 ounces cream cheese (½ cup), softened
◄ 1 cup beef broth
◄ ¼ cup heavy whipping cream
◄ ¼ cup water
◄ 1 tablespoon Worcestershire sauce
◄ Salt and ground black pepper
◄ ½ cup sour cream

1. In a large skillet over medium heat, cook the ground beef with the onions, garlic, and mushrooms, crumbling the meat with a large spoon it as cooks, until the meat is browned and the onions are softened and translucent, about 10 minutes. Drain the fat, if necessary. 2. Stir in the cream cheese and cook until melted. Add the broth, cream, water, and Worcestershire sauce and stir to combine. Continue to simmer for 5 minutes. 3. Season to taste with salt and pepper. Stir in the sour cream and serve. Leftovers can be stored in an airtight container in the refrigerator for up to 5 days.

Per Serving:

calories: 396 | fat: 32g | protein: 22g | carbs: 23g | net carbs: 2g | fiber: 0g

Pepperoni Pizza Casserole

Prep time: 10 minutes | Cook time: 30 minutes | Serves 4

◄ 1 tablespoon olive oil
◄ ¼ white onion, diced
◄ 1 pound (454 g) pepperoni, roughly chopped
◄ 2 teaspoons dried oregano
◄ 1 teaspoon red pepper flakes
◄ 2 eggs
◄ ½ cup heavy (whipping)
cream
◄ 2 tablespoons tomato paste
◄ 1 cup shredded Mozzarella cheese, divided
◄ Salt, to taste
◄ Freshly ground black pepper, to taste

1. Preheat the oven to 350ºF (180ºC). 2. In a large skillet over medium heat, heat the olive oil. 3. Add the onion and sauté for 5 to 7 minutes until softened and translucent. 4. Stir in the pepperoni, oregano, and red pepper flakes and remove from the heat. 5. In a medium bowl, whisk the eggs, cream, tomato paste, and ½ cup of Mozzarella. Season with salt and pepper and whisk again. 6. Spread the pepperoni and onions in a 7-by-11-inch baking dish. Pour the egg mixture over it. Gently shake the dish and tap it on the counter to ensure the mixture makes it through to the bottom and sides of the dish. Top with the remaining ½ cup of Mozzarella. Bake for 25 minutes. Refrigerate leftovers in an airtight container for up to 1 week.

Per Serving:

calories: 772 | fat: 68g | protein: 36g | carbs: 4g | net carbs: 3g | fiber: 1g

Easy Zucchini Beef Lasagna

Prep time: 10 minutes | Cook time: 45 minutes | Serves 4

◄ 1 pound ground beef
◄ 2 large zucchinis, sliced lengthwise
◄ 3 cloves garlic
◄ 1 medium white onion, finely chopped
◄ 3 tomatoes, chopped
◄ Salt and black pepper to
taste
◄ 2 teaspoons sweet paprika
◄ 1 teaspoon dried thyme
◄ 1 teaspoon dried basil
◄ 1 cup shredded mozzarella cheese
◄ 1 tablespoon olive oil
◄ Cooking spray

1. Preheat the oven to 370ºF and lightly grease a baking dish with cooking spray. 2. Heat the olive oil in a skillet and cook the beef for 4 minutes while breaking any lumps as you stir. Top with onion, garlic, tomatoes, salt, paprika, and pepper. Stir and continue cooking for 5 minutes. 3. Then, lay ⅓ of the zucchini slices in the baking dish. Top with ⅓ of the beef mixture and repeat the layering process two more times with the same quantities. Season with basil and thyme. 4. Finally, sprinkle the mozzarella cheese on top and tuck the baking dish in the oven. Bake for 35 minutes. Remove the lasagna and let it rest for 10 minutes before serving.

Per Serving:

calories: 396 | fat: 27g | protein: 27g | carbs: 12g | net carbs: 9g | fiber: 3g

Coconut Milk Ginger Marinated Pork Tenderloin

Prep time: 5 minutes | Cook time: 25 minutes | Serves 4

◄ ¼ cup coconut oil, divided
◄ 1½ pounds boneless pork chops, about ¾ inch thick
◄ 1 tablespoon grated fresh ginger
◄ 2 teaspoons minced garlic
◄ 1 cup coconut milk
◄ 1 teaspoon chopped fresh basil
◄ Juice of 1 lime
◄ ½ cup shredded unsweetened coconut

1. Brown the pork. In a large skillet over medium heat, warm 2 tablespoons of the coconut oil. Add the pork chops to the skillet and brown them all over, turning them several times, about 10 minutes in total. 2. Braise the pork. Move the pork to the side of the skillet and add the remaining 2 tablespoons of coconut oil. Add the ginger and garlic and sauté until they've softened, about 2 minutes. Stir in the coconut milk, basil, and lime juice and move the pork back to the center of the skillet. Cover the skillet and simmer until the pork is just cooked through and very tender, 12 to 15 minutes. 3. Serve. Divide the pork chops between four plates and top them with the shredded coconut.

Per Serving:

calories: 479 | fat: 38g | protein: 32g | carbs: 6g | net carbs: 3g | fiber: 3g

Prep time: 15 minutes | Cook time: 28 to 30 minutes | Serves 6

◀ Avocado oil spray
◀ 8 ounces (227 g) Italian sausage, casings removed
◀ ½ cup chopped mushrooms
◀ ¼ cup diced onion
◀ 1 teaspoon Italian seasoning
◀ Sea salt and freshly ground

◀ black pepper, to taste
◀ 1 cup keto-friendly marinara sauce
◀ 3 bell peppers, halved and seeded
◀ 3 ounces (85 g) provolone cheese, shredded

1. Spray a large skillet with oil and place it over medium-high heat. Add the sausage and cook for 5 minutes, breaking up the meat with a wooden spoon. Add the mushrooms, onion, and Italian seasoning, and season with salt and pepper. Cook for 5 minutes more. Stir in the marinara sauce and cook until heated through. 2. Scoop the sausage filling into the bell pepper halves. 3. Set the air fryer to 350ºF (177ºC). Arrange the peppers in a single layer in the air fryer basket, working in batches if necessary. Air fry for 15 minutes. 4. Top the stuffed peppers with the cheese and air fry for 3 to 5 minutes more, until the cheese is melted and the peppers are tender.

Per Serving:

calories: 205 | fat: 16g | protein: 10g | carbs: 6g | net carbs: 5g | fiber: 1g

Prep time: 5 minutes | Cook time: 15 minutes | Serves 4

◀ 4 (5-ounce / 142-g) pork chops
◀ 1 teaspoon salt
◀ ½ teaspoon pepper
◀ 2 tablespoons avocado oil
◀ 1 cup chopped button mushrooms
◀ ½ medium onion, sliced

◀ 1 clove garlic, minced
◀ 1 cup chicken broth
◀ ¼ cup heavy cream
◀ 4 tablespoons butter
◀ ¼ teaspoon xanthan gum
◀ 1 tablespoon chopped fresh parsley

1. Sprinkle pork chops with salt and pepper. Place avocado oil and mushrooms in Instant Pot and press the Sauté button. Sauté 3 to 5 minutes until mushrooms begin to soften. Add onions and pork chops. Sauté additional 3 minutes until pork chops reach a golden brown. 2. Add garlic and broth to Instant Pot. Click lid closed. Press the Manual button and adjust time for 15 minutes. When timer beeps, allow a 10-minute natural release. Quick-release the remaining pressure. 3. Remove lid and place pork chops on plate. Press the Sauté button and add heavy cream, butter, and xanthan gum. Reduce for 5 to 10 minutes or until sauce begins to thicken. Add pork chops back into pot. Serve warm topped with mushroom sauce and parsley.

Per Serving:

calories: 516 | fat: 40g | protein: 32g | carbs: 3g | net carbs: 2g | fiber: 1g

Prep time: 10 minutes | Cook time: 0 minutes | Serves 4

Rolls:
◀ 1 medium zucchini (about 7 ounces/200 g)
◀ 1 cup (120 g) cooked beef
Dipping Sauce:
◀ ¼ cup (60 ml) extra-virgin olive oil or refined avocado oil

◀ strips
◀ 5 medium radishes, sliced thin

◀ 2 tablespoons hot sauce
◀ 2 teaspoons fresh lime juice

1. Place the zucchini on a cutting board and, using a vegetable peeler, peel long strips from the zucchini until it is next to impossible to create a full, long strip. 2. Place a zucchini strip on a cutting board, with a short end facing you. Place a couple of pieces of beef and 3 or 4 radish slices at the short end closest to you. Roll it up, then stab with a toothpick to secure. Repeat with the remaining zucchini strips, placing the completed rolls on a serving plate. 3. In a small serving dish, whisk together the dipping sauce ingredients. Serve the dipping sauce alongside the rolls.

Per Serving:

calories: 370 | fat: 33g | protein: 14g | carbs: 4g | net carbs: 3g | fiber: 1g

Prep time: 10 minutes | Cook time: 9 minutes | Serves 2

◀ 5 ounces (142 g) ground beef
◀ 1 teaspoon ground black pepper
◀ 1 tablespoon sesame oil
◀ 1 cup lettuce, chopped
◀ ¼ cup Monterey Jack

◀ cheese, shredded
◀ 2 ounces (57 g) dill pickles, sliced
◀ 1 ounce (28 g) scallions, chopped
◀ 1 tablespoon heavy cream

1. In a mixing bowl, combine the ground beef and ground black pepper.shape the mixture into mini burgers. 2. Pour the sesame oil in the Instant Pot and heat for 3 minutes on Sauté mode. 3. Place the mini hamburgers in the hot oil and cook for 3 minutes on each side. 4. Meanwhile, in a salad bowl, mix the chopped lettuce, shredded cheese, dill pickles, scallions, and heavy cream. Toss to mix well. 5. Top the salad with cooked mini burgers. Serve immediately.

Per Serving:

calories: 284 | fat: 19g | protein: 26g | carbs: 4g | net carbs: 2g | fiber: 1g

Rib Eye with Chimichurri Sauce

Prep time: 15 minutes | Cook time: 15 minutes | Serves 4

For The Chimichurri:
- ½ cup good-quality olive oil
- ½ cup finely chopped fresh parsley
- 2 tablespoons red wine vinegar
- 2 tablespoons finely chopped fresh cilantro

For The Steak:
- 4 (5-ounce) rib eye steaks
- 1 tablespoon good-quality olive oil

- 1½ tablespoons minced garlic
- 1 tablespoon finely chopped chile pepper
- ½ teaspoon sea salt
- ¼ teaspoon freshly ground black pepper

- Sea salt, for seasoning
- Freshly ground black pepper, for seasoning

Make The Chimichurri: 1. In a medium bowl, stir together the olive oil, parsley, vinegar, cilantro, garlic, chile, salt, and pepper. Let it stand for 15 minutes to mellow the flavors. Make The Steak: 1. Prepare the steaks. Let the steaks come to room temperature and lightly oil them with the olive oil and season them with salt and pepper. 2. Grill the steaks. Preheat the grill to high heat. Grill the steaks for 6 to 7 minutes per side for medium (140°F internal temperature) or until they're done the way you like them. 3. Rest and serve. Let the steaks rest for 10 minutes and then serve them topped with generous spoonfuls of the chimichurri sauce.

Per Serving:

calories: 503 | fat: 42g | protein: 29g | carbs: 1g | net carbs: 1g | fiber: 0g

Pepper Steak Stir-Fry

Prep time: 10 minutes | Cook time: 20 minutes | Serves 3

- 1 tablespoon extra-virgin olive oil, or more as needed
- 1 red bell pepper, cored, seeded, and cut into ½-inch-wide strips
- 1 green bell pepper, cored, seeded, and cut into ½-inch-wide strips
- ½ medium onion, thinly sliced
- 2 garlic cloves, minced

- 1 pound (454 g) flank steak, cut into ½-inch-wide strips
- Pink Himalayan sea salt
- Freshly ground black pepper
- ¼ cup coconut aminos or soy sauce
- 2 tablespoons granulated erythritol
- 1 teaspoon ground ginger
- Cauliflower rice, cooked (optional)

1. In a large sauté pan or skillet, heat 1 tablespoon of olive oil over medium heat. Add the bell peppers, onion, and garlic and cook until tender, about 5 minutes. Transfer the vegetables to a bowl. 2. Season the steak with salt and pepper and transfer it to the skillet. If there is no oil left in the pan, add about 1 teaspoon olive oil. 3. Increase the temperature to medium high and cook the steak for

5 to 7 minutes, with 5 minutes being for medium and 7 minutes being for well done. 4. In a small bowl, mix the coconut aminos, erythritol, and ginger. 5. Return the pepper mixture to the pan and drizzle with the sauce. 6. Reduce the heat to medium low and simmer for about 5 minutes, until the sauce reduces by about half, then serve with the cauliflower rice, if desired.

Per Serving:

calories: 316 | fat: 16g | protein: 35g | carbs: 8g | net carbs: 6g | fiber: 2g

Filipino Pork Loin

Prep time: 10 minutes | Cook time: 40 minutes | Serves 4

- 1 pound (454 g) pork loin, chopped
- ½ cup apple cider vinegar
- 1 cup chicken broth

- 1 chili pepper, chopped
- 1 tablespoon coconut oil
- 1 teaspoon salt

1. Melt the coconut oil on Sauté mode. 2. When it is hot, and chili pepper and cook it for 2 minutes. Stir it. 3. Add chopped pork loin and salt. Cook the ingredients for 5 minutes. 4. After this, add apple cider vinegar and chicken broth. 5. Close and seal the lid and cook the Filipino pork for 30 minutes on High Pressure (Manual mode). Then make a quick pressure release.

Per Serving:

calories: 320 | fat:19 g | protein: 32g | carbs: 0g | net carbs: 0g | fiber: 0g

Eggplant Pork Lasagna

Prep time: 20 minutes | Cook time: 30 minutes | Serves 6

- 2 eggplants, sliced
- 1 teaspoon salt
- 10 ounces (283 g) ground pork
- 1 cup Mozzarella, shredded

- 1 tablespoon unsweetened tomato purée
- 1 teaspoon butter, softened
- 1 cup chicken stock

1. Sprinkle the eggplants with salt and let sit for 10 minutes, then pat dry with paper towels. 2. In a mixing bowl, mix the ground pork, butter, and tomato purée. 3. Make a layer of the sliced eggplants in the bottom of the Instant Pot and top with ground pork mixture. 4. Top the ground pork with Mozzarella and repeat with remaining ingredients. 5. Pour in the chicken stock. Close the lid. Select Manual mode and set cooking time for 30 minutes on High Pressure. 6. When timer beeps, use a natural pressure release for 10 minutes, then release the remaining pressure and open the lid. 7. Cool for 10 minutes and serve.

Per Serving:

calories: 136 | fat: 4g | protein: 16g | carbs: 12g | net carbs: 5g | fiber: 7g

Crispy Pork Lettuce Wraps

Prep time: 10 minutes | Cook time: 10 minutes | Serves 4

- 2 tablespoons olive oil
- 2 garlic cloves, minced
- ¼ cup sesame oil, divided
- 1 pound (454 g) pork, sliced thinly
- 2 to 3 tablespoons gluten-free soy sauce
- 1 teaspoon chili garlic sauce
- 2 to 3 tablespoons rice wine vinegar
- 1 large carrot, julienned
- ½ large cucumber, julienned
- 2 tablespoons chopped fresh cilantro
- 1 small head butter lettuce, or romaine lettuce

1. In a large skillet over medium heat, heat the olive oil. 2. Add the garlic and sauté for 1 to 2 minutes until fragrant. 3. Add 2 tablespoons of sesame oil and the pork. Cook for 5 to 6 minutes or until the pork is cooked through and starts to get crispy. Remove from the heat. 4. In a small bowl, whisk the remaining 2 tablespoons of sesame oil, the soy sauce, chili garlic sauce, and vinegar. 5. Add the carrot and cucumber to the dressing and toss to combine. 6. Assemble the lettuce wraps: Layer pork and veggies in lettuce cups and serve with a sprinkle of fresh cilantro.

Per Serving:

calories: 340 | fat: 24g | protein: 23g | carbs: 8g | net carbs: 7g | fiber: 1g

Weeknight Chili

Prep time: 10 minutes | Cook time: 35 minutes | Serves 6

- ¼ cup extra-virgin olive oil
- 1 small yellow onion, diced
- 1 green bell pepper, diced
- 1 pound (454 g) ground beef, preferably grass-fed
- ½ pound (227 g) ground Italian sausage (hot or sweet)
- 1 tablespoon chili powder
- 2 teaspoons ground cumin
- 1½ teaspoons salt
- 6 cloves garlic, minced
- 1 (14½-ounce / 411-g) can diced tomatoes, with juices
- 1 (6-ounce / 170-g) can tomato paste
- 2 cups water
- 2 ripe avocados, pitted, peeled, and chopped
- 1 cup sour cream

1. Heat the olive oil in a large pot over medium heat. Add the onion and bell pepper and sauté for 5 minutes, or until just tender. 2. Add the ground beef and sausage and cook until meat is browned, 5 to 6 minutes, stirring to break into small pieces. Add the chili powder, cumin, salt, and garlic and sauté, stirring frequently, for 1 minute, until fragrant. 3. Add the tomatoes and their juices, tomato paste, and water, stirring to combine well. Bring the mixture to a boil, reduce heat to low, cover, and simmer for 15 to 20 minutes, stirring occasionally. Add additional water for a thinner chili if desired. 4. Serve hot, garnished with chopped avocado and sour cream.

Per Serving:

calories: 591 | fat: 49g | protein: 25g | carbs: 18g | net carbs: 10g | fiber: 8g

Grilled Skirt Steak with Jalapeño Compound Butter

Prep time: 10 minutes | Cook time: 10 minutes | Serves 4

- ¼ cup unsalted grass-fed butter, at room temperature
- ½ jalapeño pepper, seeded and minced very finely
- Zest and juice of ½ lime
- ½ teaspoon sea salt
- 4 (4-ounce) skirt steaks
- 1 tablespoon olive oil
- Sea salt, for seasoning
- Freshly ground black pepper, for seasoning

1. Make the compound butter. In a medium bowl, stir together the butter, jalapeño pepper, lime zest, lime juice, and salt until everything is well combined. Lay a piece of plastic wrap on a clean work surface and spoon the butter mixture into the middle. Form the butter into a log about 1 inch thick by folding the plastic wrap over the butter and twisting the two ends in opposite directions. Roll the butter log on the counter to smooth the edges and put it in the freezer until it's very firm, about 4 hours. 2. Grill the steak. Preheat the grill to high heat. Lightly oil the steaks with the olive oil and season them lightly with salt and pepper. Grill the steaks for about 5 minutes per side for medium (140°F internal temperature) or until they're done the way you like them. 3. Rest and serve. Let the steaks rest for 10 minutes and serve them sliced across the grain, topped with a thick slice of the compound butter.

Per Serving:

calories: 404 | fat: 32g | protein: 29g | carbs: 0g | net carbs: 0g | fiber: 0g

Pork Goulash with Cauliflower

Prep time: 10 minutes | Cook time: 15 minutes | Serves 4

- 1 red bell pepper, seeded and chopped
- 2 tablespoons olive oil
- 1½ pounds ground pork
- Salt and black pepper, to taste
- 2 cups cauliflower florets
- 1 onion, chopped
- 14 ounces canned diced tomatoes
- ¼ teaspoon garlic powder
- 1 tablespoon tomato puree
- 1½ cups water

1. Heat olive oil in a pan over medium heat, stir in the pork, and brown for 5 minutes. Place in the bell pepper and onion, and cook for 4 minutes. Stir in the water, tomatoes, and cauliflower, bring to a simmer and cook for 5 minutes while covered. Place in the black pepper, tomato paste, salt, and garlic powder. Stir well, remove from the heat, split into bowls, and enjoy.

Per Serving:

calories: 559 | fat: 43g | protein: 31g | carbs:11 g | net carbs: 6g | fiber: 5g

North African Lamb

Prep time: 10 minutes | Cook time: 10 minutes | Serves 4

- ◄ 2 teaspoons paprika
- ◄ 2 garlic cloves, minced
- ◄ 2 teaspoons dried oregano
- ◄ 2 tablespoons sumac
- ◄ 12 lamb cutlets
- ◄ ¼ cup sesame oil
- ◄ 2 teaspoons cumin
- ◄ 4 carrots, sliced
- ◄ ¼ cup fresh parsley, chopped
- ◄ 2 teaspoons harissa paste
- ◄ 1 tablespoon red wine vinegar
- ◄ Salt and black pepper, to taste
- ◄ 2 tablespoons black olives, sliced
- ◄ 2 cucumbers, sliced

1. In a bowl, combine the cutlets with the paprika, oregano, black pepper, 2 tablespoons water, half of the oil, sumac, garlic, and salt, and rub well. Add the carrots in a pot, cover with water, bring to a boil over medium heat, cook for 2 minutes then drain before placing them in a salad bowl. 2. Place the cucumbers and olives to the carrots. In another bowl, combine the harissa with the rest of the oil, a splash of water, parsley, vinegar, and cumin. Place this to the carrots mixture, season with pepper and salt, and toss well to coat. 3. Preheat the grill to medium heat and arrange the lamb cutlets on it, grill each side for 3 minutes, and split among separate plates. Serve alongside the carrot salad.

Per Serving:

calories: 354 | fat: 23g | protein: 27g | carbs: 7g | net carbs: 4g | fiber: 3g

Five-Spice Pork Belly

Prep time: 10 minutes | Cook time: 17 minutes | Serves 4

- ◄ 1 pound (454 g) unsalted pork belly

Sauce:
- ◄ 1 tablespoon coconut oil
- ◄ 1 (1-inch) piece fresh ginger, peeled and grated
- ◄ 2 cloves garlic, minced
- ◄ ½ cup beef or chicken broth
- ◄ ¼ to ½ cup Swerve confectioners'-style sweetener or equivalent
- ◄ 2 teaspoons Chinese five-spice powder

    amount of liquid or powdered sweetener
- ◄ 3 tablespoons wheat-free tamari, or ½ cup coconut aminos
- ◄ 1 green onion, sliced, plus more for garnish

1. Spray the air fryer basket with avocado oil. Preheat the air fryer to 400ºF (204ºC). 2. Cut the pork belly into ½-inch-thick slices and season well on all sides with the five-spice powder. Place the slices in a single layer in the air fryer basket (if you're using a smaller air fryer, work in batches if necessary) and cook for 8 minutes, or until cooked to your liking, flipping halfway through. 3. While the pork belly cooks, make the sauce: Heat the coconut oil in a small saucepan over medium heat. Add the ginger and garlic and sauté for 1 minute, or until fragrant. Add the broth, sweetener, and tamari and simmer for 10 to 15 minutes, until thickened. Add the green onion and cook for another minute, until the green onion is softened. Taste and adjust the seasoning to your liking. 4. Transfer the pork belly to a large bowl. Pour the sauce over the pork belly and coat well. Place the pork belly slices on a serving platter and garnish with sliced green onions. 5. Best served fresh. Store leftovers in an airtight container in the fridge for up to 4 days. Reheat in a preheated 400ºF (204ºC) air fryer for 3 minutes, or until heated through.

Per Serving:

calories: 533 | fat: 49g | protein: 14g | carbs: 6g | net carbs: 3g | fiber: 3g

Pork Meatballs

Prep time: 10 minutes | Cook time: 12 minutes | Makes 18 meatballs

- ◄ 1 pound (454 g) ground pork
- ◄ 1 large egg, whisked
- ◄ ½ teaspoon garlic powder
- ◄ ½ teaspoon salt
- ◄ ½ teaspoon ground ginger
- ◄ ¼ teaspoon crushed red pepper flakes
- ◄ 1 medium scallion, trimmed and sliced

1. Combine all ingredients in a large bowl. Spoon out 2 tablespoons mixture and roll into a ball. Repeat to form eighteen meatballs total. 2. Place meatballs into ungreased air fryer basket. Adjust the temperature to 400ºF (204ºC) and air fry for 12 minutes, shaking the basket three times throughout cooking. Meatballs will be browned and have an internal temperature of at least 145ºF (63ºC) when done. Serve warm.

Per Serving:

calories: 77 | fat: 5g | protein: 7g | carbs: 0g | net carbs: 0g | fiber: 0g

Pork and Mushroom Bake

Prep time: 5 minutes | Cook time: 45 minutes | Serves 6

- ◄ 1 onion, chopped
- ◄ 2 (10½ ounces) cans mushroom soup
- ◄ 6 pork chops
- ◄ ½ cup sliced mushrooms
- ◄ Salt and ground pepper, to taste

1. Preheat the oven to 370ºF. 2. Season the pork chops with salt and black pepper, and place in a baking dish. Combine the mushroom soup, mushrooms, and onion, in a bowl. Pour this mixture over the pork chops. Bake for 45 minutes.

Per Serving:

calories: 302 | fat: 10g | protein: 42g | carbs: 9g | net carbs: 8g | fiber: 1g

Sloppy Joe Chili

Prep time: 20 minutes | Cook time: 40 minutes | Serves 6

Spice Blend:
- 1 tablespoon smoked paprika
- 1 teaspoon granulated garlic
- 1 teaspoon granulated onion

- ½ teaspoon sea salt
- ½ teaspoon ground black pepper

Sloppy Joe Mixture:
- 2 slices thick-cut bacon, chopped
- 1 large yellow onion, finely diced
- 1 medium green bell pepper, finely diced
- 1 medium red bell pepper, finely diced
- Sea salt and ground black pepper, to taste
- Pinch of ground cinnamon
- 1 clove garlic, minced or grated

- 4 portobello mushrooms, cut into ½-inch pieces
- 2 pounds (907 g) ground beef, 85% lean
- 1 (28-ounce / 794-g) can diced tomatoes
- 3 tablespoons coconut aminos
- 2 tablespoons ketchup, homemade or store-bought
- 1 tablespoon apple cider vinegar
- 2 teaspoons Dijon mustard

For Garnish:
- 1 small red onion, diced
- ⅓ cup full-fat sour cream

- (optional)

Make This on the Stovetop: 1. In a small bowl, mix together all the ingredients for the spice blend. Set aside. 2. Place the bacon in a large stockpot over medium-high heat. Cook, stirring occasionally, until the fat has rendered, about 4 minutes. 3. Add the onion and bell peppers, lightly season with salt and pepper, add the cinnamon, and sauté until the onions are translucent and beginning to brown, about 5 minutes. Add the garlic and cook for 1 minute more, until fragrant. 4. Turn the heat down to medium, add the mushrooms, and lightly season with salt and pepper. Cook for 5 minutes, then stir in the spice blend and add the beef. Let the meat cook for a few minutes to begin to brown, then add the diced tomatoes, coconut aminos, ketchup, vinegar, mustard, and cinnamon. Stir to combine, then turn the heat down to medium-low and simmer for 15 to 20 minutes, until the meat is cooked through. 5. To serve, spoon the sloppy joe mixture onto serving plates and garnish with the red onion and sour cream, if desired. Make This in a Slow Cooker: 1. In a small bowl, mix together all the ingredients for the spice blend. Set aside. 2. Place the bacon in a skillet or sauté pan over medium-high heat and cook, stirring occasionally, until the fat has rendered, about 4 minutes. 3. Transfer the bacon and the rendered fat to a slow cooker with all of the remaining ingredients and the spice blend. Cook on low for 3 to 4 hours. Make This in an Instant Pot or Other Multicooker: Use 1 (6-ounce / 170-g) can tomato paste instead of 1 (28-ounce / 794-g) can diced tomatoes. 1. In a small bowl, mix together all the ingredients for the spice blend. Set aside. 2. Set the Instant Pot to the sauté function (normal). Once hot, place the bacon in the pot and cook, stirring occasionally, until rendered, 3 to 4 minutes. Add the onion, bell peppers, and garlic, lightly season with salt and pepper, and sauté until translucent and beginning to brown, about 5 minutes. 3. Add the remaining ingredients and the spice blend to the pot, reset the cooker to manual, and cook on high pressure for 20 minutes. When cooking is finished, allow the cooker to depressurize on its own; don't flip

Per Serving:
calories: 421 | fat: 24g | protein: 34g | carbs: 20g | net carbs: 15g | fiber: 5g

Lemon Pork Chops with Buttered Brussels Sprouts

Prep time: 10 minutes | Cook time: 22 minutes | Serves 6

- 3 tablespoons lemon juice
- 3 cloves garlic, pureed
- 1 tablespoon olive oil
- 6 pork loin chops
- 1 tablespoon butter

- 1 pound brussels sprouts, trimmed and halved
- 2 tablespoons white wine
- Salt and black pepper to taste

1. Preheat broiler to 400ºF and mix the lemon juice, garlic, salt, black pepper, and oil in a bowl. 2. Brush the pork with the mixture, place in a baking sheet, and cook for 6 minutes on each side until browned. Share into 6 plates and make the side dish. 3. Melt butter in a small wok or pan and cook in brussels sprouts for 5 minutes until tender. Drizzle with white wine, sprinkle with salt and black pepper and cook for another 5 minutes. Ladle brussels sprouts to the side of the chops and serve with a hot sauce.

Per Serving:
calories: 300 | fat: 11g | protein: 42g | carbs: 7g | net carbs: 4g | fiber: 3g

Beef Stew with Bacon

Prep time: 15 minutes | Cook time: 1 hour 10 minutes | Serves 6

- 8 ounces bacon, chopped
- 4 pounds beef meat for stew, cubed
- 4 garlic cloves, minced
- 2 brown onions, chopped
- 2 tablespoons olive oil
- 4 tablespoons red vinegar
- 4 cups beef stock

- 2 tablespoons tomato puree
- 2 cinnamon sticks
- 3 lemon peel strips
- ½ cup fresh parsley, chopped
- 4 thyme sprigs
- 2 tablespoons butter
- Salt and black pepper, to taste

1. Set a saucepan over medium heat and warm oil, add in the garlic, bacon, and onion, and cook for 5 minutes. Stir in the beef, and cook until slightly brown. Pour in the vinegar, black pepper, butter, lemon peel strips, stock, salt, tomato puree, cinnamon sticks and thyme; stir for 3 minutes. 2. Cook for 1 hour while covered. Get rid of the thyme, lemon peel, and cinnamon sticks. Split into serving bowls and sprinkle with parsley to serve.

Per Serving:
calories: 669 | fat: 38g | protein: 63g | carbs: 11g | net carbs: 8g | fiber: 3g

Simple Liver and Onions

Prep time: 10 minutes | Cook time: 25 minutes | Serves 4

- ½ cup grass-fed butter
- ¼ cup extra-virgin olive oil
- 2 onions, thinly sliced
- ½ cup white wine
- 1 pound calf's liver, trimmed and cut into strips
- 1 tablespoon balsamic
- vinegar
- 2 tablespoons chopped fresh parsley
- Sea salt, for seasoning
- Freshly ground black pepper, for seasoning

1. Sauté the onions. In a large skillet over medium heat, warm the butter and olive oil. Add the onions to the skillet and sauté them until they've softened, about 5 minutes. Stir in the white wine and reduce the heat to medium-low. Cover the skillet and cook, stirring frequently, until the onions are very soft and lightly browned, about 15 minutes. Transfer the onions with a slotted spoon to a plate. 2. Cook the liver. Increase the heat to high and stir in the liver strips and the vinegar. Sauté the liver until it's done the way you like it, about 4 minutes for medium rare. 3. Finish the dish. Return the onions to the skillet along with the parsley, stirring to combine them. Season the liver and onions with salt, pepper. 4. Serve. Divide the liver and onions between four plates and serve immediately.

Per Serving:

calories: 497 | fat: 40g | protein: 23g | carbs: 8g | net carbs: 5g | fiber: 3g

Beef Burgers with Kale and Cheese

Prep time: 6 minutes | Cook time: 6 minutes | Serves 6

- 1 pound (454 g) ground beef
- ½ pound (227 g) beef sausage, crumbled
- 1½ cups chopped kale
- ¼ cup chopped scallions
- 2 garlic cloves, minced
- ½ cup grated Romano cheese
- ⅓ cup crumbled blue cheese
- Salt and ground black pepper, to taste
- 1 teaspoon crushed dried sage
- ½ teaspoon oregano
- ½ teaspoon dried basil
- 1 tablespoon olive oil

1. Place 1½ cups of water and a steamer basket in your Instant Pot. 2. Mix all ingredients until everything is well incorporated. 3. Shape the mixture into 6 equal sized patties. Place the burgers on the steamer basket. 4. Secure the lid. Choose Manual mode and High Pressure; cook for 6 minutes. Once cooking is complete, use a quick pressure release; carefully remove the lid. Bon appétit!

Per Serving:

calories: 323 | fat: 20g | protein: 30g | carbs: 6g | net carbs: 5g | fiber: 1g

Bacon and Cheese Stuffed Pork Chops

Prep time: 10 minutes | Cook time: 12 minutes | Serves 4

- ½ ounce (14 g) plain pork rinds, finely crushed
- ½ cup shredded sharp Cheddar cheese
- 4 slices cooked sugar-free bacon, crumbled
- 4 (4-ounce / 113-g) boneless pork chops
- ½ teaspoon salt
- ¼ teaspoon ground black pepper

1. In a small bowl, mix pork rinds, Cheddar, and bacon. 2. Make a 3-inch slit in the side of each pork chop and stuff with ¼ pork rind mixture. Sprinkle each side of pork chops with salt and pepper. 3. Place pork chops into ungreased air fryer basket, stuffed side up. Adjust the temperature to 400ºF (204ºC) and air fry for 12 minutes. Pork chops will be browned and have an internal temperature of at least 145ºF (63ºC) when done. Serve warm.

Per Serving:

calories: 357 | fat: 17g | protein: 39g | carbs: 1g | net carbs: 1g | fiber: 0g

Beef Zucchini Boats

Prep time: 10 minutes | Cook time: 33 minutes | Serves 4

- 2 garlic cloves, minced
- 1 teaspoon cumin
- 1 tablespoon olive oil
- 1 pound ground beef
- ½ cup onions, chopped
- 1 teaspoon smoked paprika
- Salt and black pepper, to taste
- 4 zucchinis
- ¼ cup fresh cilantro,
- chopped
- ½ cup Monterey Jack cheese, shredded
- 1½ cups enchilada sauce
- 1 avocado, chopped, for serving
- Green onions, chopped, for serving
- Tomatoes, chopped, for serving

1. Set a pan over high heat and warm the oil. Add the onions, and cook for 2 minutes. Stir in the beef, and brown for 4-5 minutes. Stir in the paprika, pepper, garlic, cumin, and salt; cook for 2 minutes. 2. Slice the zucchini in half lengthwise and scoop out the seeds. Set the zucchini in a greased baking pan, stuff each with the beef, scatter enchilada sauce on top, and spread with the Monterey cheese. 3. Bake in the oven at 350ºF for 20 minutes while covered. Uncover, spread with cilantro, and bake for 5 minutes. Top with tomatoes, green onions and avocado, place on serving plates and enjoy.

Per Serving:

calories: 422 | fat: 33g | protein: 39g | carbs: 15g | net carbs: 8g | fiber: 7g

Balsamic Grilled Pork Chops

Prep time: 5 minutes | Cook time: 20 minutes | Serves 6

◀ 6 pork loin chops, boneless
◀ 2 tablespoons erythritol
◀ ¼ cup balsamic vinegar
◀ 3 cloves garlic, minced
◀ ¼ cup olive oil
◀ ⅓ teaspoon salt
◀ Black pepper to taste

1. Put the pork in a plastic bag. In a bowl, mix the erythritol, balsamic vinegar, garlic, olive oil, salt, pepper, and pour the sauce over the pork. Seal the bag, shake it, and place in the refrigerator. 2. Marinate the pork for 2 hours. Preheat the grill to medium heat, remove the pork when ready, and grill covered for 10 minutes on each side. Remove and let sit for 4 minutes, and serve with parsnip sauté.

Per Serving:
calories: 267 | fat: 17g | protein: 24g | carbs: 2g | net carbs: 1g | fiber: 1g

Homemade Classic Beef Burgers

Prep time: 10 minutes | Cook time: 6 minutes | Serves 4

◀ 1 pound (454 g) ground beef
◀ ½ teaspoon onion powder
◀ ½ teaspoon garlic powder
◀ 2 tablespoons ghee
◀ 1 teaspoon Dijon mustard
◀ 4 low carb buns, halved
◀ ¼ cup mayonnaise
◀ 1 teaspoon sriracha sauce
◀ 4 tablespoons cabbage slaw
◀ Salt and black pepper to taste

1. Mix together the beef, onion powder, garlic powder, mustard, salt, and black pepper; create 4 burgers. Melt the ghee in a skillet and cook the burgers for about 3 minutes per side. 2. Serve in buns topped with mayo, sriracha, and cabbage slaw.

Per Serving:
calories: 679 | fat: 55g | protein: 39g | carbs: 7g | net carbs: 6g | fiber: 1g

Beef Provençal

Prep time: 10 minutes | Cook time: 35 minutes | Serves 4

◀ 12 ounces beef steak racks
◀ 2 fennel bulbs, sliced
◀ Salt and black pepper, to taste
◀ 3 tablespoons olive oil
◀ ½ cup apple cider vinegar
◀ 1 teaspoon herbs de Provence
◀ 1 tablespoon swerve

1. In a bowl, mix the fennel with 2 tablespoons of oil, swerve, and vinegar, toss to coat well, and set to a baking dish. Season with herbs de Provence, pepper and salt, and cook in the oven at 400ºF for 15 minutes. 2. Sprinkle black pepper and salt to the beef, place into an oiled pan over medium heat, and cook for a couple of minutes. Place the beef to the baking dish with the fennel, and bake for 20 minutes. Split everything among plates and enjoy.

Per Serving:
calories: 251 | fat: 15g | protein: 19g | carbs: 8g | net carbs: 4g | fiber: 4g

Bacon-Wrapped Pork Bites

Prep time: 15 minutes | Cook time: 20 minutes | Serves 4

◀ 3 tablespoons butter
◀ 10 ounces (283 g) pork tenderloin, cubed
◀ 6 ounces (170 g) bacon, sliced
◀ ½ teaspoon white pepper
◀ ¾ cup chicken stock

1. Melt the butter on Sauté mode in the Instant Pot. 2. Meanwhile, wrap the pork tenderloin cubes in the sliced bacon and sprinkle with white pepper. Secure with toothpicks, if necessary. 3. Put the wrapped pork tenderloin in the melted butter and cook for 3 minutes on each side. 4. Add the chicken stock and close the lid. 5. Select Manual mode and set cooking time for 14 minutes on High Pressure. 6. When timer beeps, use a natural pressure release for 5 minutes, then release any remaining pressure. Open the lid. 7. Discard the toothpicks and serve immediately.

Per Serving:
calories: 410 | fat: 29g | protein: 35g | carbs: 1g | net carbs: 1g | fiber: 0g

Coconut Pork Muffins

Prep time: 5 minutes | Cook time: 9 minutes | Serves 2

◀ 1 egg, beaten
◀ 2 tablespoons coconut flour
◀ 1 teaspoon parsley
◀ ¼ teaspoon salt
◀ 1 tablespoon coconut cream
◀ 4 ounces (113 g) ground pork, fried
◀ 1 cup water

1. Whisk together the egg, coconut flour, parsley, salt, and coconut cream. Add the fried ground pork. Mix the the mixture until homogenous. 2. Pour the mixture into a muffin pan. 3. Pour the water in the Instant Pot and place in the trivet. 4. Lower the muffin pan on the trivet and close the Instant Pot lid. 5. Set the Manual mode and set cooking time for 4 minutes on High Pressure. 6. When timer beeps, perform a natural pressure release for 5 minutes, then release any remaining pressure. Open the lid. 7. Serve warm.

Per Serving:
calories: 160 | fat: 7g | protein: 19g | carbs: 6g | net carbs: 2g | fiber: 3g

Spicy Sausage and Cabbage Skillet

Prep time: 5 minutes | Cook time: 35 minutes | Serves 4

- 1 tablespoon olive oil
- 1 small white onion, diced
- 1 garlic clove, minced
- 1 pound (454 g) hot Italian sausage, casings removed
- 1 head cabbage, chopped
- Salt, to taste
- Freshly ground black pepper, to taste
- 1 cup shredded provolone cheese

1. Preheat the oven to 350ºF (180ºC). 2. In a large cast-iron skillet over medium heat, heat the olive oil. 3. Add the onion and garlic. Sauté for 5 to 7 minutes until the onion is softened and translucent. 4. Add the sausage and cook for 7 to 10 minutes or until browned. Remove from the heat, slice the sausage, and return it to the skillet. 5. Add the cabbage and season with salt and pepper. 6. Top with the provolone and transfer the skillet to the oven. Bake for 20 minutes or until the cheese melts. Refrigerate leftovers in an airtight container for up to 6 days.

Per Serving:

calories: 602 | fat: 48g | protein: 28g | carbs: 17g | net carbs: 11g | fiber: 6g

Slow Cooker Short Rib and Chorizo Stew

Prep time: 10 minutes | Cook time: 4½ hours | Serves 12

- 1 pound (454 g) bone-in short ribs
- 1 (26-ounce / 737-g) box diced tomatoes with juices, or 3 tomatoes, chopped, with juices
- 1 cup tomato sauce
- ¼ cup chopped onions
- 1 red bell pepper, chopped
- 2 green chiles, chopped
- ½ cup beef bone broth, homemade or store-bought
- 2 teaspoons minced garlic
- 2 tablespoons chili powder

For Garnish:
- Sliced green onions
- Chopped fresh cilantro
- 2 teaspoons dried oregano leaves
- 1 teaspoon ground cumin
- ½ teaspoon cayenne pepper
- ½ teaspoon paprika
- ½ teaspoon fine sea salt
- ½ teaspoon freshly ground black pepper
- 4 slices bacon, diced
- 1 pound (454 g) 80% lean ground beef
- 1 pound (454 g) Mexican-style fresh (raw) chorizo, removed from casings

- Lime wedges

1. Place the short ribs in a 4-quart (or larger) slow cooker. Pour in the diced tomatoes and tomato sauce. Add the onions, red bell pepper, chiles, and beef broth. Season with the garlic, chili powder, oregano, cumin, cayenne pepper, paprika, salt, and black pepper. Stir to combine, then cover. Cook on low until the meat is falling off the bone, about 4 hours. 2. When the ribs are nearly done, cook the rest of the meat on the stovetop: Heat a large sauté pan over medium-high heat. Fry the diced bacon in the pan until crispy, then remove the bacon from the pan and set aside, leaving the fat in the pan. Crumble the ground beef and chorizo into the hot pan and cook until evenly browned. Remove the pan from the heat. 3. When the ribs are done, remove them from the slow cooker and place them in a large bowl or casserole dish (to catch the juices as you work). Remove the meat from the bones, discard the bones, then shred the meat using two forks. Return the shredded meat and any juices to the slow cooker. Add the ground beef, chorizo, and bacon. Cover and cook on low for at least 20 minutes, then taste and add more salt, pepper, or chili powder, if desired. The longer the stew simmers, the better it will taste. 4. Serve garnished with sliced green onions and chopped cilantro, with lime wedges on the side. Store extras in an airtight container in the fridge for up to 4 days.

Per Serving:

calories: 411 | fat: 31g | protein: 25g | carbs: 7g | net carbs: 5g | fiber: 2g

Beef Burgers with Mushroom

Prep time: 10 minutes | Cook time: 21 to 23 minutes | Serves 4

- 1 pound (454 g) ground beef, formed into 4 patties
- Sea salt and freshly ground black pepper, to taste
- 1 cup thinly sliced onion
- 8 ounces (227 g)
- mushrooms, sliced
- 1 tablespoon avocado oil
- 2 ounces (57 g) Gruyère cheese, shredded (about ½ cup)

1. Season the patties on both sides with salt and pepper. 2. Set the air fryer to 375ºF (191ºC). Place the patties in the basket and cook for 3 minutes. Flip and cook for another 2 minutes. Remove the burgers and set aside. 3. Place the onion and mushrooms in a medium bowl. Add the avocado oil and salt and pepper to taste; toss well. 4. Place the onion and mushrooms in the air fryer basket. Cook for 15 minutes, stirring occasionally. 5. Spoon the onions and mushrooms over the patties. Top with the cheese. Place the patties back in the air fryer basket and cook for another 1 to 3 minutes, until the cheese melts and an instant-read thermometer reads 160ºF (71ºC). Remove and let rest. The temperature will rise to 165ºF (74ºC), yielding a perfect medium-well burger.

Per Serving:

calories: 442 | fat: 32g | protein: 28g | carbs: 6g | net carbs: 4g | fiber: 2g

Garlic Pork Chops with Mint Pesto

Prep time: 10 minutes | Cook time: 2 hours | Serves 4

- 1 cup parsley
- 1 cup mint
- 1½ onions, chopped
- ⅓ cup pistachios
- 1 teaspoon lemon zest
- 5 tablespoons avocado oil
- Salt, to taste
- 4 pork chops
- 5 garlic cloves, minced
- Juice from 1 lemon

1. In a food processor, combine the parsley with avocado oil, mint, pistachios, salt, lemon zest, and 1 onion. Rub the pork with this mixture, place in a bowl, and refrigerate for 1 hour while covered. 2. Remove the chops and set to a baking dish, place in ½ onion, and garlic; sprinkle with lemon juice, and bake for 2 hours in the oven at 250°F. Split amongst plates and enjoy.

Per Serving:

calories: 567 | fat: 40g | protein: 37g | carbs: 7g | net carbs: 5g | fiber: 2g

Korean Ground Beef Bowl

Prep time: 5 minutes | Cook time: 10 minutes | Serves 4

- 1 tablespoon sesame oil
- 1½ pounds (680 g) ground sirloin
- 1 teaspoon dried basil
- ½ teaspoon oregano
- Sea salt and ground black pepper, to taste
- ½ cup diced onion
- 1 teaspoon minced garlic
- ¼ teaspoon ground ginger
- 1 teaspoon red pepper flakes
- ¼ teaspoon allspice
- 1 tablespoon coconut aminos
- ½ cup roughly chopped fresh cilantro leaves

1. Press the Sauté button to heat up the Instant Pot. Then, heat the sesame oil until sizzling. 2. Add ground sirloin and cook for a few minutes or until browned. Add the remaining ingredients, except for cilantro. 3. Secure the lid. Choose Manual mode and High Pressure; cook for 5 minutes. Once cooking is complete, use a natural pressure release; carefully remove the lid. 4. Divide among individual bowls and serve garnished with fresh cilantro. Bon appétit!

Per Serving:

calories: 307 | fat: 17g | protein: 34g | carbs: 4g | net carbs: 3g | fiber: 1g

Chapter 6 Fish and Seafood

Tuna Steaks with Olive Tapenade

Prep time: 10 minutes | Cook time: 10 minutes | Serves 4

- 4 (6-ounce / 170-g) ahi tuna steaks
- 1 tablespoon olive oil
- Salt and freshly ground

Olive Tapenade:
- ½ cup pitted kalamata olives
- 1 tablespoon olive oil
- 1 tablespoon chopped fresh parsley
- black pepper, to taste
- ½ lemon, sliced into 4 wedges
- 1 clove garlic
- 2 teaspoons red wine vinegar
- 1 teaspoon capers, drained

1. Preheat the air fryer to 400ºF (204ºC). 2. Drizzle the tuna steaks with the olive oil and sprinkle with salt and black pepper. Arrange the tuna steaks in a single layer in the air fryer basket. Pausing to turn the steaks halfway through the cooking time, air fry for 10 minutes until the fish is firm. 3. To make the tapenade: In a food processor fitted with a metal blade, combine the olives, olive oil, parsley, garlic, vinegar, and capers. Pulse until the mixture is finely chopped, pausing to scrape down the sides of the bowl if necessary. Spoon the tapenade over the top of the tuna steaks and serve with lemon wedges.

Per Serving:

calories: 240 | fat: 9g | protein: 36g | carbs: 2g | net carbs: 1g | fiber: 1g

Stuffed Trout

Prep time: 5 minutes | Cook time: 20 minutes | Serves 4

- 2 (7-ounce/200-g) head-off, gutted trout
- 2 tablespoons refined avocado oil or melted coconut oil
- 2 teaspoons dried dill weed
- 1 teaspoon dried thyme leaves
- ½ teaspoon ground black pepper
- ¼ teaspoon finely ground gray sea salt
- ½ lemon, sliced
- 1 green onion, green part only, sliced in half lengthwise

1. Preheat the oven to 400°F (205°C). 2. Place the fish in a large cast-iron frying pan or on an unlined rimmed baking sheet and coat with the oil. In a small bowl, mix together the dried herbs, pepper, and salt. Sprinkle the fish—top, bottom, and inside—with the herb mixture. 3. Open up the fish and place the lemon and green onion slices inside. Lay it flat on the pan or baking sheet and transfer to the oven. Bake for up to 20 minutes, until the desired doneness is reached. 4. Cut the fish in half before transferring to a serving platter.

Per Serving:

calories: 219 | fat: 12g | protein: 27g | carbs: 1g | net carbs: 1g | fiber: 0g

Parmesan Mackerel with Coriander

Prep time: 10 minutes | Cook time: 7 minutes | Serves 2

- 12 ounces (340 g) mackerel fillet
- 2 ounces (57 g) Parmesan,
- grated
- 1 teaspoon ground coriander
- 1 tablespoon olive oil

1. Sprinkle the mackerel fillet with olive oil and put it in the air fryer basket. 2. Top the fish with ground coriander and Parmesan. 3. Cook the fish at 390ºF (199ºC) for 7 minutes.

Per Serving:

calories: 504 | fat: 36g | protein: 42g | carbs: 3g | net carbs: 2g | fiber: 0g

Tuna Avocado Bites

Prep time: 10 minutes | Cook time: 7 minutes | Makes 12 bites

- 1 (10-ounce / 283-g) can tuna, drained
- ¼ cup full-fat mayonnaise
- 1 stalk celery, chopped
- 1 medium avocado, peeled,
- pitted, and mashed
- ½ cup blanched finely ground almond flour, divided
- 2 teaspoons coconut oil

1. In a large bowl, mix tuna, mayonnaise, celery, and mashed avocado. Form the mixture into balls. 2. Roll balls in almond flour and spritz with coconut oil. Place balls into the air fryer basket. 3. Adjust the temperature to 400ºF (204ºC) and set the timer for 7 minutes. 4. Gently turn tuna bites after 5 minutes. Serve warm.

Per Serving:

2 bites: calories: 170 | fat: 13g | protein: 12g | carbs: 4g | net carbs: 1g | fiber: 3g

Shrimp Scampi with Zucchini Noodles

Prep time: 5 minutes | Cook time: 10 minutes | Serves 4

- ½ cup extra-virgin olive oil, divided
- 1 pound (454 g) shrimp, peeled and deveined
- 1 teaspoon salt
- ¼ teaspoon freshly ground black pepper
- 2 tablespoons unsalted butter
- 6 garlic cloves, minced
- 2 tablespoons dry white wine or chicken broth
- ½ teaspoon red pepper flakes
- Zest and juice of 1 lemon
- ¼ cup chopped fresh Italian parsley
- 4 cups spiralized zucchini noodles (about 2 medium zucchini)

1. In a large skillet, heat ¼ cup of olive oil over medium-high heat. Add the shrimp, sprinkle with salt and pepper, and sauté for 2 to 3 minutes, or until the shrimp is just pink. Using a slotted spoon, transfer the shrimp to a bowl and cover to keep warm. 2. Reduce heat to low and add the remaining ¼ cup of olive oil, butter, and garlic. Cook the garlic, stirring frequently, until very fragrant, 3 to 4 minutes. 3. Whisk in the wine, red pepper flakes, and lemon zest and juice. Increase the heat to medium-high and bring to a simmer. Remove the skillet from the heat as soon as the liquid simmers. Return the shrimp to the skillet, add the parsley, and toss. 4. To serve, place the raw zucchini noodles in a large bowl. Add the shrimp and sauce and toss to coat.

Per Serving:

calories: 414 | fat: 34g | protein: 25g | carbs: 5g | net carbs: 3g | fiber: 2g

Firecracker Shrimp

Prep time: 10 minutes | Cook time: 7 minutes | Serves 4

- 1 pound (454 g) medium shelled and deveined shrimp
- 2 tablespoons salted butter, melted
- ½ teaspoon Old Bay seasoning
- ¼ teaspoon garlic powder
- 2 tablespoons sriracha
- ¼ teaspoon powdered erythritol
- ¼ cup full-fat mayonnaise
- ⅛ teaspoon ground black pepper

1. In a large bowl, toss shrimp in butter, Old Bay seasoning, and garlic powder. Place shrimp into the air fryer basket. 2. Adjust the temperature to 400ºF (204ºC) and set the timer for 7 minutes. 3. Flip the shrimp halfway through the cooking time. Shrimp will be bright pink when fully cooked. 4. In another large bowl, mix sriracha, powdered erythritol, mayonnaise, and pepper. Toss shrimp in the spicy mixture and serve immediately.

Per Serving:

calories: 270 | fat: 20g | protein: 19g | carbs: 3g | net carbs: 2g | fiber: 1g

Creamy Shrimp and Bacon Skillet

Prep time: 5 minutes | Cook time: 20 minutes | Serves 4

- 10 ounces (283 g) thick-cut bacon, diced
- ½ onion, diced
- 2 garlic cloves, minced
- 1 pound (454 g) shrimp, peeled, deveined, tails removed
- Salt, to taste
- Freshly ground black pepper, to taste
- 4 ounces (113 g) cream cheese
- Dash chicken broth (optional)
- ¼ cup grated Parmesan cheese

1. Preheat the broiler. 2. In a large ovenproof skillet over medium-high heat, cook the bacon in its own fat for about 5 minutes until it starts to get crispy. 3. Add the onion and garlic. Sauté for 5 to 7 minutes until the onion is softened and translucent. 4. Add the shrimp. Season with salt and pepper. Cook for 2 to 3 minutes, stirring, or until the shrimp start to turn pink. 5. Add the cream cheese and stir well to combine as it melts. If necessary, add a splash of chicken broth to thin it out. 6. Top with the Parmesan and transfer the skillet to the oven. Broil for 4 to 5 minutes until the Parmesan is lightly browned. Refrigerate leftovers in an airtight container for up to 5 days.

Per Serving:

calories: 574 | fat: 45g | protein: 36g | carbs: 5g | net carbs: 5g | fiber: 0g

Salmon & Kale

Prep time: 5 minutes | Cook time: 15 minutes | Serves 4

- 1 pound (455 g) salmon fillets, cut into 4 equal portions
- ¾ cup (180 ml) vinaigrette of choice
- 1 small red onion, sliced
- 4 cups (240 g) destemmed kale leaves
- ¼ teaspoon red pepper flakes
- ¼ teaspoon finely ground sea salt
- Lemon wedges, for serving

1. Set the salmon in a shallow dish and pour the vinaigrette over the top. Cover and set in the fridge for 2 hours to marinate. 2. When ready to cook, transfer the salmon and all the marinade to a large frying pan. Distribute the onion slices around the fish, then turn the heat to medium-low. Continue cooking the salmon for 6 minutes per side, until seared. 3. Once the salmon has cooked for a total of 12 minutes, push the fish to the sides of the pan, making room for the kale. Add the kale, red pepper flakes, and salt and toss to coat the kale in the pan drippings. Cover and cook for 3 minutes, or until the kale is wilted. 4. Divide the salmon fillets and braised kale among 4 dinner plates and serve.

Per Serving:

calories: 438 | fat: 33g | protein: 26g | carbs: 9g | net carbs: 6g | fiber: 3g

Italian Tuna Roast

Prep time: 15 minutes | Cook time: 21 to 24 minutes | Serves 8

- Cooking spray
- 1 tablespoon Italian seasoning
- ⅛ teaspoon ground black pepper
- 1 tablespoon extra-light
- olive oil
- 1 teaspoon lemon juice
- 1 tuna loin (approximately 2 pounds / 907 g, 3 to 4 inches thick)

1. Spray baking dish with cooking spray and place in air fryer basket. Preheat the air fryer to 390°F (199°C). 2. Mix together the Italian seasoning, pepper, oil, and lemon juice. 3. Using a dull table knife or butter knife, pierce top of tuna about every half inch: Insert knife into top of tuna roast and pierce almost all the way to the bottom. 4. Spoon oil mixture into each of the holes and use the knife to push seasonings into the tuna as deeply as possible. 5. Spread any remaining oil mixture on all outer surfaces of tuna. 6. Place tuna roast in baking dish and roast at 390°F (199°C) for 20 minutes. Check temperature with a meat thermometer. Cook for an additional 1 to 4 minutes or until temperature reaches 145°F (63°C). 7. Remove basket from the air fryer and let tuna sit in the basket for 10 minutes.

Per Serving:

calories: 206 | fat: 6g | protein: 35g | carbs: 1g | net carbs: 1g | fiber: 0g

Sushi

Prep time: 15 minutes | Cook time: 3 to 5 minutes | Serves 2 to 4

- 4 cups cauliflower rice
- 2 tablespoons grass-fed gelatin
- 1 tablespoon apple cider vinegar
- 1 teaspoon salt
- 2 to 4 nori sheets
- ½ pound (227 g) sushi-grade fish, thinly sliced
- 1 small avocado, halved, pitted, peeled, and thinly sliced
- 1 small cucumber (or any other vegetable you'd like), thinly sliced
- Sesame seeds, for topping (optional)
- Coconut aminos or tamari, wasabi, sugar-free pickled ginger, sliced avocado, and/or avocado oil mayonnaise mixed with sugar-free hot sauce, for serving (optional)

1. In a shallow pot with a lid, combine the cauliflower with 3 tablespoons of water. Turn the heat to medium, cover the pot, and steam for 3 to 5 minutes. 2. Drain the cauliflower and transfer to a mixing bowl. Stir in the gelatin, vinegar, and salt. Stir together until the mixture is smooth and sticky. Set aside. 3. Fold a dish towel in half lengthwise and place it on your counter. Cover the towel in plastic wrap. 4. Place a nori sheet on top of the plastic wrap, then spread with a layer of the cauliflower rice. 5. Layer slices of fish, avocado, and cucumber over the cauliflower on the end of the nori sheet closest to you. 6. Starting at the end closest to you, gently roll the nori sheet over all the ingredients, using the towel as your rolling aid. (Emphasis on the word "gently" because you don't want to tear the nori sheet.) When you're done rolling, remove the towel and plastic wrap as you slide the roll onto a plate or cutting board. Using a sharp knife, cut the roll into equal pieces. Repeat steps 4 through 7 with the remaining nori and filling ingredients. 7. Sprinkle sesame seeds on top of your sushi, if desired, and serve with any of the other optional ingredients you'd like.

Per Serving:

calories: 295 | fat: 15g | protein: 30g | carbs: 10g | net carbs: 2g | fiber: 8g

Coconut Milk-Braised Squid

Prep time: 10 minutes | Cook time: 20 minutes | Serves 3

- 1 pound (454 g) squid, sliced
- 1 teaspoon sugar-free tomato paste
- 1 cup coconut milk
- 1 teaspoon cayenne pepper
- ½ teaspoon salt

1. Put all ingredients from the list above in the instant pot. 2. Close and seal the lid and cook the squid on Manual (High Pressure) for 20 minutes. 3. When the cooking time is finished, do the quick pressure release. 4. Serve the squid with coconut milk gravy.

Per Serving:

calories: 326 | fat: 21g | protein: 25g | carbs: 10g | net carbs: 8g | fiber: 2g

Sole Asiago

Prep time: 10 minutes | Cook time: 8 minutes | Serves 4

- 4 (4 ounces) sole fillets
- ¾ cup ground almonds
- ¼ cup Asiago cheese
- 2 eggs, beaten
- 2½ tablespoons melted coconut oil

1. Preheat the oven to 350°F. Line a baking sheet with parchment paper and set aside. 2. Pat the fish dry with paper towels. 3. Stir together the ground almonds and cheese in a small bowl. 4. Place the bowl with the beaten eggs in it next to the almond mixture. 5. Dredge a sole fillet in the beaten egg and then press the fish into the almond mixture so it is completely coated. Place on the baking sheet and repeat until all the fillets are breaded. 6. Brush both sides of each piece of fish with the coconut oil. 7. Bake the sole until it is cooked through, about 8 minutes in total. 8. Serve immediately.

Per Serving:

calories: 406 | fat: 31g | protein: 29g | carbs: 6g | net carbs: 3g | fiber: 3g

Steamed Halibut with Lemon

Prep time: 10 minutes | Cook time: 9 minutes | Serves 3

◀ 3 halibut fillet
◀ ½ lemon, sliced
◀ ½ teaspoon white pepper
◀ ½ teaspoon ground coriander
◀ 1 tablespoon avocado oil
◀ 1 cup water, for cooking

1. Pour water and insert the steamer rack in the instant pot. 2. Rub the fish fillets with white pepper, ground coriander, and avocado oil. 3. Place the fillets in the steamer rack. 4. Then top the halibut with sliced lemon. Close and seal the lid. 5. Cook the meal on High Pressure for 9 minutes. Make a quick pressure release.

Per Serving:

calories: 328 | fat: 7g | protein: 60g | carbs: 1g | net carbs: 1g | fiber: 0g

Salmon with Cauliflower

Prep time: 10 minutes | Cook time: 25 minutes | Serves 4

◀ 1 pound (454 g) salmon fillet, diced
◀ 1 cup cauliflower, shredded
◀ 1 tablespoon dried cilantro
◀ 1 tablespoon coconut oil, melted
◀ 1 teaspoon ground turmeric
◀ ¼ cup coconut cream

1. Mix salmon with cauliflower, dried cilantro, ground turmeric, coconut cream, and coconut oil. 2. Transfer the salmon mixture into the air fryer and cook the meal at 350ºF (177ºC) for 25 minutes. Stir the meal every 5 minutes to avoid the burning.

Per Serving:

calories: 295 | fat: 20g | protein: 21g | carbs: 7g | net carbs: 5g | fiber: 2g

Lemon Mahi-Mahi

Prep time: 5 minutes | Cook time: 14 minutes | Serves 2

◀ Oil, for spraying
◀ 2 (6-ounce / 170-g) mahi-mahi fillets
◀ 1 tablespoon lemon juice
◀ 1 tablespoon olive oil
◀ ¼ teaspoon salt
◀ ¼ teaspoon freshly ground black pepper
◀ 1 tablespoon chopped fresh dill
◀ 2 lemon slices

1. Line the air fryer basket with parchment and spray lightly with oil. 2. Place the mahi-mahi in the prepared basket. 3. In a small bowl, whisk together the lemon juice and olive oil. Brush the mixture evenly over the mahi-mahi. 4. Sprinkle the mahi-mahi with the salt and black pepper and top with the dill. 5. Air fry at 400ºF

(204ºC) for 12 to 14 minutes, depending on the thickness of the fillets, until they flake easily. 6. Transfer to plates, top each with a lemon slice, and serve.

Per Serving:

calories: 233 | fat: 9g | protein: 35g | carbs: 2g | net carbs: 2g | fiber: 0g

Simple Fish Curry

Prep time: 10 minutes | Cook time: 25 minutes | Serves 4

◀ 2 tablespoons coconut oil
◀ 1½ tablespoons grated fresh ginger
◀ 2 teaspoons minced garlic
◀ 1 tablespoon curry powder
◀ ½ teaspoon ground cumin
◀ 2 cups coconut milk
◀ 16 ounces firm white fish, cut into 1-inch chunks
◀ 1 cup shredded kale
◀ 2 tablespoons chopped cilantro

1. Place a large saucepan over medium heat and melt the coconut oil. 2. Sauté the ginger and garlic until lightly browned, about 2 minutes. 3. Stir in the curry powder and cumin and sauté until very fragrant, about 2 minutes. 4. Stir in the coconut milk and bring the liquid to a boil. 5. Reduce the heat to low and simmer for about 5 minutes to infuse the milk with the spices. 6. Add the fish and cook until the fish is cooked through, about 10 minutes. 7. Stir in the kale and cilantro and simmer until wilted, about 2 minutes. 8. Serve.

Per Serving:

calories: 416 | fat: 31g | protein: 26g | carbs: 5g | net carbs: 4g | fiber: 1g

Foil-Packet Salmon

Prep time: 2 minutes | Cook time: 7 minutes | Serves 2

◀ 2 (3-ounce / 85-g) salmon fillets
◀ ¼ teaspoon garlic powder
◀ 1 teaspoon salt
◀ ¼ teaspoon pepper
◀ ¼ teaspoon dried dill
◀ ½ lemon
◀ 1 cup water

1. Place each filet of salmon on a square of foil, skin-side down. 2. Season with garlic powder, salt, and pepper and squeeze the lemon juice over the fish. 3. Cut the lemon into four slices and place two on each filet. Close the foil packets by folding over edges. 4. Add the water to the Instant Pot and insert a trivet. Place the foil packets on the trivet. 5. Secure the lid. Select the Steam mode and set the cooking time for 7 minutes at Low Pressure. 6. Once cooking is complete, do a quick pressure release. Carefully open the lid. 7. Check the internal temperature with a meat thermometer to ensure the thickest part of the filets reached at least 145ºF (63ºC). Salmon should easily flake when fully cooked. Serve immediately.

Per Serving:

calories: 128 | fat: 5g | protein: 19g | carbs: 0g | net carbs: 0g | fiber: 0g

Chili Lime Shrimp

Prep time: 5 minutes | Cook time: 5 minutes | Serves 4

- 1 pound (454 g) medium shrimp, peeled and deveined
- 1 tablespoon salted butter, melted
- 2 teaspoons chili powder
- ¼ teaspoon garlic powder
- ¼ teaspoon salt
- ¼ teaspoon ground black pepper
- ½ small lime, zested and juiced, divided

1. In a medium bowl, toss shrimp with butter, then sprinkle with chili powder, garlic powder, salt, pepper, and lime zest. 2. Place shrimp into ungreased air fryer basket. Adjust the temperature to 400°F (204°C) and air fry for 5 minutes. Shrimp will be firm and form a "C" shape when done. 3. Transfer shrimp to a large serving dish and drizzle with lime juice. Serve warm.

Per Serving:

calories: 129 | fat: 3g | protein: 23g | carbs: 2g | net carbs: 1g | fiber: 1g

Pan-Fried Cod with Dill Caper Sauce

Prep time: 5 minutes | Cook time: 5 minutes | Serves 6

Dill Caper Sauce:
- ¼ cup drained capers
- 1 tablespoon chopped fresh dill

Fish:
- 1½ pounds (680 g) cod fillets, or any other mild white fish
- Salt and pepper, to taste
- ¼ cup extra-virgin olive oil
- Juice from 1 small lemon
- Salt and pepper, to taste
- 1 tablespoon butter
- 2 teaspoons avocado oil
- Juice of ½ lemon

1. Prepare the sauce first, even a day or two before. Combine the capers, dill, olive oil, and lemon juice in a jar with a tight-fitting lid. Shake vigorously. If you want to make it more of a sauce than a dressing, you can also pulse the mixture a few times in a food processor or with an immersion blender. Taste and add salt and pepper as needed. 2. Season both sides of the fish with salt and pepper. Heat a large skillet over medium heat. Add the butter and avocado oil, and heat until the butter bubbles; swirl the pan to combine. Add the fish and cook about 2 minutes, depending on thickness. Carefully flip to brown the other side and squeeze the lemon juice over the fish. Cook for 1 to 2 minutes more. Do not overcook. 3. Remove the fish from pan, transfer to a serving platter, and spoon 2 tablespoons sauce over each serving.

Per Serving:

calories: 336 | fat: 24g | protein: 19g | carbs: 10g | net carbs: 9g | fiber: 1g

Seared Scallops with Chorizo and Asiago Cheese

Prep time: 10 minutes | Cook time: 15 minutes | Serves 4

- 2 tablespoons ghee
- 16 fresh scallops
- 8 ounces chorizo, chopped
- 1 red bell pepper, seeds removed, sliced
- 1 cup red onions, finely chopped
- 1 cup asiago cheese, grated
- Salt and black pepper to taste

1. Melt half of the ghee in a skillet over medium heat, and cook the onion and bell pepper for 5 minutes until tender. Add the chorizo and stir-fry for another 3 minutes. Remove and set aside. 2. Pat dry the scallops with paper towels, and season with salt and pepper. Add the remaining ghee to the skillet and sear the scallops for 2 minutes on each side to have a golden brown color. Add the chorizo mixture back and warm through. Transfer to serving platter and top with asiago cheese.

Per Serving:

calories: 570 | fat: 42g | protein: 36g | carbs: 11g | net carbs: 9g | fiber: 2g

Greek Stuffed Squid

Prep time: 15 minutes | Cook time: 30 minutes | Serves 4

- 8 ounces (227 g) frozen spinach, thawed and drained (about 1½ cup)
- 4 ounces (113 g) crumbled goat cheese
- ½ cup chopped pitted olives (I like Kalamata in this recipe)
- ½ cup extra-virgin olive oil, divided
- ¼ cup chopped sun-dried
- tomatoes
- ¼ cup chopped fresh flat-leaf Italian parsley
- 2 garlic cloves, finely minced
- ¼ teaspoon freshly ground black pepper
- 2 pounds (907 g) baby squid, cleaned and tentacles removed

1. Preheat the oven to 350°F(180°C). 2. In a medium bowl, combine the spinach, goat cheese, olives, ¼ cup olive oil, sun-dried tomatoes, parsley, garlic, and pepper. 3. Pour 2 tablespoons olive oil in the bottom of an 8-inch square baking dish and spread to coat the bottom. 4. Stuff each cleaned squid with 2 to 3 tablespoons of the cheese mixture, depending on the size of squid, and place in the prepared baking dish. 5. Drizzle the tops with the remaining 2 tablespoons olive oil and bake until the squid are cooked through, 25 to 30 minutes. Remove from the oven and allow to cool 5 to 10 minutes before serving.

Per Serving:

calories: 580 | fat: 43g | protein: 26g | carbs: 16g | net carbs: 12g | fiber: 4g

Thai Coconut Fish

Prep time: 10 minutes | Cook time: 25 to 45 minutes | Serves 4

- 1 tablespoon avocado oil, MCT oil, or extra-virgin olive oil
- 3 shallots, chopped
- 1½ tablespoons red curry paste
- 1½ cups chicken bone broth, homemade or store-bought
- 1 (13½-ounce / 383-g) can full-fat coconut milk
- ¼ teaspoon fine sea salt, plus more for the fish
- 1 pound (454 g) halibut fillets, cut into 2-inch pieces
- ¼ cup fresh cilantro leaves, chopped, plus more for garnish
- 2 green onions, cut into ½-inch pieces, plus more for garnish
- Juice of 1 lime
- 2 cups zoodles, for serving (optional)

1. Heat the oil in a cast-iron skillet over medium heat. Add the shallots and sauté until tender, about 2 minutes. Reduce the heat to low. Whisk in the curry paste, broth, coconut milk, and salt. Simmer, uncovered, until thickened a bit, 20 to 40 minutes, depending on exactly how thick you would like the soup to be. 2. Sprinkle salt all over the fish pieces and add to the soup. Cover the skillet and poach the fish until it is cooked through and opaque and flakes easily, 4 to 5 minutes, depending on how thick your pieces are. 3. Once the fish is cooked through, stir in the cilantro, green onions, and lime juice. Immediately remove from the heat and place in serving bowls over zoodles, if desired. Garnish with additional sliced green onions and cilantro leaves. 4. Store extras in an airtight container in the fridge for up to 3 days. Store any leftover zoodles separately to keep them from getting soggy. Reheat in a saucepan over medium heat for a few minutes or until warmed to your liking, then spoon over warmed zoodles.

Per Serving:

calories: 360 | fat: 22g | protein: 32g | carbs: 7g | net carbs: 6g | fiber: 1g

Tuna with Herbs

Prep time: 20 minutes | Cook time: 17 minutes | Serves 4

- 1 tablespoon butter, melted
- 1 medium-sized leek, thinly sliced
- 1 tablespoon chicken stock
- 1 tablespoon dry white wine
- 1 pound (454 g) tuna
- ½ teaspoon red pepper flakes, crushed
- Sea salt and ground black
- pepper, to taste
- ½ teaspoon dried rosemary
- ½ teaspoon dried basil
- ½ teaspoon dried thyme
- 2 small ripe tomatoes, puréed
- 1 cup Parmesan cheese, grated

1. Melt ½ tablespoon of butter in a sauté pan over medium-high

heat. Now, cook the leek and garlic until tender and aromatic. Add the stock and wine to deglaze the pan. 2. Preheat the air fryer to 370°F (188°C). 3. Grease a casserole dish with the remaining ½ tablespoon of melted butter. Place the fish in the casserole dish. Add the seasonings. Top with the sautéed leek mixture. Add the tomato purée. Cook for 10 minutes in the preheated air fryer. Top with grated Parmesan cheese; cook an additional 7 minutes until the crumbs are golden. Bon appétit!

Per Serving:

calories: 450 | fat: 22g | protein: 56g | carbs: 8g | net carbs: 6g | fiber: 2g

Pan-Seared Lemon-Garlic Salmon

Prep time: 5 minutes | Cook time: 10 minutes | Serves 2

- 1 tablespoon extra-virgin olive oil
- 2 (8-ounce / 227-g) salmon fillets
- 1 lemon, halved
- Pink Himalayan sea salt
- Freshly ground black pepper
- 2 tablespoons butter
- 1 tablespoon chopped fresh parsley
- 2 garlic cloves, minced

1. In a medium sauté pan or skillet, heat the olive oil over medium-high heat. 2. Squeeze the juice from a lemon half over the fillets. Season the salmon with salt and pepper. 3. Place the salmon skin-side up in the skillet. Cook for 4 to 5 minutes, then flip the fish and cook for an additional 2 to 3 minutes on the other side. 4. Add the butter, the juice from the other lemon half, the parsley, and garlic to the pan. Toss to combine. Allow the fish to cook for 2 to 3 more minutes, until the flesh flakes easily with a fork. 5. Transfer the fish to a serving plate, then top with the butter sauce and serve.

Per Serving:

calories: 489 | fat: 33g | protein: 45g | carbs: 0g | net carbs: 0g | fiber: 0g

Bacon Halibut Steak

Prep time: 15 minutes | Cook time: 10 minutes | Serves 4

- 24 ounces (680 g) halibut steaks (6 ounces / 170 g each fillet)
- 1 teaspoon avocado oil
- 1 teaspoon ground black pepper
- 4 ounces bacon, sliced

1. Sprinkle the halibut steaks with avocado oil and ground black pepper. 2. Then wrap the fish in the bacon slices and put in the air fryer. 3. Cook the fish at 390°F (199°C) for 5 minutes per side.

Per Serving:

calories: 430 | fat: 24g | protein: 48g | carbs: 1g | net carbs: 1g | fiber: 0g

Baked Coconut Haddock

Prep time: 10 minutes | Cook time: 12 minutes | Serves 4

◄ 4 (5-ounce) boneless haddock fillets
◄ Sea salt
◄ Freshly ground black pepper
◄ 1 cup shredded unsweetened

coconut
◄ ¼ cup ground hazelnuts
◄ 2 tablespoons coconut oil, melted

1. Preheat the oven to 400°F. Line a baking sheet with parchment paper and set aside. 2. Pat the fillets very dry with paper towels and lightly season them with salt and pepper. 3. Stir together the shredded coconut and hazelnuts in a small bowl. 4. Dredge the fish fillets in the coconut mixture so that both sides of each piece are thickly coated. 5. Place the fish on the baking sheet and lightly brush both sides of each piece with the coconut oil. 6. Bake the haddock until the topping is golden and the fish flakes easily with a fork, about 12 minutes total. 7. Serve.

Per Serving:

calories: 299 | fat: 24g | protein: 20g | carbs: 4g | net carbs: 1g | fiber: 4g

Lemon-Thyme Poached Halibut

Prep time: 5 minutes | Cook time: 15 minutes | Serves 4

◄ 1 lemon, thinly sliced
◄ ½ cup extra-virgin olive oil or MCT oil, plus more for drizzling
◄ 4 (6-ounce / 170-g) halibut steaks
◄ 1 teaspoon fine sea salt
◄ ½ teaspoon freshly ground

black pepper
◄ 1 sprig fresh thyme or other herb of choice
◄ Coarse sea salt, for garnish (preferably Hawaiian alaea sea salt for color)
◄ 1 tablespoon capers, for garnish (optional)

1. Line the bottom of a large enameled cast-iron skillet with the lemon slices. Pour the oil over the top of the lemon slices. Place the halibut steaks in the skillet and add enough water to cover the fish. Season the poaching liquid with the salt and pepper, then add the sprig of thyme. 2. Heat on medium-low until the poaching liquid is steaming but not boiling (about 165°F / 74°C). Once the liquid is steaming, poach the halibut steaks until they are cooked through and opaque, 10 to 12 minutes (depending on thickness). Remove the steaks from the poaching liquid. 3. Serve with a drizzle of olive oil and garnished with coarse sea salt and capers, if desired. 4. Store extras in an airtight container in the fridge for up to 3 days. To reheat, place the halibut in a heat-safe dish with a few tablespoons of water, cover, and place in a preheated 350°F (180°C) oven until warmed.

Per Serving:

calories: 305 | fat: 29g | protein: 9g | carbs: 2g | net carbs: 1g | fiber: 1g

Sicilian-Style Zoodle Spaghetti

Prep time: 10 minutes | Cook time: 11 minutes | Serves 2

◄ 4 cups zoodles (spiralled zucchini)
◄ 2 ounces cubed bacon
◄ 4 ounces canned sardines, chopped

◄ ½ cup canned chopped tomatoes
◄ 1 tablespoon capers
◄ 1 tablespoon parsley
◄ 1 teaspoon minced garlic

1. Pour some of the sardine oil in a pan. Add garlic and cook for 1 minute. Add the bacon and cook for 2 more minutes. Stir in the tomatoes and let simmer for 5 minutes. Add zoodles and sardines and cook for 3 minutes.

Per Serving:

calories: 290 | fat: 18g | protein: 22g | carbs: 13g | net carbs: 9g | fiber: 4g

Sushi Shrimp Rolls

Prep time: 5 minutes | Cook time: 0 minutes | Serves 5

◄ 2 cups cooked and chopped shrimp
◄ 1 tablespoon sriracha sauce

◄ ¼ cucumber, julienned
◄ 5 hand roll nori sheets
◄ ¼ cup mayonnaise

1. Combine shrimp, mayonnaise, cucumber and sriracha sauce in a bowl. Lay out a single nori sheet on a flat surface and spread about 1/5 of the shrimp mixture. Roll the nori sheet as desired. Repeat with the other ingredients. Serve with sugar-free soy sauce.

Per Serving:

calories: 180 | fat: 12g | protein: 16g | carbs: 2g | net carbs: 1g | fiber: 1g

Apple Cider Mussels

Prep time: 10 minutes | Cook time: 2 minutes | Serves 5

◄ 2 pounds (907 g) mussels, cleaned, peeled
◄ 1 teaspoon onion powder

◄ 1 teaspoon ground cumin
◄ 1 tablespoon avocado oil
◄ ¼ cup apple cider vinegar

1. Mix mussels with onion powder, ground cumin, avocado oil, and apple cider vinegar. 2. Put the mussels in the air fryer and cook at 395°F (202°C) for 2 minutes.

Per Serving:

calories: 210 | fat: 9g | protein: 23g | carbs: 7g | net carbs: 6g | fiber: 1g

Prep time: 10 minutes | Cook time: 18 minutes | Serves 4

- 4 tilapia fillets
- 2 garlic cloves, minced
- 2 teaspoons oregano
- 14 ounces diced tomatoes
- 1 tablespoon olive oil
- ½ red onion, chopped
- 2 tablespoons parsley
- ¼ cup kalamata olives

1. Heat olive oil in a skillet over medium heat and cook the onion for 3 minutes. Add garlic and oregano and cook for 30 seconds. Stir in tomatoes and bring the mixture to a boil. 2 Reduce the heat and simmer for 5 minutes. Add olives and tilapia, and cook for about 8 minutes. Serve the tilapia with tomato sauce.

Per Serving:

calories: 230 | fat: 9g | protein: 29g | carbs: 9g | net carbs: 7g | fiber: 2g

Prep time: 10 minutes | Cook time: 6 minutes | Serves 4

- 4 lobster tails, peeled
- 2 tablespoons lime juice
- ½ teaspoon dried basil
- ½ teaspoon coconut oil, melted

1. Mix lobster tails with lime juice, dried basil, and coconut oil. 2. Put the lobster tails in the air fryer and cook at 380°F (193°C) for 6 minutes.

Per Serving:

calories: 110 | fat: 2g | protein: 22g | carbs: 1g | net carbs: 1g | fiber: 0g

Prep time: 15 minutes | Cook time: 12 minutes | Serves 6

- 3 pounds mussels, cleaned, de-bearded
- 1 cup minced shallots
- 3 tablespoons minced garlic
- 1½ cups coconut milk
- 2 cups dry white wine
- 2 teaspoons red curry powder
- ⅓ cup coconut oil
- ⅓ cup chopped green onions
- ⅓ cup chopped parsley

1. Pour the wine into a large saucepan and cook the shallots and garlic over low heat. Stir in the coconut milk and red curry powder and cook for 3 minutes. 2. Add the mussels and steam for 7 minutes or until their shells are opened. Then, use a slotted spoon to

remove to a bowl leaving the sauce in the pan. Discard any closed mussels at this point. 3. Stir the coconut oil into the sauce, turn the heat off, and stir in the parsley and green onions. Serve the sauce immediately with a butternut squash mash.

Per Serving:

calories: 275 | fat: 19g | protein: 23g | carbs: 3g | net carbs: 2g | fiber: 1g

Prep time: 7 minutes | Cook time: 10 minutes | Serves 2

- 2 eggs, beaten
- 12 ounces (340 g) haddock fillet, chopped
- 1 tablespoon cream cheese
- ¾ teaspoon dried rosemary
- 2 ounces (57 g) Parmesan, grated
- 1 teaspoon butter

1. Whisk the beaten eggs until homogenous. Add the cream cheese, dried rosemary, and dill. 2. Grease the springform with the butter and place the haddock inside. 3. Pour the egg mixture over the fish and add sprinkle with Parmesan. 4. Set the Manual mode (High Pressure) and cook for 5 minutes. Then make a natural release pressure for 5 minutes.

Per Serving:

calories: 380 | fat: 16g | protein: 56g | carbs: 18g | net carbs: 18g | fiber: 0g

Prep time: 10 minutes | Cook time: 8 to 10 minutes | Serves 2

- 1 pound (454 g) salmon fillet
- 1½ tablespoons olive oil, divided
- 1 tablespoon sherry vinegar
- 1 tablespoon capers, rinsed and drained
- 1 seedless cucumber, thinly
- sliced
- ¼ Vidalia onion, thinly sliced
- 2 tablespoons chopped fresh parsley
- Salt and freshly ground black pepper, to taste

1. Preheat the air fryer to 400°F (204°C). 2. Lightly coat the salmon with ½ tablespoon of the olive oil. Place skin-side down in the air fryer basket and air fry for 8 to 10 minutes until the fish is opaque and flakes easily with a fork. Transfer the salmon to a plate and let cool to room temperature. Remove the skin and carefully flake the fish into bite-size chunks. 3. In a small bowl, whisk the remaining 1 tablespoon olive oil and the vinegar until thoroughly combined. Add the flaked fish, capers, cucumber, onion, and parsley. Season to taste with salt and freshly ground black pepper. Toss gently to coat. Serve immediately or cover and refrigerate for up to 4 hours.

Per Serving:

calories: 470 | fat: 35g | protein: 30g | carbs: 6g | net carbs: 5g | fiber: 1g

Rosemary Catfish

Prep time: 10 minutes | Cook time: 20 minutes | Serves 4

◀ 16 ounces (454 g) catfish fillet
◀ 1 tablespoon dried rosemary
◀ 1 teaspoon garlic powder
◀ 1 tablespoon avocado oil
◀ 1 teaspoon salt
◀ 1 cup water, for cooking

1. Cut the catfish fillet into 4 steaks. 2. Then sprinkle them with dried rosemary, garlic powder, avocado oil, and salt. 3. Place the fish steak in the baking mold in one layer. 4. After this, pour water and insert the steamer rack in the instant pot. 5. Put the baking mold with fish on the rack. Close and seal the lid. 6. Cook the meal on Manual (High Pressure) for 20 minutes. Make a quick pressure release.

Per Serving:

calories: 163 | fat: 9g | protein: 18g | carbs: 1g | net carbs: 1g | fiber: 0g

Paprika Shrimp

Prep time: 5 minutes | Cook time: 6 minutes | Serves 2

◀ 8 ounces (227 g) medium shelled and deveined shrimp
◀ 2 tablespoons salted butter, melted
◀ 1 teaspoon paprika
◀ ½ teaspoon garlic powder
◀ ¼ teaspoon onion powder
◀ ½ teaspoon Old Bay seasoning

1. Toss all ingredients together in a large bowl. Place shrimp into the air fryer basket. 2. Adjust the temperature to 400°F (204°C) and set the timer for 6 minutes. 3. Turn the shrimp halfway through the cooking time to ensure even cooking. Serve immediately.

Per Serving:

calories: 155 | fat: 9g | protein: 16g | carbs: 3g | net carbs: 2g | fiber: 1g

Dilled Salmon in Creamy Sauce

Prep time: 5 minutes | Cook time: 8 minutes | Serves 2

◀ 2 salmon fillets
◀ ¾ teaspoon dried tarragon
◀ 2 tablespoons olive oil
◀ ¾ teaspoon dried dill
◀ Sauce
◀ 2 tablespoons butter
◀ ½ teaspoon dill
◀ ½ teaspoon tarragon
◀ ¼ cup heavy cream
◀ Salt and black pepper to taste

1. Season the salmon with dill and tarragon. Warm the olive oil in a pan over medium heat. Add salmon and cook for about 4 minutes on both sides. Set aside. 2. To make the sauce: melt the butter and add the dill and tarragon. Cook for 30 seconds to infuse the flavors. Whisk in the heavy cream, season with salt and black pepper, and cook for 2-3 minutes. Serve the salmon topped with the sauce.

Per Serving:

calories: 391 | fat: 31g | protein: 26g | carbs: 2g | net carbs: 2g | fiber: 0g

Tuna Stuffed Poblano Peppers

Prep time: 15 minutes | Cook time: 12 minutes | Serves 4

◀ 7 ounces (198 g) canned tuna, shredded
◀ 1 teaspoon cream cheese
◀ ¼ teaspoon minced garlic
◀ 2 ounces (57 g) Provolone cheese, grated
◀ 4 poblano pepper
◀ 1 cup water, for cooking

1. Remove the seeds from poblano peppers. 2. In the mixing bowl, mix up shredded tuna, cream cheese, minced garlic, and grated cheese. 3. Then fill the peppers with tuna mixture and put it in the baking pan. 4. Pour water and insert the baking pan in the instant pot. 5. Cook the meal on Manual mode (High Pressure) for 12 minutes. Then make a quick pressure release.

Per Serving:

calories: 153 | fat: 8g | protein: 17g | carbs: 2g | net carbs: 1g | fiber: 1g

Paprika Crab Burgers

Prep time: 30 minutes | Cook time: 14 minutes | Serves 3

◀ 2 eggs, beaten
◀ 1 shallot, chopped
◀ 2 garlic cloves, crushed
◀ 1 tablespoon olive oil
◀ 1 teaspoon yellow mustard
◀ 1 teaspoon fresh cilantro, chopped
¾ cup Parmesan cheese
◀ 10 ounces (283 g) crab meat
◀ 1 teaspoon smoked paprika
◀ ½ teaspoon ground black pepper
◀ Sea salt, to taste

1. In a mixing bowl, thoroughly combine the eggs, shallot, garlic, olive oil, mustard, cilantro, crab meat, paprika, black pepper, and salt. Mix until well combined. 2. Shape the mixture into 6 patties. Roll the crab patties over grated Parmesan cheese, coating well on all sides. Place in your refrigerator for 2 hours. 3. Spritz the crab patties with cooking oil on both sides. Cook in the preheated air fryer at 360°F (182°C) for 14 minutes. Serve on dinner rolls if desired. Bon appétit!

Per Serving:

calories: 410 | fat: 26g | protein: 36g | carbs: 7g | net carbs: 6g | fiber: 1g

Prep time: 5 minutes | Cook time: 20 minutes | Serves 4

- ¼ cup plus 2 tablespoons (75 ml) avocado oil, divided
- ¼ cup (60 ml) coconut aminos
- 2 tablespoons plus 2 teaspoons tomato paste
- 2 tablespoons apple cider vinegar
- 1 (2-in/5-cm) piece fresh ginger root, grated
- 4 cloves garlic, minced
- ½ teaspoon finely ground sea salt

- 1 pound (455 g) salmon fillets, cut into 4 equal portions
- 2 (7-ounce/198-g) packages konjac noodles or equivalent amount of other low-carb noodles of choice
- 2 green onions, sliced
- Handful of fresh cilantro leaves, roughly chopped
- 1 teaspoon sesame seeds

1. Heat 2 tablespoons of the oil in a large frying pan over medium heat. 2. While the oil is heating, make the sauce: In a small bowl, whisk together the remaining ¼ cup of oil, the coconut aminos, tomato paste, vinegar, ginger, garlic, and salt. 3. Place the salmon in the hot pan, reduce the heat to low, and slather with the sauce. Drizzle any remaining sauce directly into the pan. Cover and cook on low for 15 minutes, until seared and lightly cooked through. 4. Once the salmon is done, pile the salmon up on one side of the pan, leaving enough space for the noodles. Add the noodles and green onions to the pan and toss to coat in the remaining sauce. Then place the cooked salmon on top of the noodles. Cook for another 3 to 5 minutes, just long enough to heat the noodles. 5. Sprinkle the cilantro and sesame seeds over the top of the salmon. Divide the noodles and salmon among 4 dinner plates, drizzling each portion with the leftover pan sauce, and enjoy.

Per Serving:

calories: 333 | fat: 22g | protein: 25g | carbs: 8g | net carbs: 5g | fiber: 4g

Chicken-Pecan Salad Cucumber Bites

Prep time: 15 minutes | Cook time: 0 minutes | Serves 2

- ◀ 1 cup diced cooked chicken breast
- ◀ 2 tablespoons mayonnaise
- ◀ ¼ cup chopped pecans
- ◀ ¼ cup diced celery
- ◀ Pink Himalayan salt
- ◀ Freshly ground black pepper
- ◀ 1 cucumber, peeled and cut into ¼-inch slices

1. In a medium bowl, mix together the chicken, mayonnaise, pecans, and celery. Season with pink Himalayan salt and pepper. 2. Lay the cucumber slices out on a plate, and add a pinch of pink Himalayan salt to each. 3. Top each cucumber slice with a spoonful of the chicken-salad mixture and serve.

Per Serving:

calories: 323 | fat: 24g | protein: 23g | carbs: 6g | net carbs: 4g | fiber: 3g

Tapenade

Prep time: 5 minutes | Cook time: 0 minutes | Serves 2

- ◀ 1 cup pitted black olives
- ◀ 1 cup pitted green olives
- ◀ ¼ cup sun-dried tomatoes in oil, drained
- ◀ 6 fresh basil leaves
- ◀ 1 tablespoon capers
- ◀ 1 tablespoon fresh parsley leaves
- ◀ 2 teaspoons fresh thyme
- leaves
- ◀ Leaves from 1 sprig fresh oregano
- ◀ 1 clove garlic
- ◀ 1 anchovy fillet
- ◀ ¼ cup olive oil
- ◀ 6 medium celery stalks, cut into sticks, for serving

1. Place all the ingredients, except the olive oil and celery sticks, in a blender or food processor. Pulse until roughly chopped. 2. Add the olive oil and pulse a couple more times, just to combine. 3. Transfer to a 16-ounce (475-ml) or larger serving dish and enjoy with celery sticks. Store it: :Keep in an airtight container in the fridge for up to 5 days.

Per Serving:

calories: 167 | fat: 16g | protein: 1g | carbs: 4g | net carbs: 3g | fiber: 1g

Savory Mackerel & Goat'S Cheese "Paradox" Balls

Prep time: 10 minutes | Cook time: 0 minutes | Makes 10 fat bombs

- ◀ 2 smoked or cooked mackerel fillets, boneless, skin removed
- ◀ 4.4 ounces (125 g) soft goat's cheese
- ◀ 1 tablespoon fresh lemon juice
- ◀ 1 teaspoon Dijon or yellow
- mustard
- ◀ 1 small red onion, finely diced
- ◀ 2 tablespoons chopped fresh chives or herbs of choice
- ◀ ¾ cup pecans, crushed
- ◀ 10 leaves baby gem lettuce

1. In a food processor, combine the mackerel, goat's cheese, lemon juice, and mustard. Pulse until smooth. Transfer to a bowl, add the onion and herbs, and mix with a spoon. Refrigerate for 20 to 30 minutes, or until set. 2. Using a large spoon or an ice cream scoop, divide the mixture into 10 balls, about 40 g/1.4 ounces each. Roll each ball in the crushed pecans. Place each ball on a small lettuce leaf and serve. Keep the fat bombs refrigerated in a sealed container for up to 5 days.

Per Serving:

1 fat bomb: calories: 150 | fat: 13g | protein: 7g | carbs: 3g | net carbs: 2g | fiber: 1g

Strawberry Shortcake Coconut Ice

Prep time: 5 minutes | Cook time: 0 minutes | Serves 5

- ◀ 9 hulled strawberries (fresh or frozen and defrosted)
- ◀ ⅓ cup (85 g) coconut cream
- ◀ 1 tablespoon apple cider
- vinegar
- ◀ 2 drops liquid stevia, or 2 teaspoons erythritol
- ◀ 3 cups (420 g) ice cubes

1. Place the strawberries, coconut cream, vinegar, and sweetener in a blender or food processor. Blend until smooth. 2. Add the ice and pulse until crushed. 3. Divide among four ¾-cup (180-ml) or larger bowls and serve immediately.

Per Serving:

calories: 61 | fat: 5g | protein: 0g | carbs: 3g | net carbs: 2g | fiber: 1g

Classy Crudités and Dip

Prep time: 15 minutes | Cook time: 0 minutes | Serves 8

Vegetables
- 1 cup whole cherry tomatoes
- 1 cup green beans, trimmed
- 2 cups broccoli florets
- 2 cups cauliflower florets
- 1 bunch asparagus, trimmed
- 1 large green bell pepper, seeded and chopped

Sour Cream Dip
- 2 cups full-fat sour cream
- 3 tablespoons dry chives
- 1 tablespoon lemon juice
- ½ cup dried parsley
- ½ teaspoon garlic powder
- ⅛ teaspoon salt
- ⅛ teaspoon black pepper

1. Cut vegetables into bite-sized uniform pieces. Arrange in like groups around outside edge of a large serving platter, leaving room in middle for dip. 2. Make dip by combining dip ingredients in a medium-sized decorative bowl and mixing well. 3. Place dip bowl in the center of platter and serve.

Per Serving:

calories: 146| fat: 10g | protein: 4g | carbs: 9g | net carbs: 6g | fiber: 3g

Keto Asian Dumplings

Prep time: 20 minutes | Cook time: 20 minutes | Serves 4

Dipping Sauce:
- ¼ cup gluten-free soy sauce
- 2 tablespoons sesame oil

Filling:
- 1 tablespoon sesame oil
- 2 garlic cloves
- 1 teaspoon grated fresh ginger
- 1 celery stalk, minced
- ½ onion, minced
- 1 carrot, minced
- 8 ounces (227 g) ground pork
- 8 ounces (227 g) shrimp, peeled, deveined, and finely
- 1 tablespoon rice vinegar
- 1 teaspoon chili garlic sauce

 chopped
- 2 tablespoons gluten-free soy sauce
- ½ teaspoon fish sauce
- Salt and freshly ground black pepper, to taste
- 3 scallions, green parts only, chopped
- 1 head napa cabbage, rinsed, leaves separated (about 12 leaves)

Make the Dipping Sauce; 1. In a small bowl, whisk together the soy sauce, sesame oil, vinegar, and chili garlic sauce. Set aside. Make the Filling: 2. In a large skillet over medium heat, heat the sesame oil. 3. Add the garlic, ginger, celery, onion, and carrot. Sauté for 5 to 7 minutes until softened. 4. Add the pork. Cook for 5 to 6 minutes, breaking it up with a spoon, until it starts to brown. 5. Add the shrimp and stir everything together well. 6. Stir in the soy sauce and fish sauce. Season with a little salt and pepper. Give it a stir and add the scallions. Keep it warm over low heat until ready to fill the dumplings. 7. Steam the cabbage leaves: Place the leaves in

a large saucepan with just 1 to 2 inches of boiling water. Cook for about 5 minutes or until the leaves become tender. Remove from the water and set aside to drain. 8. Lay each leaf out flat. Put about 2 tablespoons of filling in the center of one leaf. Wrap the leaf over itself, tucking the sides in so the whole thing is tightly wrapped. Secure with a toothpick. Continue with the remaining leaves and filling. Serve with the dipping sauce. Refrigerate leftovers in an airtight container for up to 3 days.

Per Serving:

3 dumplings: calories: 305 | fat: 17g | protein: 27g | carbs: 11g | net carbs: 8g | fiber: 3g

Goat Cheese–Mackerel Pâté

Prep time: 10 minutes | Cook time: 0 minutes | Serves 4

- 4 ounces (113 g) olive oil-packed wild-caught mackerel
- 2 ounces (57 g) goat cheese
- Zest and juice of 1 lemon
- 2 tablespoons chopped fresh parsley
- 2 tablespoons chopped fresh arugula
- 1 tablespoon extra-virgin olive oil
- 2 teaspoons chopped capers
- 1 to 2 teaspoons fresh horseradish (optional)
- Crackers, cucumber rounds, endive spears, or celery, for serving (optional)

1. In a food processor, blender, or large bowl with immersion blender, combine the mackerel, goat cheese, lemon zest and juice, parsley, arugula, olive oil, capers, and horseradish (if using). Process or blend until smooth and creamy. 2. Serve with crackers, cucumber rounds, endive spears, or celery. 3. Store covered in the refrigerator for up to 1 week.

Per Serving:

calories: 190 | fat: 15g | protein: 11g | carbs: 3g | net carbs: 2g | fiber: 1g

Chipped Artichokes

Prep time: 5 minutes | Cook time: 35 minutes | Serves 4

- ½ teaspoon salt, divided
- 2 large artichokes, trimmed
- 2 tablespoons lemon juice
- ½ cup full-fat mayonnaise

1. In a large pot, prepare 1" water with ¼ teaspoon salt. 2. Put artichokes in a steamer basket inside pot, stem-side up, and cover pot. When boiling starts, reduce heat to medium-low and leave untouched 25 minutes. 3. Test to see if done by pulling off outer leaf using tongs. If it doesn't come off easily, add additional water to pot and steam 5–10 more minutes. Let cool. 4. Serve with dip made by combining lemon juice, mayonnaise, and remaining salt.

Per Serving:

calories: 219 | fat: 20g | protein: 2g | carbs: 8g | net carbs: 3g | fiber: 5g

Grandma's Meringues

Prep time: 10 minutes | Cook time: 1 hour | Makes 12 meringues

- 2 large egg whites, room temperature
- ¼ teaspoon cream of tartar
- Pinch of finely ground sea salt
For Serving:
- 24 fresh strawberries, sliced
- ¾ cup (190 g) coconut

- salt
- ½ cup (80 g) confectioners'-style erythritol
- ½ teaspoon vanilla extract
- cream
- 12 fresh mint leaves

1. Preheat the oven to 225°F (108°C). Line a rimmed baking sheet with parchment paper or a silicone baking mat. 2. Place the egg whites, cream of tartar, and salt in a very clean large bowl. Make sure that the bowl does not have any oil residue in it. Using a handheld electric mixer or stand mixer, mix on low speed until the mixture becomes foamy. 3. Once foamy, increase the speed to high. Slowly add the erythritol, 1 tablespoon at a time, mixing all the while. Add a tablespoon about every 20 seconds. 4. Keep beating until the mixture is shiny and thick and peaks have formed; it should be nearly doubled in volume. (The peaks won't be as stiff as in a traditional meringue.) Fold in the vanilla. 5. Using a large spoon, dollop the meringue mixture onto the lined baking sheet, making a total of 12 meringues. 6. Bake for 1 hour without opening the oven door. After 1 hour, turn off the oven and keep the meringues in the cooling oven for another hour, then remove. 7. To serve, place 2 meringues on each plate. Top each serving with 4 sliced strawberries, 2 tablespoons of coconut cream, and 2 mint leaves.

Per Serving:

calories: 100 | fat: 8g | protein: 2g | carbs: 6g | net carbs: 4g | fiber: 2g

Loaded Bacon and Cheddar Cheese Balls

Prep time: 10 minutes | Cook time: 0 minutes | Makes 16 balls

- 7 bacon slices, cooked until crisp, cooled, and crumbled
- 1 tablespoon chopped chives
- 8 ounces (227 g) cream cheese
- 1½ cups finely shredded

- Cheddar cheese
- ½ teaspoon smoked paprika
- 1 teaspoon onion powder
- ½ teaspoon sea salt
- Olive oil or butter, for greasing

1. Line a plate or storage container with parchment paper. 2. In a small bowl, toss together the crumbled bacon and chives and set aside. 3. In a food processor or blender, mix together the cream cheese, Cheddar, paprika, onion powder, and salt. 4. Grease your hands with olive oil or butter to avoid sticking, and form 16 balls of cheese. Roll each ball in the bacon and chive "batter" as you go, and set them on the prepared plate or storage container. 5. Serve right away, or store in an airtight container in the refrigerator for up to 5 days.

Per Serving:

2 cheese balls: calories: 228 | fat: 20g | protein: 10g | carbs: 2g | net carbs: 2g | fiber: 0g

Cheddar Cauliflower Rice

Prep time: 3 minutes | Cook time: 1 minute | Serves 4

- 1 head fresh cauliflower, chopped into florets
- 1 cup water
- 3 tablespoons butter
- 1 tablespoon heavy cream

- 1 cup shredded sharp Cheddar cheese
- ½ teaspoon salt
- ¼ teaspoon pepper
- ¼ teaspoon garlic powder

1. Place cauliflower in steamer basket. Pour water into Instant Pot and lower steamer rack into pot. Click lid closed. Press the Steam button and adjust time for 1 minute. When timer beeps, quick-release the pressure. 2. Remove steamer basket and place cauliflower in food processor. Pulse until cauliflower is broken into small pearls. Place cauliflower into large bowl, and add remaining ingredients. Gently fold until fully combined.

Per Serving:

calories: 241 | fat: 18g | protein: 10g | carbs: 8g | net carbs: 5g | fiber: 3g

Brussels Sprouts with Aioli Sauce

Prep time: 5 minutes | Cook time: 7 minutes | Serves 4

- 1 tablespoon butter
- ½ cup chopped scallions
Aioli Sauce:
- ¼ cup mayonnaise
- 1 tablespoon fresh lemon juice

- ¾ pound (340 g) Brussels sprouts
- 1 garlic clove, minced
- ½ teaspoon Dijon mustard

1. Set your Instant Pot to Sauté and melt the butter. 2. Add the scallions and sauté for 2 minutes until softened. Add the Brussels sprouts and cook for another 1 minute. 3. Lock the lid. Select the Manual mode and set the cooking time for 4 minutes at High Pressure. 4. Meanwhile, whisk together all the ingredients for the Aioli sauce in a small bowl until well incorporated. 5. When the timer beeps, perform a quick pressure release. Carefully remove the lid. 6. Serve the Brussels sprouts with the Aioli sauce on the side.

Per Serving:

calories: 167 | fat: 14g | protein: 3g | carbs: 9g | net carbs: 5g | fiber: 3g

Low-Carb Zucchini Fritters

Prep time: 20 minutes | Cook time: 20 minutes | Serves 4

◀ 3 or 4 medium zucchini
◀ Salt, to taste
◀ 1 or 2 garlic cloves, minced
◀ ¼ cup almond flour
◀ 2 eggs, whisked

◀ Freshly ground black pepper, to taste
◀ 2 tablespoons butter
◀ 2 tablespoons sliced scallion, green parts only

1. In a food processor or with a cheese grater, shred the zucchini into hash brown–like pieces. Transfer to a colander and sprinkle liberally with salt. Let sit in the sink for 15 to 20 minutes. Carefully rinse and drain the zucchini, pat dry with a paper towel, and place in a large bowl. 2. Add the garlic, almond flour, and eggs to the bowl. Season with pepper. Stir until well incorporated. 3. In a large skillet over medium-high heat, melt the butter. Spoon 2 to 3 tablespoons of the zucchini mixture into your hand and create a patty about half the size of your palm. Repeat with the remaining zucchini mixture. Carefully place the patties into the butter (you may have to cook these in batches). Cook for about 3 minutes until browned on one side. Flip and cook the other side for about 3 minutes until browned. Serve topped with the sliced scallion.

Per Serving:
calories: 101 | fat: 9g | protein: 4g | carbs: 1g | net carbs: 1g | fiber: 0g

Lemon Pepper Wings

Prep time: 5 minutes | Cook time: 16 minutes | Serves 6

◀ 1 to 2 cups coconut oil or other Paleo fat, for frying
◀ 1 pound (454 g) chicken wings (about 12 wings)
Sauce:
◀ ¼ cup MCT oil or extra-virgin olive oil

◀ ½ teaspoon fine sea salt, divided
◀ 1 teaspoon freshly ground black pepper, divided
◀ Grated zest of 1 lemon
◀ Juice of 1 lemon

1. Preheat the oil to 350°F (180°C) in a deep-fryer or in a 4-inch-deep (or deeper) cast-iron skillet over medium heat. The oil should be at least 3 inches deep; add more oil if needed. 2. While the oil is heating, make the sauce: Place the MCT oil in a small dish. Add the lemon zest and juice and whisk to combine. 3. Fry the wings in the hot oil, about six at a time, until golden brown on all sides and cooked through, about 8 minutes. Remove the wings from the oil and sprinkle with half of the salt and pepper. Repeat with the remaining wings, salt, and pepper. 4. Place the wings on a serving platter and serve with the sauce. They are best served fresh. Store extra wings and sauce separately in airtight containers in the fridge for up to 3 days. To reheat, place the wings on a rimmed baking sheet and heat in a preheated 400°F (205°C) oven for 4 minutes, or until the chicken is warm.

Per Serving:

calories: 286 | fat: 24g | protein: 16g | carbs: 1g | net carbs: 1g | fiber: 0g

Roasted Spiced Nut Mix

Prep time: 10 minutes | Cook time: 10 minutes | Serves 8

◀ 1 teaspoon vanilla extract
◀ 1 teaspoon ground cinnamon
◀ 1 teaspoon ground allspice
◀ ½ teaspoon ground ginger
◀ ½ teaspoon ground nutmeg
◀ 1 teaspoon liquid stevia

(optional)
◀ 4 tablespoons butter
◀ 1 cup pecans
◀ ½ cup almonds
◀ ½ cup macadamia nuts

1. Preheat the oven to 375°F (190°C). 2. In a small bowl, combine the vanilla, cinnamon, allspice, ginger, nutmeg, and stevia (if using). Set aside. 3. In a large nonstick skillet over medium-low heat, melt the butter. 4. Add the pecans, almonds, and macadamias. Sprinkle the spice mixture over the nuts and stir to combine, ensuring the nuts are thoroughly coated in butter and spices. Cook for about 10 minutes or until the nuts are golden brown. Remove from the heat and cool slightly before serving. 5. Store in an airtight container on the counter for a few days or refrigerate for up to 1 week.

Per Serving:
¼ cup: calories: 279 | fat: 27g | protein: 4g | carbs: 5g | net carbs: 2g | fiber: 3g

Herbed Shrimp

Prep time: 5 minutes | Cook time: 5 minutes | Serves 4

◀ 2 tablespoons olive oil
◀ ¾ pound (340 g) shrimp, peeled and deveined
◀ 1 teaspoon paprika
◀ 1 teaspoon garlic powder
◀ 1 teaspoon onion powder
◀ 1 teaspoon dried parsley flakes

◀ ½ teaspoon dried oregano
◀ ½ teaspoon dried thyme
◀ ½ teaspoon dried basil
◀ ½ teaspoon dried rosemary
◀ ¼ teaspoon red pepper flakes
◀ Coarse sea salt and ground black pepper, to taste
◀ 1 cup chicken broth

1. Set your Instant Pot to Sauté and heat the olive oil. 2. Add the shrimp and sauté for 2 to 3 minutes. 3. Add the remaining ingredients to the Instant Pot and stir to combine. 4. Secure the lid. Select the Manual mode and set the cooking time for 2 minutes at Low Pressure. 5. When the timer beeps, perform a quick pressure release. Carefully remove the lid. 6. Transfer the shrimp to a plate and serve.

Per Serving:
calories: 146 | fat: 8g | protein: 19g | carbs: 3g | net carbs: 2g | fiber: 1g

Salmon-Stuffed Cucumbers

Prep time: 10 minutes | Cook time: 0 minutes | Serves 4

- 2 large cucumbers, peeled
- 1 (4 ounces / 113 g) can red salmon
- 1 medium very ripe avocado, peeled, pitted, and mashed
- 1 tablespoon extra-virgin olive oil
- Zest and juice of 1 lime
- 3 tablespoons chopped fresh cilantro
- ½ teaspoon salt
- ¼ teaspoon freshly ground black pepper

1. Slice the cucumber into 1-inch-thick segments and using a spoon, scrape seeds out of center of each segment and stand up on a plate. 2. In a medium bowl, combine the salmon, avocado, olive oil, lime zest and juice, cilantro, salt, and pepper and mix until creamy. 3. Spoon the salmon mixture into the center of each cucumber segment and serve chilled.

Per Serving:
calories: 174 | fat: 12g | protein: 10g | carbs: 9g | net carbs: 6g | fiber: 3g

Zucchini Cakes with Lemon Aioli

Prep time: 20 minutes | Cook time: 22 minutes | Makes 8 small cakes

Cakes:
- 3 lightly packed cups (450 g) shredded zucchini (about 3 medium zucchinis)
- 4 strips bacon (about 4 ounces/110 g)
- 1 teaspoon finely ground sea salt
- 1 large egg
- 1 tablespoon coconut flour

Lemon Aioli:
- ¼ cup (52 g) mayonnaise
- Grated zest of ½ lemon
- 1 tablespoon plus 1 teaspoon lemon juice
- 1 teaspoon Dijon mustard

- 1 tablespoon arrowroot starch or tapioca starch
- ¾ teaspoon garlic powder
- ¾ teaspoon onion powder
- ½ teaspoon dried oregano leaves
- ¼ teaspoon ground black pepper

- 1 clove garlic, minced
- ¼ teaspoon finely ground sea salt
- ⅛ teaspoon ground black pepper

1. Cut the cucumber in half lengthwise, scoop out the seeds, and then cut each piece in half crosswise. Set aside. 2. Place the remaining ingredients in a medium-sized bowl and mix until incorporated. 3. Spoon the tuna mixture into the hollowed-out cucumber pieces, piling it high. Set on a plate and 1. Place the shredded zucchini in a strainer set over the sink. Sprinkle with the salt and allow to sit for 15 minutes. 2. Meanwhile, cook the bacon in a large frying pan over medium heat until crispy, about 10 minutes. Remove the bacon from the pan, leaving the grease in the pan. When the bacon has cooled, crumble it. 3. While the bacon is cooking, make the aioli: Put the mayonnaise, lemon zest, lemon juice, mustard, garlic, salt, and pepper in a small bowl and whisk to incorporate. Set aside. 4. When the zucchini is ready, squeeze it over and over again to get out as much of the water as you can. 5. Transfer the zucchini to a large mixing bowl and add the remaining ingredients for the cakes. Stir until fully incorporated. 6. Set the frying pan with the bacon grease over medium-low heat. Scoop up 2 tablespoons of the zucchini mixture, roll it into a ball between your hands, and place in the hot pan. Repeat with the remaining mixture, making a total of 8 balls. Press each ball with the back of a fork until the cakes are about ½ inch (1.25 cm) thick. 7. Cook the cakes for 4 to 6 minutes per side, until golden. Serve with the aioli.

Per Serving:
calories: 636 | fat: 53g | protein: 28g | carbs: 12g | net carbs: 9g | fiber: 3g

Baked Brie with Pecans

Prep time: 5 minutes | Cook time: 10 minutes | Serves 6

- 1 (¾ pound / 340 g) wheel Brie cheese
- 3 ounces (85 g) pecans, chopped
- 2 garlic cloves, minced
- 2 tablespoons minced fresh rosemary leaves
- 1½ tablespoons olive oil
- Salt and freshly ground black pepper, to taste

1. Preheat the oven to 400°F (205°C). 2. Line a baking sheet with parchment paper and place the Brie on it. 3. In a small bowl, stir together the pecans, garlic, rosemary, and olive oil. Season with salt and pepper. Spoon the mixture in an even layer over the Brie. Bake for about 10 minutes until the cheese is warm and the nuts are lightly browned. 4. Remove and let it cool for 1 to 2 minutes before serving.

Per Serving:
calories: 318 | fat: 29g | protein: 13g | carbs: 3g | net carbs: 2g | fiber: 1g

Buttered Cabbage

Prep time: 5 minutes | Cook time: 5 minutes | Serves 4

- 1 medium head white cabbage, sliced into strips
- 4 tablespoons butter
- ½ teaspoon salt
- ¼ teaspoon pepper
- 1 cup water

1. Place cabbage in 7-cup glass bowl with butter, salt, and pepper. 2. Pour water into Instant Pot and place steam rack on bottom. Place bowl on steam rack. Click lid closed. Press the Manual button and adjust time for 5 minutes. When timer beeps, quick-release the pressure.

Per Serving:
calories: 158 | fat: 10g | protein: 3g | carbs: 13g | net carbs: 8g | fiber: 5g

Deviled Eggs with Tuna

Prep time: 10 minutes | Cook time: 8 minutes | Serves 3

◁ 1 cup water
◁ 6 eggs
◁ 1 (5 ounces / 142 g) can tuna, drained
◁ 4 tablespoons mayonnaise
◁ 1 teaspoon lemon juice
◁ 1 celery stalk, diced finely
◁ ¼ teaspoon Dijon mustard
◁ ¼ teaspoon chopped fresh dill
◁ ¼ teaspoon salt
◁ ⅛ teaspoon garlic powder

1. Add water to Instant Pot. Place steam rack or steamer basket inside pot. Carefully put eggs into steamer basket. Click lid closed. Press the Manual button and adjust time for 8 minutes. 2. Add remaining ingredients to medium bowl and mix. 3. When timer beeps, quick-release the steam and remove eggs. Place in bowl of cool water for 10 minutes, then remove shells. 4. Cut eggs in half and remove hard-boiled yolks, setting whites aside. Place yolks in food processor and pulse until smooth, or mash with fork. Add yolks to bowl with tuna and mayo, mixing until smooth. 5. Spoon mixture into egg-white halves. Serve chilled.

Per Serving:

calories: 303 | fat: 22g | protein: 20g | carbs: 2g | net carbs: 2g | fiber: 0g

Pickled Herring

Prep time: 4 minutes | Cook time: 5 minutes | Serves 12

◁ 4 pounds (1.8 kg) herring or skinned Northern Pike
Saltwater Brine:
◁ 10 cups water
Pickling Brine:
◁ ½ cup thinly sliced red onions
◁ Handful of fresh dill
◁ 2 cups water
◁ 2½ cups coconut vinegar
◁ ½ cup Swerve confectioners'-style sweetener or equivalent amount of liquid or
For Serving:
◁ Hard-boiled eggs, halved or quartered
◁ Pickled ginger
◁ Capers

fillets, cut into 2-inch pieces

◁ ½ cup fine sea salt

powdered sweetener
◁ 2 teaspoons ground allspice
◁ 1 teaspoon dry mustard or mustard seeds
◁ ½ teaspoon grated fresh ginger
◁ ½ teaspoon prepared horseradish
◁ ½ teaspoon peppercorns

◁ Fermented pickles
◁ Sliced red onions
◁ Fresh dill sprigs

1. Place the fish in a large bowl with the 10 cups of water. Add the salt and stir. Cover and refrigerate for 24 hours, then drain the fish and rinse it well. 2. Place the drained and rinsed fish in a clean 2-liter glass jar, layering it with the sliced onions and dill. 3. In a large pot over medium heat, heat the 2 cups of water, coconut vinegar, sweetener, allspice, mustard, ginger, horseradish, and peppercorns. Once the sweetener has dissolved, about 5 minutes, allow the brine to cool a little, then pour over the fish packed in the jar. Cover and refrigerate overnight to allow the flavors to meld; the longer the better for stronger flavors. If you let it sit for 5 days, the bones will dissolve. The pickled fish will keep in an airtight container in the fridge for up to 1 month. 4. To serve, arrange the pickled fish on a platter with hard-boiled eggs, pickled ginger, capers, fermented pickles, sliced red onions, and fresh dill.

Per Serving:

calories: 240 | fat: 14g | protein: 27g | carbs: 2g | net carbs: 2g | fiber: 0g

Bacon-Wrapped Jalapeños

Prep time: 10 minutes | Cook time: 20 minutes | Serves 4

◁ 10 jalapeños
◁ 8 ounces cream cheese, at room temperature
◁ 1 pound bacon (you will use about half a slice per popper)

1. Preheat the oven to 450°F. Line a baking sheet with aluminum foil or a silicone baking mat. 2. Halve the jalapeños lengthwise, and remove the seeds and membranes (if you like the extra heat, leave them in). Place them on the prepared pan cut-side up. 3. Spread some of the cream cheese inside each jalapeño half. 4. Wrap a jalapeño half with a slice of bacon (depending on the size of the jalapeño, use a whole slice of bacon, or half). 5. Secure the bacon around each jalapeño with 1 to 2 toothpicks so it stays put while baking. 6. Bake for 20 minutes, until the bacon is done and crispy. 7. Serve hot or at room temperature. Either way, they are delicious!

Per Serving:

calories: 164 | fat: 13g | protein: 9g | carbs: 1g | net carbs: 1g | fiber: 0g

Whoops They're Gone Walnuts 'n Dark Chocolate Snack Bag

Prep time: 5 minutes | Cook time: 0 minutes | Makes about 2 cups

◁ 1 (3½-ounce / 99-g) bar of dark chocolate
◁ 1½ cups shelled walnuts
◁ 6 tablespoons large coconut flakes (optional)

1. Break up the bar while it is still in the package, then pour the pieces into a zippered plastic bag. Add the walnuts and shake. 2. If desired, add the coconut flakes to the bag as well.

Per Serving:

calories: 305 | fat: 27g | protein: 7g | carbs: 9g | net carbs: 6g | fiber: 3g

Smoky "Hummus" and Veggies

Prep time: 15 minutes | Cook time: 20 minutes | serves 6

- ◄ Nonstick coconut oil cooking spray
- ◄ 1 cauliflower head, cut into florets
- ◄ ¼ cup tahini
- ◄ ¼ cup cold-pressed olive oil, plus extra for drizzling
- ◄ Juice of 1 lemon
- ◄ 1 tablespoon ground paprika
- ◄ 1 teaspoon sea salt
- ◄ ¼ cup chopped fresh parsley, for garnish
- ◄ 2 tablespoons pine nuts (optional)
- ◄ Flax crackers, for serving
- ◄ Sliced cucumbers, for serving
- ◄ Celery pieces, for serving

1. Preheat the oven to 400°F and grease a baking sheet with cooking spray. 2. Spread the cauliflower florets out on the prepared baking sheet and bake for 20 minutes. 3. Remove the cauliflower from the oven and allow it to cool for 10 minutes. 4. In a food processor or high-powered blender, combine the cauliflower with the tahini, olive oil, lemon juice, paprika, and salt. Blend on high until a fluffy, creamy texture is achieved. If the mixture seems too thick, slowly add a few tablespoons of water until smooth. 5. Scoop the "hummus" into an airtight container and chill in the refrigerator for about 20 minutes. 6. Transfer the "hummus" to a serving bowl and drizzle with olive oil. Garnish with the parsley and pine nuts (if using). 7. Serve with your favorite flax crackers and sliced cucumbers and celery.

Per Serving:

calories: 169 | fat: 15g | protein: 4g | carbs: 9g | net carbs: 5g | fiber: 4g

Colby Cheese and Pepper Dip

Prep time: 5 minutes | Cook time: 5 minutes | Serves 8

- ◄ 1 tablespoon butter
- ◄ 2 red bell peppers, sliced
- ◄ 2 cups shredded Colby cheese
- ◄ 1 cup cream cheese, room temperature
- ◄ 1 cup chicken broth
- ◄ 2 garlic cloves, minced
- ◄ 1 teaspoon red Aleppo pepper flakes
- ◄ 1 teaspoon sumac
- ◄ Salt and ground black pepper, to taste

1. Set your Instant Pot to Sauté and melt the butter. 2. Add the bell peppers and sauté for about 2 minutes until just tender. 3. Add the remaining ingredients to the Instant Pot and gently stir to incorporate. 4. Lock the lid. Select the Manual mode and set the cooking time for 3 minutes at High Pressure. 5. When the timer beeps, perform a quick pressure release. Carefully remove the lid. 6. Allow to cool for 5 minutes and serve warm.

Per Serving:

calories: 241 | fat: 21g | protein: 11g | carbs: 3g | net carbs: 3g | fiber: 0g

Charlie's Energy Balls

Prep time: 10 minutes | Cook time: 20 minutes | Makes 20 balls

- ◄ ½ cup natural almond butter, room temperature
- ◄ ¼ cup coconut oil, melted
- ◄ 1 large egg
- ◄ ½ cup coconut flour
- ◄ 2 tablespoons unflavored beef gelatin powder
- ◄ 1 scoop chocolate-flavored whey protein powder

1. Preheat the oven to 350°F and grease a rimmed baking sheet with coconut oil spray. 2. In a large mixing bowl, mix together the almond butter, coconut oil, and egg using a fork. In a small bowl, whisk together the coconut flour, gelatin, and protein powder. 3. Pour the dry ingredients into the wet mixture and mash with a fork until you have a cohesive dough. It should not be too sticky. Note: If the dough doesn't come together well or is very sticky, add a little coconut flour until it combines well. 4. Using your hands, form the dough into 20 even-sized balls, about 1½ inches in diameter, and put them on the prepared baking sheet. 5. Bake for 20 minutes, until slightly browned and hardened. Allow to cool on the baking sheet for 10 minutes prior to serving. 6. Store in a zip-top plastic bag in the refrigerator for up to a week.

Per Serving:

calories: 91 | fat: 7g | protein: 4g | carbs: 3g | net carbs: 2g | fiber: 1g

Salami, Pepperoncini, and Cream Cheese Pinwheels

Prep time: 20 minutes | Cook time: 0 minutes | Serves 2

- ◄ 8 ounces cream cheese, at room temperature
- ◄ ¼ pound salami, thinly sliced
- ◄ 2 tablespoons sliced pepperoncini (I use Mezzetta)

1. Lay out a sheet of plastic wrap on a large cutting board or counter. 2. Place the cream cheese in the center of the plastic wrap, and then add another layer of plastic wrap on top. Using a rolling pin, roll the cream cheese until it is even and about ¼ inch thick. Try to make the shape somewhat resemble a rectangle. 3. Pull off the top layer of plastic wrap. 4. Place the salami slices so they overlap to completely cover the cream-cheese layer. 5. Place a new piece of plastic wrap on top of the salami layer so that you can flip over your cream cheese–salami rectangle. Flip the layer so the cream cheese side is up. 6. Remove the plastic wrap and add the sliced pepperoncini in a layer on top. 7. Roll the layered ingredients into a tight log, pressing the meat and cream cheese together. (You want it as tight as possible.) Then wrap the roll with plastic wrap and refrigerate for at least 6 hours so it will set. 8. Use a sharp knife to cut the log into slices and serve.

Per Serving:

calories: 583 | fat: 54g | protein: 19g | carbs: 7g | net carbs: 7g | fiber: 0g

Crispy Grilled Kale Leaves

Prep time: 10 minutes | Cook time: 5 minutes | Serves 4

- ½ cup good-quality olive oil
- 2 teaspoons freshly squeezed lemon juice
- ½ teaspoon garlic powder
- 7 cups large kale leaves,
- thoroughly washed and patted dry
- Sea salt, for seasoning
- Freshly ground black pepper, for seasoning

1. Preheat the grill. Set the grill to medium-high heat. 2. Mix the dressing. In a large bowl, whisk together the olive oil, lemon juice, and garlic powder until it thickens. 3. Prepare the kale. Add the kale leaves to the bowl and use your fingers to massage the dressing thoroughly all over the leaves. Season the leaves lightly with salt and pepper. 4. Grill and serve. Place the kale leaves in a single layer on the preheated grill. Grill for 1 to 2 minutes, turn the leaves over, and grill the other side for 1 minute, until they're crispy. Put the leaves on a platter and serve.

Per Serving:

calories: 282 | fat: 28g | protein: 3g | carbs: 9g | net carbs: 6g | fiber: 3g

Cauliflower Patties

Prep time: 10 minutes | Cook time: 10 minutes | Makes 10 patties

- 1 medium head cauliflower (about 1½ pounds/680 g), or 3 cups (375 g) pre-riced cauliflower
- 2 large eggs
- ⅔ cup (75 g) blanched almond flour
- ¼ cup (17 g) nutritional yeast
- 1 tablespoon dried chives
- 1 teaspoon finely ground sea salt
- 1 teaspoon garlic powder
- ½ teaspoon turmeric powder
- ¼ teaspoon ground black pepper
- 3 tablespoons coconut oil or ghee, for the pan

1. If you're using pre-riced cauliflower, skip ahead to Step 2. Otherwise, cut the base off the head of cauliflower and remove the florets. Transfer the florets to a food processor or blender and pulse 3 or 4 times to break them up into small (¼-inch/6-mm) pieces. 2. Transfer the riced cauliflower to a medium-sized saucepan and add enough water to the pan to completely cover the cauliflower. Cover with the lid and bring to a boil over medium heat. Boil, covered, for 3½ minutes. 3. Meanwhile, place a fine-mesh strainer over a bowl. 4. Pour the hot cauliflower into the strainer, allowing the bowl to catch the boiling water. With a spoon, press down on the cauliflower to remove as much water as possible. 5. Discard the cooking water and place the cauliflower in the bowl, then add the eggs, almond flour, nutritional yeast, chives, salt, and spices. Stir until everything is incorporated. 6. Heat a large frying pan over medium-low heat. Add the oil and allow to melt completely. 7. Using a ¼-cup (60-ml) scoop, scoop up a portion of the mixture and roll between your hands to form a ball about 1¾ inches (4.5 cm) in diameter. Place in the hot oil and flatten the ball with the back of a fork until it is

a patty about ½ inch (1.25 cm) thick. Repeat with the remaining cauliflower mixture, making a total of 10 patties. 8. Cook the patties for 5 minutes per side, or until golden brown. Transfer to a serving plate and enjoy!

Per Serving:

calories: 164 | fat: 12g | protein: 7g | carbs: 7g | net carbs: 3g | fiber: 4g

Quick Salsa

Prep time: 5 minutes | Cook time: 0 minutes | Makes about 3 cups

- ¼ cup fresh cilantro, stems and leaves, finely chopped
- 1 small red onion, finely chopped
- 8 roma tomatoes or other small to medium tomatoes, finely chopped
- 1 small jalapeño pepper, minced, seeded if desired for less heat (optional)
- Juice of 1 to 2 limes
- Sea salt and ground black pepper, to taste

1. Toss together all the ingredients in a large mixing bowl. Alternatively, place all the ingredients in a food processor and pulse until the desired consistency is reached. 2. Season with salt and pepper to taste. 3. Store in an airtight container in the refrigerator for up to 5 days.

Per Serving:

calories: 12 | fat: 3g | protein: 1g | carbs: 3g | net carbs: 2g | fiber 1g

Cheese Chips and Guacamole

Prep time: 10 minutes | Cook time: 10 minutes | Serves 2

For The Cheese Chips:
- 1 cup shredded cheese (I use Mexican blend)
- For The Guacamole:
- 1 avocado, mashed
- Juice of ½ lime
- 1 teaspoon diced jalapeño
- 2 tablespoons chopped fresh cilantro leaves
- Pink Himalayan salt
- Freshly ground black pepper

Make The Cheese Chips: 1. Preheat the oven to 350°F. Line a baking sheet with parchment paper or a silicone baking mat. 2. Add ¼-cup mounds of shredded cheese to the pan, leaving plenty of space between them, and bake until the edges are brown and the middles have fully melted, about 7 minutes. 3. Set the pan on a cooling rack, and let the cheese chips cool for 5 minutes. The chips will be floppy when they first come out of the oven but will crisp as they cool. Make The Guacamole: 1. In a medium bowl, mix together the avocado, lime juice, jalapeño, and cilantro, and season with pink Himalayan salt and pepper. 2. Top the cheese chips with the guacamole, and serve.

Per Serving:

calories: 323 | fat: 27g | protein: 15g | carbs: 8g | net carbs: 3g | fiber: 5g

Salami Chips with Buffalo Chicken Dip

Prep time: 10 minutes | Cook time: 10 minutes | Serves 6

◀ 8 ounces (227 g) salami, cut crosswise into 24 slices
Buffalo Chicken Dip:
◀ 1 cup full-fat coconut milk
◀ ¾ cup shredded cooked chicken
◀ ⅓ cup nutritional yeast
◀ 1 tablespoon coconut aminos
◀ 1 tablespoon hot sauce
◀ 2 teaspoons onion powder
◀ 1½ teaspoons garlic powder
◀ 1 teaspoon turmeric powder
◀ ½ teaspoon finely ground sea salt
◀ ¼ teaspoon ground black pepper
◀ ¼ cup roughly chopped fresh parsley

1. Preheat the oven to 400ºF (205ºC). Line 2 rimmed baking sheets with parchment paper or silicone baking mats. 2. Set the salami slices on the lined baking sheets. Bake for 8 to 10 minutes, until the centers look crisp and the edges are just slightly turned up. Meanwhile, make the dip: 1. Place the dip ingredients in a small saucepan. Bring to a simmer over medium-high heat, then reduce the heat to medium-low and cook, uncovered, for 6 minutes, or until thickened, stirring often. 2. Transfer the salami chips to a serving plate and the dip to a serving bowl. Stir the parsley into the dip and dig in! Storage: Store in an airtight container in the fridge for up to 3 days or in the freezer for up to 3 months.

Per Serving:
calories: 294 | fat: 21g | protein: 20g | carbs: 7g | net carbs: 5g | fiber: 2g

Mac Fatties

Prep time: 10 minutes | Cook time: 0 minutes | Makes 20 fat cups

◀ 1¾ cups (280 g) roasted and salted macadamia nuts
◀ ⅓ cup (70 g) coconut oil
◀ Rosemary Lemon Flavor:
Spicy Cumin Flavor:
◀ ½ teaspoon ground cumin
Turmeric Flavor:
◀ ½ teaspoon turmeric powder
◀ ¼ teaspoon ginger powder
◀ Garlic Herb Flavor:
◀ 1¼ teaspoons dried oregano
◀ 1 teaspoon finely chopped fresh rosemary
◀ ¼ teaspoon lemon juice
◀ ¼ teaspoon cayenne pepper leaves
◀ ½ teaspoon paprika
◀ ½ teaspoon garlic powder

1. Place the macadamia nuts and oil in a blender or food processor. Blend until smooth, or as close to smooth as you can get it with the equipment you're using. 2. Divide the mixture among 4 small bowls, placing ¼ cup (87 g) in each bowl. 3. To the first bowl, add the rosemary and lemon juice and stir to combine. 4. To the second bowl, add the cumin and cayenne and stir to combine. 5. To the third bowl, add the turmeric and ginger and stir to combine. 6. To the fourth bowl, add the oregano, paprika, and garlic powder and stir to combine. 7. Set a 24-well silicone or metal mini muffin pan on the counter. If using a metal pan, line 20 of the wells with mini foil liners. (Do not use paper; it would soak up all the fat.) Spoon the mixtures into the wells, using about 1 tablespoon per well. 8. Place in the freezer for 1 hour, or until firm. Enjoy directly from the freezer.

Per Serving:
calories: 139 | fat: 14g | protein: 1g | carbs: 2g | net carbs: 1g | fiber: 1g

Creamy Mashed Cauliflower

Prep time: 3 minutes | Cook time: 1 minute | Serves 4

◀ 1 head cauliflower, chopped into florets
◀ 1 cup water
◀ 1 clove garlic, finely minced
◀ 3 tablespoons butter
◀ 2 tablespoons sour cream
◀ ½ teaspoon salt
◀ ¼ teaspoon pepper

1. Place cauliflower on steamer rack. Add water and steamer rack to Instant Pot. Press the Steam button and adjust time to 1 minute. When timer beeps, quick-release the pressure. 2. Place cooked cauliflower into food processor and add remaining ingredients. Blend until smooth and creamy. Serve warm.

Per Serving:
calories: 125 | fat: 9g | protein: 3g | carbs: 8g | net carbs: 5g | fiber: 3g

Garlic Meatballs

Prep time: 20 minutes | Cook time: 15 minutes | Serves 6

◀ 7 ounces (198 g) ground beef
◀ 7 ounces (198 g) ground pork
◀ 1 teaspoon minced garlic
◀ 3 tablespoons water
◀ 1 teaspoon chili flakes
◀ 1 teaspoon dried parsley
◀ 1 tablespoon coconut oil
◀ ¼ cup beef broth

1. In the mixing bowl, mix up ground beef, ground pork, minced garlic, water, chili flakes, and dried parsley. 2. Make the medium size meatballs from the mixture. 3. After this, heat up coconut oil in the instant pot on Sauté mode. 4. Put the meatballs in the hot coconut oil in one layer and cook them for 2 minutes from each side. 5. Then add beef broth and close the lid. 6. Cook the meatballs for 10 minutes on Manual mode (High Pressure). 7. Then make a quick pressure release and transfer the meatballs on the plate.

Per Serving:
calories: 131 | fat: 6g | protein: 19g | carbs: 0g | net carbs: 0g | fiber: 0g

BLT Dip

Prep time: 10 minutes | Cook time: 15 minutes | Serves 10

- 8 strips bacon (about 8 oz/225 g)

Blt Dip:
- Warm bacon grease, reserved from cooking bacon (above)
- 1½ cups raw cashews, soaked in water for 12 hours, drained, and rinsed
- ⅓ cup mayonnaise
- ¼ cup collagen peptides or protein powder (optional)
- 2 tablespoons apple cider vinegar

Toppinhs:
- 1 cup sliced iceberg lettuce
- 1 small tomato, diced
- Crumbled bacon (from above)
- 2 green onions, sliced

- 2 tablespoons lemon juice
- 2 teaspoons paprika or smoked paprika
- 2 tablespoons diced yellow onions
- 1 clove garlic
- ½ teaspoon finely ground sea salt
- ¼ teaspoon ground black pepper

- 1 English cucumber (about 12 in/30.5 cm long), sliced crosswise into coins, for serving

1. Cook the bacon in a large frying pan over medium heat until crispy, about 15 minutes, then remove from the pan. When the bacon has cooled, crumble it. 2. Make the dip: Pour the warm bacon grease into a food processor or high-powered blender. Add the soaked cashews, mayonnaise, collagen (if using), vinegar, lemon juice, paprika, onions, garlic, salt, and pepper. Pulse until smooth, about 2 minutes. 3. Transfer the mixture to a 9-inch (23-cm) pie plate. Top with the lettuce, tomato, bacon, and green onions. Serve with the cucumber coins.

Per Serving:

calories: 378 | fat: 28g | protein: 20g | carbs: 13g | net carbs: 11g | fiber: 2g

Buffalo Chicken Meatballs

Prep time: 5 minutes | Cook time: 10 minutes | Serves 4

- 1 pound (454 g) ground chicken
- ½ cup almond flour
- 2 tablespoons cream cheese
- 1 packet dry ranch dressing mix
- ½ teaspoon salt

- ¼ teaspoon pepper
- ¼ teaspoon garlic powder
- 1 cup water
- 2 tablespoons butter, melted
- ⅓ cup hot sauce
- ¼ cup crumbled feta cheese
- ¼ cup sliced green onion

1. In large bowl, mix ground chicken, almond flour, cream cheese, ranch, salt, pepper, and garlic powder. Roll mixture into 16 balls. 2. Place meatballs on steam rack and add 1 cup water to Instant Pot. Click lid closed. Press the Meat/Stew button and set time for 10 minutes. 3. Combine butter and hot sauce. When timer beeps,

remove meatballs and place in clean large bowl. Toss in hot sauce mixture. Top with sprinkled feta and green onions to serve.

Per Serving:

calories: 367 | fat: 25g | protein: 25g | carbs: 9g | net carbs: 7g | fiber: 2g

Creamed Onion Spinach

Prep time: 3 minutes | Cook time: 5 minutes | Serves 6

- 4 tablespoons butter
- ¼ cup diced onion
- 8 ounces (227 g) cream cheese
- 1 (12 ounces / 340 g) bag

- frozen spinach
- ½ cup chicken broth
- 1 cup shredded whole-milk Mozzarella cheese

1. Press the Sauté button and add butter. Once butter is melted, add onion to Instant Pot and sauté for 2 minutes or until onion begins to turn translucent. 2. Break cream cheese into pieces and add to Instant Pot. Press the Cancel button. Add frozen spinach and broth. Click lid closed. Press the Manual button and adjust time for 5 minutes. When timer beeps, quick-release the pressure and stir in shredded Mozzarella. If mixture is too watery, press the Sauté button and reduce for additional 5 minutes, stirring constantly.

Per Serving:

calories: 273 | fat: 24g | protein: 9g | carbs: 5g | net carbs: 3g | fiber: 2g

Greens Chips with Curried Yogurt Sauce

Prep time: 10 minutes | Cook time: 5 to 6 minutes | Serves 4

- 1 cup low-fat Greek yogurt
- 1 tablespoon freshly squeezed lemon juice
- 1 tablespoon curry powder
- ½ bunch curly kale, stemmed, ribs removed and discarded, leaves cut into 2-

- to 3-inch pieces
- ½ bunch chard, stemmed, ribs removed and discarded, leaves cut into 2- to 3-inch pieces
- 1½ teaspoons olive oil

1. In a small bowl, stir together the yogurt, lemon juice, and curry powder. Set aside. 2. In a large bowl, toss the kale and chard with the olive oil, working the oil into the leaves with your hands. This helps break up the fibers in the leaves so the chips are tender. 3. Air fry the greens in batches at 390°F (199°C) for 5 to 6 minutes, until crisp, shaking the basket once during cooking. Serve with the yogurt sauce.

Per Serving:

calories: 76 | fat: 2g | protein: 6g | carbs: 11g | net carbs: 10g | fiber: 2g

Caponata Dip

Prep time: 15 minutes | Cook time: 35 minutes | Makes about 2 cups

◀ 1 large eggplant (about 1¼ pounds / 567 g), cut into ½-inch pieces
◀ 1 large yellow onion, cut into ½-inch pieces
◀ 4 large cloves garlic, peeled and smashed with the side of a knife
◀ 4 tablespoons extra-virgin olive oil, divided, plus extra

For Garnish:
◀ Extra-virgin olive oil
◀ Fresh cilantro leaves
◀ Pinch of paprika (optional)
◀ Pine nuts (optional)

for garnish
◀ ½ teaspoon sea salt
◀ ¼ teaspoon ground black pepper
◀ ¼ teaspoon ground cumin
◀ 1 medium tomato, chopped into 1-inch chunks
◀ Juice of 1 lemon
◀ 2 tablespoons chopped fresh cilantro leaves

◀ For Serving (Optional):
◀ Low-carb flax crackers
◀ Sliced vegetables

1. Preheat the oven to 375°F (190°C). 2. Place the eggplant, onion, garlic, 2 tablespoons of the olive oil, salt, pepper, and cumin in a large bowl and toss to combine. 3. Spread the mixture out on a rimmed baking sheet and bake for 30 to 35 minutes, until the eggplant is softened and browned, tossing halfway through. 4. Remove the eggplant mixture from the oven and transfer it to a food processor. Add the tomato, lemon juice, cilantro, and remaining 2 tablespoons of olive oil. Pulse until the mixture is just slightly chunky. Add salt and pepper to taste. 5. Scoop the dip into a serving dish and garnish with additional olive oil, cilantro, paprika (if desired), and pine nuts (optional). Serve with low-carb crackers and sliced vegetables, if desired.

Per Serving:
calories: 90 | fat: 7g | protein: 1g | carbs: 7g | net carbs: 4g | fiber: 3g

Liver Bites

Prep time: 5 minutes | Cook time: 28 minutes | Makes 24 bites

◀ 8 ounces (225 g) chicken livers
◀ 1 tablespoon apple cider vinegar
◀ 4 strips bacon (about 4½ oz/130 g)
◀ 1 pound (455 g) ground beef
◀ 1 cup (75 g) crushed pork rinds

◀ 12 cloves garlic, minced
◀ 1 tablespoon plus 1 teaspoon onion powder
◀ 1 teaspoon ground black pepper
◀ 1 teaspoon dried thyme leaves
◀ ½ teaspoon finely ground sea salt

1. Place the chicken livers in a medium-sized bowl and cover with water. Add the vinegar. Cover and place in the fridge for 24 to 48 hours. Rinse and drain the livers. 2. Preheat the oven to 375°F (190°C). Line a rimmed baking sheet with parchment paper or a silicone baking mat. 3. Place the livers and bacon in a high-

powered blender and pulse until smooth. If using a regular blender or food processor, roughly chop the bacon beforehand. 4. Transfer the liver mixture to a medium-sized bowl and add the remaining ingredients. Mix with your hands until fully incorporated. 5. Pinch a tablespoon of the mixture, roll it into a ball between your hands, and place on the lined baking sheet. Repeat with the remaining liver mixture, making a total of 24 balls. 6. Bake the liver balls for 25 to 28 minutes, until the internal temperature reaches 165°F (74°C).

Per Serving:
calories: 116 | fat: 7g | protein: 11g | carbs: 1g | net carbs: 1g | fiber: 0g

Chicken and Cabbage Salad

Prep time: 15 minutes | Cook time: 10 minutes | Serves 4

◀ 12 ounces (340 g) chicken fillet, chopped
◀ 1 teaspoon Cajun seasoning
◀ 1 tablespoon coconut oil

◀ 1 cup chopped Chinese cabbage
◀ 1 tablespoon avocado oil
◀ 1 teaspoon sesame seeds

1. Sprinkle the chopped chicken with the Cajun seasoning. 2. Set your Instant Pot to Sauté and heat the coconut oil. Add the chicken and cook for 10 minutes, stirring occasionally. 3. When the chicken is cooked, transfer to a salad bowl. Add the cabbage, avocado oil, and sesame seeds and gently toss to combine. Serve immediately.

Per Serving:
calories: 207 | fat: 11g | protein: 25g | carbs: 1g | net carbs: 0g | fiber: 0g

Lemon-Cheese Cauliflower Bites

Prep time: 5 minutes | Cook time: 8 minutes | Serves 6

◀ 1 cup water
◀ 1 pound (454 g) cauliflower, broken into florets
◀ Sea salt and ground black pepper, to taste

◀ 2 tablespoons extra-virgin olive oil
◀ 2 tablespoons lemon juice
◀ 1 cup grated Cheddar cheese

1. Pour the water into the Instant Pot and insert a steamer basket. Place the cauliflower florets in the basket. 2. Lock the lid. Select the Manual mode and set the cooking time for 3 minutes at Low Pressure. 3. When the timer beeps, perform a quick pressure release. Carefully remove the lid. 4. Season the cauliflower with salt and pepper. Drizzle with olive oil and lemon juice. Sprinkle the grated cheese all over the cauliflower. 5. Press the Sauté button to heat the Instant Pot. Allow to cook for about 5 minutes, or until the cheese melts. Serve warm.

Per Serving:
calories: 136 | fat: 10g | protein: 7g | carbs: 5g | net carbs: 3g | fiber: 2g

Lemon-Pepper Chicken Drumsticks

Prep time: 30 minutes | Cook time: 30 minutes | Serves 2

◄ 2 teaspoons freshly ground coarse black pepper
◄ 1 teaspoon baking powder
◄ ½ teaspoon garlic powder
◄ 4 chicken drumsticks (4 ounces / 113 g each)
◄ Kosher salt, to taste
◄ 1 lemon

1. In a small bowl, stir together the pepper, baking powder, and garlic powder. Place the drumsticks on a plate and sprinkle evenly with the baking powder mixture, turning the drumsticks so they're well coated. Let the drumsticks stand in the refrigerator for at least 1 hour or up to overnight. 2. Sprinkle the drumsticks with salt, then transfer them to the air fryer, standing them bone-end up and leaning against the wall of the air fryer basket. Air fry at 375°F (191°C) until cooked through and crisp on the outside, about 30 minutes. 3. Transfer the drumsticks to a serving platter and finely grate the zest of the lemon over them while they're hot. Cut the lemon into wedges and serve with the warm drumsticks.

Per Serving:

calories: 200 | fat: 9g | protein: 28g | carbs: 5g | net carbs: 4g | fiber: 1g

Cauliflower Cheesy Garlic Bread

Prep time: 10 minutes | Cook time: 30 minutes | Serves 6

◄ Butter, or olive oil, for the baking sheet
◄ 1 head cauliflower, roughly chopped into florets
◄ 3 cups shredded Mozzarella cheese, divided
◄ ½ cup grated Parmesan cheese
◄ ¼ cup cream cheese, at room temperature
◄ 3 teaspoons garlic powder,

plus more for sprinkling
◄ 1 teaspoon onion powder
◄ ½ teaspoon red pepper flakes
◄ 1 tablespoon salt, plus more for seasoning
◄ Freshly ground black pepper, to taste
◄ 2 eggs, whisked
◄ Sugar-free marinara sauce, warmed, for dipping

1. Preheat the oven to 400°F (205°C). 2. Grease a baking sheet with butter. Set aside. Alternatively, use a pizza stone. 3. In a food processor, pulse the cauliflower until fine. Transfer to a microwave-safe bowl and microwave on high power, uncovered, for 2 minutes. Cool slightly. Place the cauliflower in a thin cloth or piece of cheesecloth and twist to remove any water (not a lot will come out but the little that's there needs to be removed). Transfer to a large bowl. 4. Add 2 cups of Mozzarella, the Parmesan, cream cheese, garlic powder, onion powder, red pepper flakes, and salt. Season generously with black pepper. Stir well to combine. 5. Add the eggs and use your hands to mix, ensuring everything is coated with egg. Transfer to the prepared baking sheet. Spread the mixture out into a large rectangle, about 1 inch thick. Sprinkle with more salt, pepper, and garlic powder. Bake for 20 minutes or until the bread starts to turn golden brown. 6. Remove from the oven, top with the remaining 1 cup of Mozzarella, and bake for about 10 minutes more or until the cheese melts. Cool slightly and cut into breadsticks. Serve with the marinara sauce for dipping. Refrigerate leftovers in an airtight container for up to 4 days.

Per Serving:

calories: 296 | fat: 20g | protein: 21g | carbs: 10g | net carbs: 7g | fiber: 3g

Pimento Cheese

Prep time: 20 minutes | Cook time: 0 minutes | serves 8

◄ 1 (8-ounce) block sharp cheddar cheese
◄ 1 (8-ounce) block mild cheddar cheese
◄ 1 cup mayonnaise
◄ 1 (4-ounce) jar diced pimentos, drained
◄ 3 ounces cream cheese (6

tablespoons), softened
◄ 1 tablespoon finely chopped onions
◄ 1 tablespoon dill relish
◄ ½ teaspoon onion powder
◄ ¼ teaspoon garlic powder
◄ ¼ teaspoon ground black pepper

Serving Suggestions:
◄ Sliced bell peppers or celery
◄ Pork rinds

1. Using the large holes on the side of a box grater, shred the cheeses into a large bowl. 2. Add the rest of the ingredients to the bowl with the shredded cheese and mix with a spoon until well combined. Refrigerate for at least 1 hour before serving. Leftovers can be stored in an airtight container in the refrigerator for up to a week.

Per Serving:

calories: 464 | fat: 46g | protein: 14g | carbs: 3g | net carbs: 3g | fiber: 0g

Everything Bagel Cream Cheese Dip

Prep time: 10 minutes | Cook time: 0 minutes | Serves 4

◄ 1 (8-ounce / 227-g) package cream cheese, at room temperature
◄ ½ cup sour cream
◄ 1 tablespoon garlic powder
◄ 1 tablespoon dried onion, or onion powder
◄ 1 tablespoon sesame seeds
◄ 1 tablespoon kosher salt

1. In a small bowl, combine the cream cheese, sour cream, garlic powder, dried onion, sesame seeds, and salt. Stir well to incorporate everything together. Serve immediately or cover and refrigerate for up to 6 days.

Per Serving:

calories: 291 | fat: 27g | protein: 6g | carbs: 6g | net carbs: 5g | fiber: 1g

Blueberry Crumble with Cream Topping

Prep time: 5 minutes | Cook time: 25 minutes | Serves 6

- ◄ 18 ounces (510 g) fresh or frozen blueberries
- ◄ 1 cup (110 g) blanched almond flour
- ◄ ⅓ cup (70 g) coconut oil or ghee, room temperature
- ◄ ⅓ cup (65 g) erythritol
- ◄ 2 tablespoons coconut flour
- ◄ 1 teaspoon ground cinnamon
- ◄ 1 cup (250 g) coconut cream, or 1 cup (240 ml) full-fat coconut milk, for serving

1. Preheat the oven to 350°F (177°C). 2. Place the blueberries in an 8-inch (20-cm) square baking pan. 3. Place the almond flour, oil, erythritol, coconut flour, and cinnamon in a medium-sized bowl and mix with a fork until crumbly. Crumble over the top of the blueberries. 4. Bake for 22 to 25 minutes, until the top is golden. 5. Remove from the oven and let sit for 10 minutes before dividing among 6 serving bowls. Top each bowl with 2 to 3 tablespoons of coconut cream.

Per Serving:

calories: 388 | fat: 33g | protein: 5g | carbs: 17g | net carbs: 13g | fiber: 4g

Edana's Macadamia Crack Bars

Prep time: 15 minutes | Cook time: 35 minutes | Makes 12 bars

Base:
- ◄ 1¼ cups (140 g) blanched almond flour
- ◄ ⅓ cup (65 g) erythritol
- ◄ ⅓ cup (70 g) coconut oil, ghee, or cacao butter, melted
- ◄ 1 teaspoon vanilla extract
- ◄ ¼ teaspoon finely ground sea salt

Toppings:
- ◄ 1 cup (160 g) raw macadamia nuts, roughly chopped

- ◄ Coconut Cream Layer:
- ◄ ½ cup (95 g) erythritol
- ◄ ½ cup (125 g) coconut cream
- ◄ ¼ cup (55 g) coconut oil, ghee, or cacao butter, melted
- ◄ 2 large egg yolks
- ◄ 1 teaspoon vanilla extract

- ◄ 1 cup (100 g) unsweetened shredded coconut

1. Preheat the oven to 350°F (177°C). Line an 8-inch (20 cm) square baking pan with parchment paper, draping it over two opposite sides of the pan for easy lifting. 2. Place the base ingredients in a large mixing bowl and stir to combine. Press into the prepared pan and par-bake for 10 to 12 minutes, until the top is only lightly browned. Remove from the oven and lower the oven temperature to 300°F (150°C). 3. Meanwhile, make the coconut cream layer: Place the erythritol, coconut cream, melted oil, egg yolks, and vanilla in a large mixing bowl. Whisk until smooth. 4.

Pour the coconut cream mixture over the par-baked base. Top with the macadamia nuts, then the shredded coconut. 5. Return the pan to the oven and bake for 25 minutes, or until the edges are lightly browned. 6. Let cool in the pan on the counter for 1 hour before transferring to the fridge to chill for another hour. Once chilled, cut into 2-inch (5 cm) squares.

Per Serving:

calories: 303 | fat: 31g | protein: 2g | carbs: 6g | net carbs: 2g | fiber: 3g

Herbed Zucchini Slices

Prep time: 5 minutes | Cook time: 5 minutes | Serves 4

- ◄ 2 tablespoons olive oil
- ◄ 2 garlic cloves, chopped
- ◄ 1 pound (454 g) zucchini, sliced
- ◄ ½ cup water
- ◄ ½ cup sugar-free tomato purée
- ◄ 1 teaspoon dried thyme
- ◄ ½ teaspoon dried rosemary
- ◄ ½ teaspoon dried oregano

1. Set your Instant Pot to Sauté and heat the olive oil. 2. Add the garlic and sauté for 2 minutes until fragrant. 3. Add the remaining ingredients to the Instant Pot and stir well. 4. Lock the lid. Select the Manual mode and set the cooking time for 3 minutes at Low Pressure. 5. When the timer beeps, perform a quick pressure release. Carefully remove the lid. 6. Serve warm.

Per Serving:

calories: 87 | fat: 8g | protein: 2g | carbs: 5g | net carbs: 3g | fiber: 2g

Zucchini Chips

Prep time: 10 minutes | Cook time: 2 hours | serves 6

- ◄ 1 large zucchini, cut into thin disks
- ◄ 1 teaspoon sea salt
- ◄ 2 tablespoons coconut oil
- ◄ 1 teaspoon dried dill
- ◄ 1 tablespoon freshly ground black pepper

1. Preheat the oven to 225°F. 2. Line a baking sheet with parchment paper. If you don't have parchment paper, use aluminum foil or a greased pan. 3. Sprinkle the zucchini slices with the salt and spread them out on paper towels. 4. With a separate paper towel, firmly press the zucchini slices and pat them dry (the dryer the better). 5. Toss the zucchini slices in the coconut oil, dill, and pepper, then spread them out on the prepared baking sheet. 6. Bake for 2 hours, or until they are golden and crisp. Check every 30 minutes or so for burn marks. If you begin to see them burn, remove the chips immediately. 7. Remove the chips from the oven and cool. 8. Once the chips have cooled, transfer them to a serving bowl or store in an airtight container for up to 3 days.

Per Serving:

calories: 52 | fat: 5g | protein: 1g | carbs: 3g | net carbs: 1g | fiber: 1g

Superpower Fat Bombs

Prep time: 10 minutes | Cook time: 0 minutes | Makes 8 bombs

- ⅔ cup (145 g) coconut oil, cacao butter, or ghee, melted
- ¼ cup (40 g) collagen peptides or protein powder
- ¼ cup (25 g) unflavored MCT oil powder
- 2 tablespoons cocoa powder
- 2 tablespoons roughly ground flax seeds
- 1 tablespoon cacao nibs
- 1 teaspoon instant coffee granules
- 4 drops liquid stevia, or 1 tablespoon plus 1 teaspoon confectioners'-style erythritol
- Pinch of finely ground sea salt

Special Equipment (Optional):
- Silicone mold with eight 2-tablespoon or larger cavities

1. Have on hand your favorite silicone mold. I like to use a large silicone ice cube tray and spoon 2 tablespoons of the mixture into each well, If you do not have a silicone mold, making this into a bark works well, too. Simply use an 8-inch (20 cm) square silicone or metal baking pan; if using a metal pan, line it with parchment paper, draping some over the sides for easy removal. 2. Place all the ingredients in a medium-sized bowl and stir until well mixed and smooth. 3. Divide the mixture evenly among 8 cavities in the silicone mold or pour into the baking pan. Transfer to the fridge and allow to set for 15 minutes if using cacao butter or 30 minutes if using ghee or coconut oil. If using a baking pan, break the bark into 8 pieces for serving.

Per Serving:

calories: 136 | fat: 12g | protein: 6g | carbs: 3g | net carbs: 1g | fiber: 2g

Baked Crab Dip

Prep time: 15 minutes | Cook time: 25 minutes | Serves 4 to 6

- 4 ounces cream cheese, softened
- ½ cup shredded Parmesan cheese, plus ½ cup extra for topping (optional) ⅓ cup mayonnaise
- ¼ cup sour cream
- 1 tablespoon chopped fresh parsley
- 2 teaspoons fresh lemon juice
- 1½ teaspoons Sriracha sauce
- ½ teaspoon garlic powder
- 8 ounces fresh lump crabmeat
- Salt and pepper

1. Preheat the oven to 375°F. 2. Combine all the ingredients except for the crabmeat in a mixing bowl and use a hand mixer to blend until smooth. 3. Put the crabmeat in a separate bowl, check for shells, and rinse with cold water, if needed. Pat dry or allow to rest in a strainer until most of the water has drained. 4. Add the crabmeat to the bowl with the cream cheese mixture and gently fold to combine. Taste for seasoning and add salt and pepper to taste, if needed. Pour into an 8-inch round or square baking dish and bake for 25 minutes, until the cheese has melted and the dip is warm throughout. 5. If desired, top the dip with another ½ cup of Parmesan cheese and broil for 2 to 3 minutes, until the cheese has melted and browned slightly.

Per Serving:

calories: 275 | fat: 23g | protein: 16g | carbs: 1g | net carbs: 1g | fiber: 0g

Peanut Butter Keto Fudge

Prep time: 5 minutes | Cook time: 10 minutes | Serves 12

- ½ cup (1 stick) butter
- 8 ounces (227 g) cream cheese
- 1 cup unsweetened peanut butter
- 1 teaspoon vanilla extract (or the seeds from 1 vanilla bean)
- 1 teaspoon liquid stevia (optional)

1. Line an 8 or 9-inch square or 9-by-13-inch rectangular baking dish with parchment paper. Set aside. 2. In a saucepan over medium heat, melt the butter and cream cheese together, stirring frequently, for about 5 minutes. 3. Add the peanut butter and continue to stir until smooth. Remove from the heat. 4. Stir in the vanilla and stevia (if using). Pour the mixture into the prepared dish and spread into an even layer. Refrigerate for about 1 hour until thickened and set enough to cut and handle. Cut into small squares and enjoy! Refrigerate, covered, for up to 1 week.

Per Serving:

1 fudge square: calories: 261 | fat: 24g | protein: 8g | carbs: 5g | net carbs: 4g | fiber: 1g

Salsa Shrimp-Stuffed Avocados

Prep time: 10 minutes | Cook time: 15 minutes | Serves 4

- 2 avocados, halved and pitted
- 12 large precooked shrimp, peeled and deveined
- 3 tablespoons salsa
- ¼ cup shredded Mexican cheese blend
- Finely chopped fresh cilantro, for garnish (optional)
- Sour cream, for garnish (optional)

1 Preheat the oven to 350°F. Line a rimmed baking sheet with parchment paper. 2 Rinse the shrimp and halve lengthwise. Place in a bowl and top with the salsa. Stir to coat the shrimp evenly with the salsa. 3 Place the avocado halves cut side up on the lined baking sheet. Fill each half with salsa-coated shrimp and top with the cheese. 4 Bake for 15 minutes, until the cheese is melted. 5 Serve garnished with cilantro and/or topped with sour cream, if desired.

Per Serving:

calories: 185 | fat: 13g | protein: 11g | carbs: 7g | net carbs: 6g | fiber: 1g

Buffalo Bill's Chicken Dip

Prep time: 15 minutes | Cook time: 30 minutes | Serves 10

- 2 (4.2-ounce) chicken breasts from cooked rotisserie chicken
- 1 (8-ounce) package full-fat cream cheese, softened
- 2 cups shredded whole milk mozzarella cheese
- 1 cup shredded Cheddar cheese
- 1 (1-ounce) package ranch
- powder seasoning mix
- 1 cup full-fat mayonnaise
- 1 cup full-fat sour cream
- ½ cup finely chopped green onion
- ¼ cup buffalo wing sauce
- 1 teaspoon garlic powder
- ½ pound no-sugar-added bacon, cooked and crumbled

1. Preheat oven to 350°F. Grease a 2-quart (8" × 8") baking dish. 2. In a small bowl, finely shred chicken. 3. Combine chicken with remaining ingredients, except bacon, in baking dish, stirring to mix well. 4. Bake 25–30 minutes; stop when bubbling and browned on top. 5. Take out of the oven and stir again to mix all the melted ingredients. Top with the crumbled bacon. Serve immediately.

Per Serving:
calories: 539| fat: 43g | protein: 25g | carbs: 5g | net carbs: 5g | fiber: 0g

N'Oatmeal Bars

Prep time: 25 minutes | Cook time: 0 minutes | Makes 16 bars

- 1 cup (180 g) coconut oil
- ½ cup (95 g) erythritol, divided
- 2 cups (300 g) hulled hemp seeds
- ½ cup (50 g) unsweetened shredded coconut
- ⅓ cup (33 g) coconut flour
- ½ teaspoon vanilla extract
- 10 ounces (285 g) unsweetened baking chocolate, roughly chopped
- ½ cup (120 ml) full-fat coconut milk

1. Line a 9-inch (23 cm) square baking pan with parchment paper, draping it over all sides of the pan for easy lifting. 2. Place the coconut oil and half of the erythritol in a medium-sized saucepan and melt over medium heat, about 2 minutes. Continue to Step 3 if using confectioners'-style erythritol; if using granulated erythritol, continue to cook until the granules can no longer be felt on the back of the spoon. 3. Add the hulled hemp seeds, shredded coconut, coconut flour, and vanilla, stirring until coated. Set aside half of the mixture for the topping. Press the remaining half of the mixture into the prepared pan. 4. Transfer the pan with the base layer to the refrigerator for at least 10 minutes, until set. 5. Meanwhile, prepare the chocolate layer: Place the remaining erythritol, the baking chocolate, and coconut milk in a small saucepan over low heat. Stir frequently until melted and smooth. 6. Take the base out of the fridge and spoon the chocolate mixture over the base layer, spreading it evenly with a knife or the back of a spoon. If the base hasn't totally set, a couple of hulled hemp seeds will lift up and

mix in with the chocolate, so don't rush it. 7. Crumble the reserved hemp seed mixture over the chocolate layer, pressing in gently. Cover and refrigerate for 2 to 3 hours or overnight. 8. Cut into 16 bars and enjoy!

Per Serving:
calories: 311 | fat: 30g | protein: 8g | carbs: 10g | net carbs: 4g | fiber: 5g

90-Second Bread

Prep time: 5 minutes | Cook time: 90 seconds | Serves 1

- 1 heaping tablespoon coconut flour
- ½ teaspoon baking powder
- 1 large egg
- 1½ tablespoons butter, melted
- Pinch salt

1. In a small, 3- to 4-inch diameter, microwave-safe bowl, combine the coconut flour, baking powder, egg, butter, and salt, and mix until well combined. 2. Place the bowl in the microwave and cook on high for 90 seconds. 3. Dump the bread from the bowl and allow to cool for a couple of minutes. 4. With a serrated knife, cut the bread in half horizontally to make two halves, if desired.

Per Serving:
calories: 204 | fat: 17g | protein: 8g | carbs: 5g | net carbs: 2g | fiber: 3g

Antipasto Skewers

Prep time: 10 minutes | Cook time: 0 minutes | Makes 8 skewers

- 8 ounces (227 g) fresh whole Mozzarella
- 16 fresh basil leaves
- 16 slices salami (4 ounces / 113 g)
- 16 slices coppa or other cured meat like prosciutto (4 ounces / 113 g)
- 8 artichoke hearts, packed in water (8 ounces / 227 g)
- ¼ cup vinaigrette made with olive oil or avocado oil and apple cider vinegar
- Flaky salt and freshly ground black pepper, to taste

1. Cut the Mozzarella into 16 small chunks. 2. Skewer 2 pieces each of the Mozzarella, basil leaves, salami slices, and coppa slices, along with one artichoke heart, on each skewer. You'll probably want to fold the basil leaves in half and the salami and coppa in fourths (or more depending on size) before skewering. 3. Place the skewers in a small shallow dish and drizzle with the dressing, turning to coat. If possible, let them marinate for 30 minutes or more. Sprinkle lightly with flaky salt and the pepper before serving.

Per Serving:
calories: 200 | fat: 15g | protein: 11g | carbs: 4g | net carbs: 4g | fiber: 0g

Cheesy Sausage Balls

Prep time: 10 minutes | Cook time: 25 minutes | serves 6

- ◄ 1 pound bulk breakfast sausage
- ◄ 1½ cups shredded sharp cheddar cheese
- ◄ 1 cup finely ground blanched almond flour
- ◄ 1 tablespoon baking powder

1. Preheat the oven to 375°F. Line a sheet pan with parchment paper. 2. Place all the ingredients in a large bowl. Using your hands, mix everything together until well combined but not overmixed. 3. Using a tablespoon or small cookie scoop, form the mixture into 1-inch balls and place on the lined sheet pan. Bake for 20 to 25 minutes, until the sausage balls are crispy around the edges and golden brown on top. Leftovers can be stored in an airtight container in the refrigerator for up to 5 days.

Per Serving:

calories: 527 | fat: 45g | protein: 22g | carbs: 6g | net carbs: 3g | fiber: 3g

Asiago Shishito Peppers

Prep time: 5 minutes | Cook time: 10 minutes | Serves 4

- ◄ Oil, for spraying
- ◄ 6 ounces (170 g) shishito peppers
- ◄ 1 tablespoon olive oil
- ◄ ½ teaspoon salt
- ◄ ½ teaspoon lemon pepper
- ◄ ⅓ cup grated Asiago cheese, divided

1. Line the air fryer basket with parchment and spray lightly with oil. 2. Rinse the shishitos and pat dry with paper towels. 3. In a large bowl, mix together the shishitos, olive oil, salt, and lemon pepper. Place the shishitos in the prepared basket. 4. Roast at 350ºF (177ºC) for 10 minutes, or until blistered but not burned. 5. Sprinkle with half of the cheese and cook for 1 more minute. 6. Transfer to a serving plate. Immediately sprinkle with the remaining cheese and serve.

Per Serving:

calories: 90 | fat: 6g | protein: 3g | carbs: 7g | net carbs: 6g | fiber: 1g

Prosciutto-Wrapped Asparagus

Prep time: 5 minutes | Cook time: 12 minutes | Serves 6

- ◄ 18 asparagus spears, ends trimmed
- ◄ 2 tablespoons coconut oil,
- melted
- ◄ 6 slices prosciutto
- ◄ 1 teaspoon garlic powder

1. Preheat the oven to 400°F. Line a rimmed baking sheet with parchment paper. 2. Place the asparagus and coconut oil in a large zip-top plastic bag. Seal and toss until the asparagus is evenly coated. 3. Wrap a slice of prosciutto around 3 grouped asparagus spears. Repeat with the remaining prosciutto and asparagus, making a total of 6 bundles. Arrange the bundles in a single layer on the lined baking sheet. Sprinkle the garlic powder over the bundles. 4. Bake for 8 to 12 minutes, until the asparagus is tender.

Per Serving:

calories: 122 | fat: 10g | protein: 8g | carbs: 3g | net carbs: 2g | fiber: 1g

Queso Dip

Prep time: 5 minutes | Cook time: 10 minutes | Serves 6

- ◄ ½ cup coconut milk
- ◄ ½ jalapeño pepper, seeded and diced
- ◄ 1 teaspoon minced garlic
- ◄ ½ teaspoon onion powder
- ◄ 2 ounces goat cheese
- ◄ 6 ounces sharp Cheddar cheese, shredded
- ◄ ¼ teaspoon cayenne pepper

1. Place a medium pot over medium heat and add the coconut milk, jalapeño, garlic, and onion powder. 2. Bring the liquid to a simmer and then whisk in the goat cheese until smooth. 3. Add the Cheddar cheese and cayenne and whisk until the dip is thick, 30 seconds to 1 minute. 4. Pour into a serving dish and serve with keto crackers or low-carb vegetables.

Per Serving:

calories: 213 | fat: 19g | protein: 10g | carbs: 2g | net carbs: 2g | fiber: 0g

Sausage Balls

Prep time: 5 minutes | Cook time: 25 minutes | Makes 2 dozen

- ◄ 1 pound (454 g) bulk Italian sausage (not sweet)
- ◄ 1 cup almond flour
- ◄ 1½ cups finely shredded Cheddar cheese
- ◄ 1 large egg
- ◄ 2 teaspoons baking powder
- ◄ 1 teaspoon onion powder
- ◄ 1 teaspoon fennel seed (optional)
- ◄ ½ teaspoon cayenne pepper (optional)

1. Preheat the oven to 350ºF (180ºC) and line a rimmed baking sheet with aluminum foil. 2. In a large bowl, combine all the ingredients. Use a fork to mix until well blended. 3. Form the sausage mixture into 1½-inch balls and place 1 inch apart on the prepared baking sheet. 4. Bake for 20 to 25 minutes, or until browned and cooked through.

Per Serving:

calories: 241 | fat: 21g | protein: 11g | carbs: 3g | net carbs: 2g | fiber: 1g

Coconut Cajun Shrimp

Prep time: 10 minutes | Cook time: 6 minutes | Serves 2

◀ 4 Royal tiger shrimps
◀ 3 tablespoons coconut shred
◀ 2 eggs, beaten

◀ ½ teaspoon Cajun seasoning
◀ 1 teaspoon olive oil

1. Heat up olive oil in the instant pot on Sauté mode. 2. Meanwhile, mix up Cajun seasoning and coconut shred. 3. Dip the shrimps in the eggs and coat in the coconut shred mixture. 4. After this, place the shrimps in the hot olive oil and cook them on Sauté mode for 3 minutes from each side.

Per Serving:

calories: 292 | fat: 54g | protein: 40g | carbs: 2g | net carbs: 1g | fiber: 1g

Chapter 8 Vegearian Mains

Broccoli with Garlic Sauce

Prep time: 19 minutes | Cook time: 15 minutes | Serves 4

- 2 tablespoons olive oil
- Kosher salt and freshly ground black pepper, to taste
Dipping Sauce:
- 2 teaspoons dried rosemary, crushed
- 3 garlic cloves, minced
- ⅓ teaspoon dried marjoram,

- taste
- 1 pound (454 g) broccoli florets

- crushed
- ¼ cup sour cream
- ⅓ cup mayonnaise

1. Lightly grease your broccoli with a thin layer of olive oil. Season with salt and ground black pepper. 2. Arrange the seasoned broccoli in the air fryer basket. Bake at 395°F (202°C) for 15 minutes, shaking once or twice. In the meantime, prepare the dipping sauce by mixing all the sauce ingredients. Serve warm broccoli with the dipping sauce and enjoy!

Per Serving:
calories: 250 | fat: 23g | protein: 3g | carbs: 10g | net carbs: 9g | fiber: 1g

Green Vegetable Stir-Fry with Tofu

Prep time: 15 minutes | Cook time: 15 minutes | Serves 2

- 3 tablespoons avocado oil, divided
- 1 cup Brussels sprouts, halved
- ½ onion, diced
- ½ leek, white and light green parts diced
- ½ head green cabbage, diced
- ¼ cup water, plus more if needed
- ½ cup kale, coarsely

- chopped
- 1 cup spinach, coarsely chopped
- 8 ounces (227 g) tofu, diced
- 2 teaspoons garlic powder
- Salt and freshly ground black pepper, to taste
- ½ avocado, pitted, peeled, and diced
- MCT oil (optional)

1. In a large skillet with a lid (or a wok if you have one), heat 2 tablespoons of avocado oil over medium-high heat. Add the Brussels sprouts, onion, leek, and cabbage and stir together. Add the water, cover, lower the heat to medium, and cook for about 5 minutes. 2. Toss in the kale and spinach and cook for 3 minutes, stirring constantly, until the onion, leek, and cabbage are

caramelized. 3. Add the tofu to the stir-fry, then season with the garlic, salt, pepper, and the remaining tablespoon of avocado oil. 4. Turn the heat back up to medium-high and cook for about 10 minutes, stirring constantly, until the tofu is nice and caramelized on all sides. If you experience any burning, turn down the heat and add 2 to 3 tablespoons of water. 5. Divide the stir-fry between two plates and sprinkle with diced avocado. Feel free to drizzle algae oil or MCT oil over the top for a little extra fat.

Per Serving:
calories: 473 | fat: 33g | protein: 17g | carbs: 27g | net carbs: 15g | fiber: 12g

Buffalo Cauliflower Bites with Blue Cheese

Prep time: 10 minutes | Cook time: 8 to 10 minutes | Serves 4

- 1 large head cauliflower, chopped into florets
- 1 tablespoon olive oil
- Salt and freshly ground
Garlic Blue Cheese Dip:
- ½ cup mayonnaise
- ¼ cup sour cream
- 2 tablespoons heavy cream
- 1 tablespoon fresh lemon juice

- black pepper, to taste
- ¼ cup unsalted butter, melted
- ¼ cup hot sauce

- 1 clove garlic, minced
- ¼ cup crumbled blue cheese
- Salt and freshly ground black pepper, to taste

1. Preheat the air fryer to 400°F (204°C). 2. In a large bowl, combine the cauliflower and olive oil. Season to taste with salt and black pepper. Toss until the vegetables are thoroughly coated. 3. Working in batches, place half of the cauliflower in the air fryer basket. Pausing halfway through the cooking time to shake the basket, air fry for 8 to 10 minutes until the cauliflower is evenly browned. Transfer to a large bowl and repeat with the remaining cauliflower. 4. In a small bowl, whisk together the melted butter and hot sauce. 5. To make the dip: In a small bowl, combine the mayonnaise, sour cream, heavy cream, lemon juice, garlic, and blue cheese. Season to taste with salt and freshly ground black pepper. 6. Just before serving, pour the butter mixture over the cauliflower and toss gently until thoroughly coated. Serve with the dip on the side.

Per Serving:
calories: 420 | fat: 39g | protein: 9g | carbs: 14g | net carbs: 11g | fiber: 3g

Crispy Eggplant Rounds

Prep time: 15 minutes | Cook time: 10 minutes | Serves 4

- ◀ 1 large eggplant, ends trimmed, cut into ½-inch slices
- ◀ ½ teaspoon salt
- ◀ 2 ounces (57 g) Parmesan
- 100% cheese crisps, finely ground
- ◀ ½ teaspoon paprika
- ◀ ¼ teaspoon garlic powder
- ◀ 1 large egg

1. Sprinkle eggplant rounds with salt. Place rounds on a kitchen towel for 30 minutes to draw out excess water. Pat rounds dry. 2. In a medium bowl, mix cheese crisps, paprika, and garlic powder. In a separate medium bowl, whisk egg. Dip each eggplant round in egg, then gently press into cheese crisps to coat both sides. 3. Place eggplant rounds into ungreased air fryer basket. Adjust the temperature to 400ºF (204ºC) and air fry for 10 minutes, turning rounds halfway through cooking. Eggplant will be golden and crispy when done. Serve warm.

Per Serving:

calories: 133 | fat: 8g | protein: 10g | carbs: 6g | net carbs: 4g | fiber: 3g

Almond-Cauliflower Gnocchi

Prep time: 5 minutes | Cook time: 25 to 30 minutes | Serves 4

- ◀ 5 cups cauliflower florets
- ◀ ⅔ cup almond flour
- ◀ ½ teaspoon salt
- ◀ ¼ cup unsalted butter,
- melted
- ◀ ¼ cup grated Parmesan cheese

1. In a food processor fitted with a metal blade, pulse the cauliflower until finely chopped. Transfer the cauliflower to a large microwave-safe bowl and cover it with a paper towel. Microwave for 5 minutes. Spread the cauliflower on a towel to cool. 2. When cool enough to handle, draw up the sides of the towel and squeeze tightly over a sink to remove the excess moisture. Return the cauliflower to the food processor and whirl until creamy. Sprinkle in the flour and salt and pulse until a sticky dough comes together. 3. Transfer the dough to a workspace lightly floured with almond flour. Shape the dough into a ball and divide into 4 equal sections. Roll each section into a rope 1 inch thick. Slice the dough into squares with a sharp knife. 4. Preheat the air fryer to 400ºF (204ºC). 5. Working in batches if necessary, place the gnocchi in a single layer in the basket of the air fryer and spray generously with olive oil. Pausing halfway through the cooking time to turn the gnocchi, air fry for 25 to 30 minutes until golden brown and crispy on the edges. Transfer to a large bowl and toss with the melted butter and Parmesan cheese.

Per Serving:

calories: 220 | fat: 20g | protein: 7g | carbs: 8g | net carbs: 5g | fiber: 3g

Mediterranean Filling Stuffed Portobello Mushrooms

Prep time: 10 minutes | Cook time: 35 minutes | Serves 4

- ◀ 4 large portobello mushroom caps
- ◀ 3 tablespoons good-quality olive oil, divided
- ◀ 1 cup chopped fresh spinach
- ◀ 1 red bell pepper, chopped
- ◀ 1 celery stalk, chopped
- ◀ ½ cup chopped sun-dried tomato
- ◀ ¼ onion, chopped
- ◀ 2 teaspoons minced garlic
- ◀ 1 teaspoon chopped fresh oregano
- ◀ 2 cups chopped pecans
- ◀ ¼ cup balsamic vinaigrette
- ◀ Sea salt, for seasoning
- ◀ Freshly ground black pepper, for seasoning

1. Preheat the oven. Set the oven temperature to 350°F. Line a baking sheet with parchment paper. 2. Prepare the mushrooms. Use a spoon to scoop the black gills out of the mushrooms. Massage 2 tablespoons of the olive oil all over the mushroom caps and place the mushrooms on the prepared baking sheet. Set them aside. 3. Prepare the filling. In a large skillet over medium-high heat, warm the remaining 1 tablespoon of olive oil. Add the spinach, red bell pepper, celery, sun-dried tomato, onion, garlic, and oregano and sauté until the vegetables are tender, about 10 minutes. Stir in the pecans and balsamic vinaigrette and season the mixture with salt and pepper. 4. Assemble and bake. Stuff the mushroom caps with the filling and bake for 20 to 25 minutes until they're tender and golden. 5. Serve. Place one stuffed mushroom on each of four plates and serve them hot.

Per Serving:

calories: 595 | fat: 56g | protein: 10g | carbs: 18g | net carbs: 9g | fiber: 9g

Cheese Stuffed Peppers

Prep time: 20 minutes | Cook time: 15 minutes | Serves 2

- ◀ 1 red bell pepper, top and seeds removed
- ◀ 1 yellow bell pepper, top and seeds removed
- ◀ Salt and pepper, to taste
- ◀ 1 cup Cottage cheese
- ◀ 4 tablespoons mayonnaise
- ◀ 2 pickles, chopped

1. Arrange the peppers in the lightly greased air fryer basket. Cook in the preheated air fryer at 400ºF (204ºC) for 15 minutes, turning them over halfway through the cooking time. 2. Season with salt and pepper. Then, in a mixing bowl, combine the cream cheese with the mayonnaise and chopped pickles. Stuff the pepper with the cream cheese mixture and serve. Enjoy!

Per Serving:

calories: 250 | fat: 20g | protein: 11g | carbs: 8g | net carbs: 6g | fiber: 2g

Sweet Pepper Nachos

Prep time: 10 minutes | Cook time: 5 minutes | Serves 2

- ◄ 6 mini sweet peppers, seeded and sliced in half
- ◄ ¾ cup shredded Colby jack cheese
- ◄ ¼ cup sliced pickled

jalapeños
- ◄ ½ medium avocado, peeled, pitted, and diced
- ◄ 2 tablespoons sour cream

1. Place peppers into an ungreased round nonstick baking dish. Sprinkle with Colby and top with jalapeños. 2. Place dish into air fryer basket. Adjust the temperature to 350ºF (177ºC) and bake for 5 minutes. Cheese will be melted and bubbly when done. 3. Remove dish from air fryer and top with avocado. Drizzle with sour cream. Serve warm.

Per Serving:

calories: 255 | fat: 21g | protein: 11g | carbs: 9g | net carbs: 5g | fiber: 4g

Basic Spaghetti Squash

Prep time: 10 minutes | Cook time: 45 minutes | Serves 2

- ◄ ½ large spaghetti squash
- ◄ 1 tablespoon coconut oil
- ◄ 2 tablespoons salted butter,

melted
- ◄ ½ teaspoon garlic powder
- ◄ 1 teaspoon dried parsley

1. Brush shell of spaghetti squash with coconut oil. Place the skin side down and brush the inside with butter. Sprinkle with garlic powder and parsley. 2. Place squash with the skin side down into the air fryer basket. 3. Adjust the temperature to 350ºF (177ºC) and air fry for 30 minutes. 4. Flip the squash so skin side is up and cook an additional 15 minutes or until fork tender. Serve warm.

Per Serving:

calories: 180 | fat: 17g | protein: 1g | carbs: 8g | net carbs: 5g | fiber: 3g

Loaded Cauliflower Steak

Prep time: 5 minutes | Cook time: 7 minutes | Serves 4

- ◄ 1 medium head cauliflower
- ◄ ¼ cup hot sauce
- ◄ 2 tablespoons salted butter,

melted
- ◄ ¼ cup blue cheese crumbles
- ◄ ¼ cup full-fat ranch dressing

1. Remove cauliflower leaves. Slice the head in ½-inch-thick slices. 2. In a small bowl, mix hot sauce and butter. Brush the mixture over the cauliflower. 3. Place each cauliflower steak into the air fryer, working in batches if necessary. 4. Adjust the temperature to 400ºF (204ºC) and air fry for 7 minutes. 5. When cooked, edges will begin turning dark and caramelized. 6. To serve, sprinkle steaks with crumbled blue cheese. Drizzle with ranch dressing.

Per Serving:

calories: 140 | fat: 12g | protein: 5g | carbs: 6g | net carbs: 5g | fiber: 1g

Baked Zucchini

Prep time: 10 minutes | Cook time: 8 minutes | Serves 4

- ◄ 2 tablespoons salted butter
- ◄ ¼ cup diced white onion
- ◄ ½ teaspoon minced garlic
- ◄ ½ cup heavy whipping cream
- ◄ 2 ounces (57 g) full-fat

cream cheese
- ◄ 1 cup shredded sharp Cheddar cheese
- ◄ 2 medium zucchini, spiralized

1. In a large saucepan over medium heat, melt butter. Add onion and sauté until it begins to soften, 1 to 3 minutes. Add garlic and sauté for 30 seconds, then pour in cream and add cream cheese. 2. Remove the pan from heat and stir in Cheddar. Add the zucchini and toss in the sauce, then put into a round baking dish. Cover the dish with foil and place into the air fryer basket. 3. Adjust the temperature to 370ºF (188ºC) and set the timer for 8 minutes. 4. After 6 minutes remove the foil and let the top brown for remaining cooking time. Stir and serve.

Per Serving:

calories: 346 | fat: 32g | protein: 11g | carbs: 6g | net carbs: 5g | fiber: 1g

Italian Baked Egg and Veggies

Prep time: 10 minutes | Cook time: 10 minutes | Serves 2

- ◄ 2 tablespoons salted butter
- ◄ 1 small zucchini, sliced lengthwise and quartered
- ◄ ½ medium green bell pepper, seeded and diced
- ◄ 1 cup fresh spinach, chopped
- ◄ 1 medium Roma tomato,

diced
- ◄ 2 large eggs
- ◄ ¼ teaspoon onion powder
- ◄ ¼ teaspoon garlic powder
- ◄ ½ teaspoon dried basil
- ◄ ¼ teaspoon dried oregano

1. Grease two ramekins with 1 tablespoon butter each. 2. In a large bowl, toss zucchini, bell pepper, spinach, and tomatoes. Divide the mixture in two and place half in each ramekin. 3. Crack an egg on top of each ramekin and sprinkle with onion powder, garlic powder, basil, and oregano. Place into the air fryer basket. 4. Adjust the temperature to 330ºF (166ºC) and bake for 10 minutes. 5. Serve immediately.

Per Serving:

calories: 260 | fat: 21g | protein: 10g | carbs: 8g | net carbs: 5g | fiber: 3g

Eggplant Parmesan

Prep time: 15 minutes | Cook time: 17 minutes | Serves 4

- ◁ 1 medium eggplant, ends trimmed, sliced into ½-inch rounds
- ◁ ¼ teaspoon salt
- ◁ 2 tablespoons coconut oil
- ◁ ½ cup grated Parmesan cheese
- ◁ 1 ounce (28 g) 100% cheese crisps, finely crushed
- ◁ ½ cup low-carb marinara sauce
- ◁ ½ cup shredded Mozzarella cheese

1. Sprinkle eggplant rounds with salt on both sides and wrap in a kitchen towel for 30 minutes. Press to remove excess water, then drizzle rounds with coconut oil on both sides. 2. In a medium bowl, mix Parmesan and cheese crisps. Press each eggplant slice into mixture to coat both sides. 3. Place rounds into ungreased air fryer basket. Adjust the temperature to 350ºF (177ºC) and air fry for 15 minutes, turning rounds halfway through cooking. They will be crispy around the edges when done. 4. Spoon marinara over rounds and sprinkle with Mozzarella. Continue cooking an additional 2 minutes at 350ºF (177ºC) until cheese is melted. Serve warm.

Per Serving:

calories: 330 | fat: 24g | protein: 18g | carbs: 13g | net carbs: 9g | fiber: 4g

Asparagus and Fennel Frittata

Prep time: 10 minutes | Cook time: 30 minutes | Serves 4

- ◁ 1 teaspoon coconut or regular butter, plus more for greasing
- ◁ 8 asparagus spears, diced
- ◁ ½ cup diced fennel
- ◁ ½ cup mushrooms, sliced (optional)
- ◁ 8 eggs
- ◁ ½ cup full-fat regular milk or coconut milk
- ◁ 1 tomato, sliced
- ◁ 1 teaspoon salt
- ◁ ½ teaspoon freshly ground black pepper
- ◁ Grated cheese (optional)

1. Preheat the oven to 350ºF (180ºC). Grease a pie dish with butter. 2. Melt 1 teaspoon of butter in a shallow skillet over medium-high heat and sauté the asparagus, fennel, and mushrooms (if using) for about 5 minutes, or until fork-tender. 3. Transfer the vegetables to the prepared pie dish. 4. Crack the eggs into a mixing bowl and pour in the milk. Whisk together until fully combined. 5. Pour the egg mixture over the vegetables in the pie dish, season with salt and pepper, and carefully and lightly mix everything together. Lay the tomato slices on top. 6. Bake the frittata for about 30 minutes. 7. Remove from the oven and let cool for 5 to 10 minutes. Slice into wedges and sprinkle with grated cheese, if desired.

Per Serving:

calories: 188 | fat: 12g | protein: 14g | carbs: 6g | net carbs: 4g | fiber: 2g

Vegetable Vodka Sauce Bake

Prep time: 10 minutes | Cook time: 30 minutes | Serves 4

- ◁ 3 tablespoons melted grass-fed butter, divided
- ◁ 4 cups mushrooms, halved
- ◁ 4 cups cooked cauliflower florets
- ◁ 1½ cups purchased vodka sauce
- ◁ ¾ cup heavy (whipping) cream
- ◁ ½ cup grated Asiago cheese
- ◁ Sea salt, for seasoning
- ◁ Freshly ground black pepper, for seasoning
- ◁ 1 cup shredded provolone cheese
- ◁ 2 tablespoons chopped fresh oregano

1. Preheat the oven. Set the oven temperature to 350°F and use 1 tablespoon of the melted butter to grease a 9-by-13-inch baking dish. 2. Mix the vegetables. In a large bowl, combine the mushrooms, cauliflower, vodka sauce, cream, Asiago, and the remaining 2 tablespoons of butter. Season the vegetables with salt and pepper. 3. Bake. Transfer the vegetable mixture to the baking dish and top it with the provolone cheese. Bake for 30 to 35 minutes until it's bubbly and heated through. 4. Serve. Divide the mixture between four plates and top with the oregano.

Per Serving:

calories: 537 | fat: 45g | protein: 19g | carbs: 14g | net carbs: 8g | fiber: 19g

Pesto Spinach Flatbread

Prep time: 10 minutes | Cook time: 8 minutes | Serves 4

- ◁ 1 cup blanched finely ground almond flour
- ◁ 2 ounces (57 g) cream cheese
- ◁ 2 cups shredded Mozzarella
- cheese
- ◁ 1 cup chopped fresh spinach leaves
- ◁ 2 tablespoons basil pesto

1. Place flour, cream cheese, and Mozzarella in a large microwave-safe bowl and microwave on high 45 seconds, then stir. 2. Fold in spinach and microwave an additional 15 seconds. Stir until a soft dough ball forms. 3. Cut two pieces of parchment paper to fit air fryer basket. Separate dough into two sections and press each out on ungreased parchment to create 6-inch rounds. 4. Spread 1 tablespoon pesto over each flatbread and place rounds on parchment into ungreased air fryer basket. Adjust the temperature to 350ºF (177ºC) and air fry for 8 minutes, turning crusts halfway through cooking. Flatbread will be golden when done. 5. Let cool 5 minutes before slicing and serving.

Per Serving:

calories: 506 | fat: 43g | protein: 27g | carbs: 9g | net carbs: 5g | fiber: 4g

Stuffed Eggplant

Prep time: 20 minutes | Cook time: 1 hour | Serves 2 to 4

◄ 1 small eggplant, halved lengthwise
◄ 3 tablespoons olive, avocado, or macadamia nut oil
◄ 1 onion, diced
◄ 12 asparagus spears or green beans, diced
◄ 1 red bell pepper, diced
◄ 1 large tomato, chopped
◄ 2 garlic cloves, minced
◄ ½ block (8 ounces / 227 g)

extra-firm tofu (optional)
◄ 3 tablespoons chopped fresh basil leaves
◄ Salt and freshly ground black pepper, to taste
◄ ¼ cup water
◄ 2 eggs
◄ Chopped fresh parsley, for garnish (optional)
◄ Shredded cheese, for garnish (optional)

1. Preheat the oven to 350°F (180°C). 2. Scoop out the flesh from the halved eggplant and chop it into cubes. Reserve the eggplant skin. 3. In a sauté pan with a lid, heat the oil over medium-high heat. Add the eggplant, onion, asparagus, bell pepper, tomato, garlic, and tofu (if using) and stir. Stir in the basil, season with salt and pepper, and cook for about 5 minutes. 4. Add the water, cover the pan, reduce the heat to medium, and cook for about 15 minutes longer. 5. Put the eggplant "boats" (the reserved skin) on a baking sheet. Scoop some of the cooked eggplant mixture into each boat (you may have some filling left over, which is fine—you can roast it alongside the eggplant). 6. Crack an egg into each eggplant boat, on top of the filling, then bake for about 40 minutes, or until desired doneness. 7. Remove the eggplant from the oven and, if desired, sprinkle parsley and cheese over the top. Let the cheese melt and cool for about 5 minutes, then serve them up!

Per Serving:

calories: 380 | fat: 26g | protein: 12g | carbs: 25g | net carbs: 15g | fiber: 10g

White Cheddar and Mushroom Soufflés

Prep time: 15 minutes | Cook time: 12 minutes | Serves 4

◄ 3 large eggs, whites and yolks separated
◄ ½ cup sharp white Cheddar cheese
◄ 3 ounces (85 g) cream cheese, softened

◄ ¼ teaspoon cream of tartar
◄ ¼ teaspoon salt
◄ ¼ teaspoon ground black pepper
◄ ½ cup cremini mushrooms, sliced

1. In a large bowl, whip egg whites until stiff peaks form, about 2 minutes. In a separate large bowl, beat Cheddar, egg yolks, cream cheese, cream of tartar, salt, and pepper together until combined.

2. Fold egg whites into cheese mixture, being careful not to stir. Fold in mushrooms, then pour mixture evenly into four ungreased ramekins. Place ramekins into air fryer basket. Adjust the temperature to 350°F (177°C) and bake for 12 minutes. Eggs will be browned on the top and firm in the center when done. Serve warm.

Per Serving:

calories: 228 | fat: 19g | protein: 13g | carbs: 2g | net carbs: 2g | fiber: 0g

Cauliflower Rice-Stuffed Peppers

Prep time: 10 minutes | Cook time: 15 minutes | Serves 4

◄ 2 cups uncooked cauliflower rice
◄ ¾ cup drained canned petite diced tomatoes
◄ 2 tablespoons olive oil
◄ 1 cup shredded Mozzarella cheese

◄ ¼ teaspoon salt
◄ ¼ teaspoon ground black pepper
◄ 4 medium green bell peppers, tops removed, seeded

1. In a large bowl, mix all ingredients except bell peppers. Scoop mixture evenly into peppers. 2. Place peppers into ungreased air fryer basket. Adjust the temperature to 350°F (177°C) and air fry for 15 minutes. Peppers will be tender and cheese will be melted when done. Serve warm.

Per Serving:

calories: 309 | fat: 23g | protein: 16g | carbs: 11g | net carbs: 7g | fiber: 4g

Mediterranean Pan Pizza

Prep time: 5 minutes | Cook time: 8 minutes | Serves 2

◄ 1 cup shredded Mozzarella cheese
◄ ¼ medium red bell pepper, seeded and chopped
◄ ½ cup chopped fresh spinach

leaves
◄ 2 tablespoons chopped black olives
◄ 2 tablespoons crumbled feta cheese

1. Sprinkle Mozzarella into an ungreased round nonstick baking dish in an even layer. Add remaining ingredients on top. 2. Place dish into air fryer basket. Adjust the temperature to 350°F (177°C) and bake for 8 minutes, checking halfway through to avoid burning. Top of pizza will be golden brown and the cheese melted when done. 3. Remove dish from fryer and let cool 5 minutes before slicing and serving.

Per Serving:

calories: 239 | fat: 17g | protein: 17g | carbs: 6g | net carbs: 5g | fiber: 1g

Roasted Spaghetti Squash

Prep time: 10 minutes | Cook time: 45 minutes | Serves 6

- ◁ 1 (4 pounds / 1.8 kg) spaghetti squash, halved and seeded
- ◁ 2 tablespoons coconut oil
- ◁ 4 tablespoons salted butter, melted
- ◁ 1 teaspoon garlic powder
- ◁ 2 teaspoons dried parsley

1. Brush shell of spaghetti squash with coconut oil. Brush inside with butter. Sprinkle inside with garlic powder and parsley. 2. Place squash skin side down into ungreased air fryer basket, working in batches if needed. Adjust the temperature to 350ºF (177ºC) and set the timer for 30 minutes. When the timer beeps, flip squash and cook an additional 15 minutes until fork-tender. 3. Use a fork to remove spaghetti strands from shell and serve warm.

Per Serving:

calories: 210 | fat: 19g | protein: 2g | carbs: 11g | net carbs: 8g | fiber: 3g

Fettuccine Alfredo (2 Variations)

Prep time: 5 minutes | Cook time: 10 minutes | Serves 4 to 6

For Both Variations:
- ◁ 2 (7 ounces / 198 g) packages shirataki noodles or 5 cups spaghetti squash or hearts of palm noodles

For the Dairy Variation:
- ◁ 2 tablespoons grass-fed butter or ghee
- ◁ 2 teaspoons garlic powder or 2 small garlic cloves, minced
- ◁ 1½ cups grass-fed heavy

For the Vegan Variation:
- ◁ 2 tablespoons butter-flavored coconut oil
- ◁ 2 teaspoons garlic powder or 2 small garlic cloves, minced
- ◁ 1½ cups heavy coconut

- ◁ 1 tablespoon chopped fresh parsley, chives, or basil, for serving (optional)

- (whipping) cream
- ◁ 1 cup grated Parmesan cheese
- ◁ Salt and freshly ground black pepper, to taste

- cream (shake the can well before measuring)
- ◁ 4 tablespoons nutritional yeast
- ◁ Salt and freshly ground black pepper, to taste

1. If you're making the dairy version, melt the butter in a skillet over medium heat, add the garlic, and stir together. Add the cream and cheese, season with salt and pepper, and whisk everything together. Cook for about 10 minutes, or until the cheese is melted. 2. If you're making the vegan version, melt the coconut oil in a skillet over medium heat, add the garlic, and stir together. Add the coconut cream and nutritional yeast, season with salt and pepper, and whisk everything together. Cook for about 10 minutes. 3. Add the noodles to the skillet and cook, stirring, for 1 minute to coat in the sauce. 4. Dish up in bowls and sprinkle with chopped parsley, chives, or

basil, if desired.

Per Serving:

calories: 510 | fat: 46g | protein: 12g | carbs: 12g | net carbs: 10g | fiber: 2g

Caprese Eggplant Stacks

Prep time: 5 minutes | Cook time: 12 minutes | Serves 4

- ◁ 1 medium eggplant, cut into ¼-inch slices
- ◁ 2 large tomatoes, cut into ¼-inch slices
- ◁ 4 ounces (113 g) fresh
- Mozzarella, cut into ½-ounce / 14-g slices
- ◁ 2 tablespoons olive oil
- ◁ ¼ cup fresh basil, sliced

1. In a baking dish, place four slices of eggplant on the bottom. Place a slice of tomato on top of each eggplant round, then Mozzarella, then eggplant. Repeat as necessary. 2. Drizzle with olive oil. Cover dish with foil and place dish into the air fryer basket. 3. Adjust the temperature to 350ºF (177ºC) and bake for 12 minutes. 4. When done, eggplant will be tender. Garnish with fresh basil to serve.

Per Serving:

calories: 203 | fat: 16g | protein: 8g | carbs: 10g | net carbs: 7g | fiber: 3g

Vegetarian Chili with Avocado and Sour Cream

Prep time: 10 minutes | Cook time: 25 minutes | Serves 8

- ◁ 2 tablespoons good-quality olive oil
- ◁ ½ onion, finely chopped
- ◁ 1 red bell pepper, diced
- ◁ 2 jalapeño peppers, chopped
- ◁ 1 tablespoon minced garlic
- ◁ 2 tablespoons chili powder
- ◁ 1 teaspoon ground cumin
- ◁ 4 cups canned diced tomatoes
- ◁ 2 cups pecans, chopped
- ◁ 1 cup sour cream
- ◁ 1 avocado, diced
- ◁ 2 tablespoons chopped fresh cilantro

1. Sauté the vegetables. In a large pot over medium-high heat, warm the olive oil. Add the onion, red bell pepper, jalapeño peppers, and garlic and sauté until they've softened, about 4 minutes. Stir in the chili powder and cumin, stirring to coat the vegetables with the spices. 2. Cook the chili. Stir in the tomatoes and pecans and bring the chili to a boil, then reduce the heat to low and simmer until the vegetables are soft and the flavors mellow, about 20 minutes. 3. Serve. Ladle the chili into bowls and serve it with the sour cream, avocado, and cilantro.

Per Serving:

calories: 332 | fat: 32g | protein: 5g | carbs: 11g | net carbs: 5g | fiber: 6g

Greek Vegetable Briam

Prep time: 10 minutes | Cook time: 30 minutes | Serves 4

◄ ⅓ cup good-quality olive oil, divided
◄ 1 onion, thinly sliced
◄ 1 tablespoon minced garlic
◄ ¾ small eggplant, diced
◄ 2 zucchini, diced
◄ 2 cups chopped cauliflower
◄ 1 red bell pepper, diced
◄ 2 cups diced tomatoes
◄ 2 tablespoons chopped fresh

◄ parsley
◄ 2 tablespoons chopped fresh oregano
◄ Sea salt, for seasoning
◄ Freshly ground black pepper, for seasoning
◄ 1½ cups crumbled feta cheese
◄ ¼ cup pumpkin seeds

1. Preheat the oven. Set the oven to broil and lightly grease a 9-by-13-inch casserole dish with olive oil. 2. Sauté the aromatics. In a medium stockpot over medium heat, warm 3 tablespoons of the olive oil. Add the onion and garlic and sauté until they've softened, about 3 minutes. 3. Sauté the vegetables. Stir in the eggplant and cook for 5 minutes, stirring occasionally. Add the zucchini, cauliflower, and red bell pepper and cook for 5 minutes. Stir in the tomatoes, parsley, and oregano and cook, giving it a stir from time to time, until the vegetables are tender, about 10 minutes. Season it with salt and pepper. 4. Broil. Transfer the vegetable mixture to the casserole dish and top with the crumbled feta. Broil for about 4 minutes until the cheese is golden. 5. Serve. Divide the casserole between four plates and top it with the pumpkin seeds. Drizzle with the remaining olive oil.

Per Serving:
calories: 356 | fat: 28g | protein: 11g | carbs: 18g | net carbs: 11g | fiber: 7g

Zucchini Pasta with Spinach, Olives, and Asiago

Prep time: 10 minutes | Cook time: 10 minutes | Serves 4

◄ 3 tablespoons good-quality olive oil
◄ 1 tablespoon grass-fed butter
◄ 1½ tablespoons minced garlic
◄ 1 cup packed fresh spinach
◄ ½ cup sliced black olives
◄ ½ cup halved cherry tomatoes

◄ 2 tablespoons chopped fresh basil
◄ 3 zucchini, spiralized
◄ Sea salt, for seasoning
◄ Freshly ground black pepper, for seasoning
◄ ½ cup shredded Asiago cheese

1. Sauté the vegetables. In a large skillet over medium-high heat, warm the olive oil and butter. Add the garlic and sauté until it's tender, about 2 minutes. Stir in the spinach, olives, tomatoes, and basil and sauté until the spinach is wilted, about 4 minutes. Stir in the zucchini noodles, toss to combine them with the sauce, and

cook until the zucchini is tender, about 2 minutes. 2. Serve. Season with salt and pepper. Divide the mixture between four bowls and serve topped with the Asiago.

Per Serving:
calories: 199 | fat: 18g | protein: 6g | carbs: 4g | net carbs: 3g | fiber: 1g

Tangy Asparagus and Broccoli

Prep time: 25 minutes | Cook time: 22 minutes | Serves 4

◄ ½ pound (227 g) asparagus, cut into 1½-inch pieces
◄ ½ pound (227 g) broccoli, cut into 1½-inch pieces
◄ 2 tablespoons olive oil

◄ Salt and white pepper, to taste
◄ ½ cup vegetable broth
◄ 2 tablespoons apple cider vinegar

1. Place the vegetables in a single layer in the lightly greased air fryer basket. Drizzle the olive oil over the vegetables. 2. Sprinkle with salt and white pepper. 3. Cook at 380°F (193°C) for 15 minutes, shaking the basket halfway through the cooking time. 4. Add ½ cup of vegetable broth to a saucepan; bring to a rapid boil and add the vinegar. Cook for 5 to 7 minutes or until the sauce has reduced by half. 5. Spoon the sauce over the warm vegetables and serve immediately. Bon appétit!

Per Serving:
calories: 89 | fat: 7g | protein: 3g | carbs: 7g | net carbs: 4g | fiber: 3g

Three-Cheese Zucchini Boats

Prep time: 15 minutes | Cook time: 20 minutes | Serves 2

◄ 2 medium zucchini
◄ 1 tablespoon avocado oil
◄ ¼ cup low-carb, no-sugar-added pasta sauce
◄ ¼ cup full-fat ricotta cheese
◄ ¼ cup shredded Mozzarella

◄ cheese
◄ ¼ teaspoon dried oregano
◄ ¼ teaspoon garlic powder
◄ ½ teaspoon dried parsley
◄ 2 tablespoons grated vegetarian Parmesan cheese

1. Cut off 1 inch from the top and bottom of each zucchini. Slice zucchini in half lengthwise and use a spoon to scoop out a bit of the inside, making room for filling. Brush with oil and spoon 2 tablespoons pasta sauce into each shell. 2. In a medium bowl, mix ricotta, Mozzarella, oregano, garlic powder, and parsley. Spoon the mixture into each zucchini shell. Place stuffed zucchini shells into the air fryer basket. 3. Adjust the temperature to 350°F (177°C) and air fry for 20 minutes. 4. To remove from the basket, use tongs or a spatula and carefully lift out. Top with Parmesan. Serve immediately.

Per Serving:
calories: 245 | fat: 18g | protein: 12g | carbs: 9g | net carbs: 7g | fiber: 2g

Roasted Veggie Bowl

Prep time: 10 minutes | Cook time: 15 minutes | Serves 2

- 1 cup broccoli florets
- 1 cup quartered Brussels sprouts
- ½ cup cauliflower florets
- ¼ medium white onion, peeled and sliced ¼ inch thick
- ½ medium green bell pepper, seeded and sliced ¼ inch thick

- 1 tablespoon coconut oil
- 2 teaspoons chili powder
- ½ teaspoon garlic powder
- ½ teaspoon cumin

1. Toss all ingredients together in a large bowl until vegetables are fully coated with oil and seasoning. 2. Pour vegetables into the air fryer basket. 3. Adjust the temperature to 360°F (182°C) and roast for 15 minutes. 4. Shake two or three times during cooking. Serve warm.

Per Serving:

calories: 168 | fat: 11g | protein: 4g | carbs: 15g | net carbs: 9g | fiber: 6g

Spinach-Artichoke Stuffed Mushrooms

Prep time: 10 minutes | Cook time: 10 to 14 minutes | Serves 4

- 2 tablespoons olive oil
- 4 large portobello mushrooms, stems removed and gills scraped out
- ½ teaspoon salt
- ¼ teaspoon freshly ground pepper

- 4 ounces (113 g) goat cheese, crumbled
- ½ cup chopped marinated artichoke hearts
- 1 cup frozen spinach, thawed and squeezed dry
- ½ cup grated Parmesan cheese
- 2 tablespoons chopped fresh parsley

1. Preheat the air fryer to 400°F (204°C). 2. Rub the olive oil over the portobello mushrooms until thoroughly coated. Sprinkle both sides with the salt and black pepper. Place top-side down on a clean work surface. 3. In a small bowl, combine the goat cheese, artichoke hearts, and spinach. Mash with the back of a fork until thoroughly combined. Divide the cheese mixture among the mushrooms and sprinkle with the Parmesan cheese. 4. Air fry for 10 to 14 minutes until the mushrooms are tender and the cheese has begun to brown. Top with the fresh parsley just before serving.

Per Serving:

calories: 255 | fat: 20g | protein: 13g | carbs: 7g | net carbs: 4g | fiber: 3g

Chapter 9 Desserts

Strawberry Panna Cotta

Prep time: 10 minutes | Cook time: 10 minutes | Serves 4

- 2 tablespoons warm water
- 2 teaspoons gelatin powder
- 2 cups heavy cream
- 1 cup sliced strawberries, plus more for garnish
- 1 to 2 tablespoons sugar-free sweetener of choice (optional)
- 1½ teaspoons pure vanilla extract
- 4 to 6 fresh mint leaves, for garnish (optional)

1. Pour the warm water into a small bowl. Sprinkle the gelatin over the water and stir well to dissolve. Allow the mixture to sit for 10 minutes. 2. In a blender or a large bowl, if using an immersion blender, combine the cream, strawberries, sweetener (if using), and vanilla. Blend until the mixture is smooth and the strawberries are well puréed. 3. Transfer the mixture to a saucepan and heat over medium-low heat until just below a simmer. Remove from the heat and cool for 5 minutes. 4. Whisking constantly, add in the gelatin mixture until smooth. Divide the custard between ramekins or small glass bowls, cover and refrigerate until set, 4 to 6 hours. 5. Serve chilled, garnishing with additional sliced strawberries or mint leaves (if using).

Per Serving:

calories: 540 | fat: 57g | protein: 6g | carbs: 8g | net carbs: 7g | fiber: 1g

Pecan Butter Cookies

Prep time: 5 minutes | Cook time: 24 minutes | Makes 12 cookies

- 1 cup chopped pecans
- ½ cup salted butter, melted
- ½ cup coconut flour
- ¾ cup erythritol, divided
- 1 teaspoon vanilla extract

1. In a food processor, blend together pecans, butter, flour, ½ cup erythritol, and vanilla 1 minute until a dough forms. 2. Form dough into twelve individual cookie balls, about 1 tablespoon each. 3. Cut three pieces of parchment to fit air fryer basket. Place four cookies on each ungreased parchment and place one piece parchment with cookies into air fryer basket. Adjust air fryer temperature to 325ºF (163ºC) and set the timer for 8 minutes. Repeat cooking with remaining batches. 4. When the timer goes off, allow cookies to cool 5 minutes on a large serving plate until cool enough to handle. While still warm, dust cookies with remaining erythritol. Allow to cool completely, about 15 minutes, before serving.

Per Serving:

calories: 121 | fat: 13g | protein: 1g | carbs: 2g | net carbs: 1g | fiber: 1g

Traditional Cheesecake

Prep time: 30 minutes | Cook time: 45 minutes | Serves 8

For Crust:
- 1½ cups almond flour
- 4 tablespoons butter, melted
- 1 tablespoon Swerve
- 1 tablespoon granulated erythritol
- ½ teaspoon ground cinnamon

For Filling:
- 16 ounces (454 g) cream cheese, softened
- ½ cup granulated erythritol
- 2 eggs
- 1 teaspoon vanilla extract
- ½ teaspoon lemon extract
- 1½ cups water

1. To make the crust: In a medium bowl, combine the almond flour, butter, Swerve, erythritol, and cinnamon. Use a fork to press it all together. When completed, the mixture should resemble wet sand. 2. Spray the springform pan with cooking spray and line the bottom with parchment paper. 3. Press the crust evenly into the pan. Work the crust up the sides of the pan, about halfway from the top, and make sure there are no bare spots on the bottom. 4. Place the crust in the freezer for 20 minutes while you make the filling. 5. To make the filling: In the bowl of a stand mixer using the whip attachment, combine the cream cheese and erythritol on medium speed until the cream cheese is light and fluffy, 2 to 3 minutes. 6. Add the eggs, vanilla extract, and lemon extract. Mix until well combined. 7. Remove the crust from the freezer and pour in the filling. Cover the pan tightly with aluminum foil and place it on the trivet. 8. Add the water to the pot and carefully lower the trivet into the pot. 9. Close the lid. Select Manual mode and set cooking time for 45 minutes on High Pressure. 10. When timer beeps, use a quick pressure release and open the lid. 11. Remove the trivet and cheesecake from the pot. Remove the foil from the pan. The center of the cheesecake should still be slightly jiggly. If the cheesecake is still very jiggly in the center, cook for an additional 5 minutes on High pressure until the appropriate doneness is reached. 12. Let the cheesecake cool for 30 minutes on the counter before placing it in the refrigerator to set. Leave the cheesecake in the refrigerator for at least 6 hours before removing the sides of the pan, slicing, and serving.

Per Serving:

calories: 437 | fat: 35g | protein: 10g | carbs: 7g | net carbs: 4g | fiber: 2g

County Fair Cinnamon Donuts

Prep time: 10 minutes | Cook time: 25 minutes | Makes 6 donuts

- ◀ 11½ ounces cream cheese (1 cup plus 7 tablespoons), room temperature
- ◀ ½ cup extra-virgin olive oil
- ◀ ¼ cup heavy whipping cream
- ◀ 4 large eggs
- ◀ ½ teaspoon liquid stevia
- ◀ ½ teaspoon maple extract

Topping:
- ◀ ¼ cup granular erythritol
- ◀ ¼ cup ground cinnamon

- ◀ ½ teaspoon vanilla extract
- ◀ ¼ cup plus 2 tablespoons coconut flour
- ◀ 2 teaspoons ground cinnamon
- ◀ 1 teaspoon baking powder
- ◀ 1 teaspoon xanthan gum
- ◀ ¼ teaspoon pink Himalayan salt

- ◀ Special equipment:
- ◀ 6-cavity silicone donut pan

1. Preheat the oven to 400°F and grease a 6-cavity donut pan with coconut oil spray. 2. In a large bowl, beat the cream cheese, olive oil, cream, eggs, stevia, and extracts using a hand mixer until smooth and fully incorporated. Set aside. 3. In a small bowl, whisk together the coconut flour, cinnamon, baking powder, xanthan gum, and salt using a whisk. Add the dry mixture to the wet ingredients and combine using the hand mixer. Fill the greased cavities of the donut mold to the brim, making sure not to overfill. 4. Bake for 25 minutes, until the donuts are puffed up and a toothpick comes out clean. 5. Meanwhile, put the ingredients for the topping on a plate and combine using your fingers. After removing the donuts from the oven, allow to cool in the pan for 5 minutes, then toss them, one at a time, in the cinnamon-sugar mixture. Set the coated donuts on a wire baking rack to cool for an additional 10 minutes prior to eating. 6. Store leftovers in a sealed container in the refrigerator for up to 4 days.

Per Serving:

calories: 461 | fat: 45g | protein: 9g | carbs: 7g | net carbs: 4g | fiber: 3g

Lemon Drops

Prep time: 5 minutes | Cook time: 0 minutes | Serves 4

- ◀ ¼ cup (60 ml) melted (but not hot) cacao butter
- ◀ ¼ cup (60 ml) melted (but not hot) coconut oil
- ◀ 1½ teaspoons confectioners'-style erythritol
- ◀ 2 teaspoons lemon-flavored

- magnesium powder (optional)
- ◀ 1 teaspoon lemon extract
- ◀ Special Equipment:
- ◀ Silicone mold(s) with 20 (½-ounce/15-ml) round cavities

1. Set the silicone mold(s) on a baking sheet. 2. Place the cacao butter, coconut oil, and erythritol in a small bowl. Whisk until the erythritol has dissolved. 3. If using magnesium powder, add it to the bowl along with the lemon extract. Whisk to combine. 4. Pour the mixture into the silicone mold(s), filling to the top. Transfer the

baking sheet to the fridge to harden for 1 hour. 5. Once hardened, remove the lemon drops from the molds and enjoy! Serve directly from the fridge.

Per Serving:

calories: 258 | fat: 29g | protein: 0g | carbs: 0g | net carbs: 0g | fiber: 0g

Lemon-Poppyseed Cookies

Prep time: 5 minutes | Cook time: 10 minutes | serves 4

- ◀ Nonstick cooking spray
- ◀ 1 cup almond butter
- ◀ ¾ cup monk fruit sweetener
- ◀ 4 tablespoons chia seeds

- ◀ 3 tablespoons fresh grated lemon zest
- ◀ Juice of 1 lemon
- ◀ 1 tablespoon poppy seeds

1. Preheat the oven to 350°F. Grease a baking sheet with cooking spray and set aside. 2. In a large mixing bowl, combine the almond butter with the monk fruit sweetener, chia seeds, lemon zest, lemon juice, and poppy seeds. Mix well, kneading the mixture with your hands. 3. Roll pieces of the dough into cookie-size balls and place them on the prepared baking sheet, spacing them evenly, as some spreading will occur during baking. 4. Bake the cookies for 8 minutes, until golden. 5. Transfer the cookies to a cooling rack. 6. Serve as is or paired with your favorite unsweetened, plant-based milk.

Per Serving:

calories: 460 | fat: 39g | protein: 13g | carbs: 21g | net carbs: 9g | fiber: 12g

Cream Cheese Shortbread Cookies

Prep time: 30 minutes | Cook time: 20 minutes | Makes 12 cookies

- ◀ ¼ cup coconut oil, melted
- ◀ 2 ounces (57 g) cream cheese, softened
- ◀ ½ cup granular erythritol

- ◀ 1 large egg, whisked
- ◀ 2 cups blanched finely ground almond flour
- ◀ 1 teaspoon almond extract

1. Combine all ingredients in a large bowl to form a firm ball. 2. Place dough on a sheet of plastic wrap and roll into a 12-inch-long log shape. Roll log in plastic wrap and place in refrigerator 30 minutes to chill. 3. Remove log from plastic and slice into twelve equal cookies. Cut two sheets of parchment paper to fit air fryer basket. Place six cookies on each ungreased sheet. Place one sheet with cookies into air fryer basket. Adjust the temperature to 320°F (160°C) and bake for 10 minutes, turning cookies halfway through cooking. They will be lightly golden when done. Repeat with remaining cookies. 4. Let cool 15 minutes before serving to avoid crumbling.

Per Serving:

1 cookie: calories: 154 | fat: 14g | protein: 4g | carbs: 4g | net carbs: 2g | fiber: 2g

Coconut Cupcakes

Prep time: 5 minutes | Cook time: 10 minutes | Serves 6

- ◄ 4 eggs, beaten
- ◄ 4 tablespoons coconut milk
- ◄ 4 tablespoons coconut flour
- ◄ ½ teaspoon vanilla extract
- ◄ 2 tablespoons erythritol
- ◄ 1 teaspoon baking powder
- ◄ 1 cup water

1. In the mixing bowl, mix up eggs, coconut milk, coconut flour, vanilla extract, erythritol, and baking powder. 2. Then pour the batter in the cupcake molds. 3. Pour the water and insert the trivet in the instant pot. 4. Place the cupcakes on the trivet. 5. Lock the lid. Select the Manual mode and set the cooking time for 10 minutes on High Pressure. Once the timer goes off, perform a natural pressure release for 5 minutes, then release any remaining pressure. Carefully open the lid. 6. Serve immediately.

Per Serving:

calories: 85 | fat: 6g | protein: 5g | carbs: 9g | net carbs: 7g | fiber: 2g

Halle Berries-and-Cream Cobbler

Prep time: 10 minutes | Cook time: 25 minutes | Serves 4

- ◄ 12 ounces (340 g) cream cheese (1½ cups), softened
- ◄ 1 large egg
- ◄ ¾ cup Swerve confectioners'-style sweetener or equivalent

Biscuits:
- ◄ 3 large egg whites
- ◄ ¾ cup blanched almond flour
- ◄ 1 teaspoon baking powder

Frosting:
- ◄ 2 ounces (57 g) cream cheese (¼ cup), softened
- ◄ 1 tablespoon Swerve confectioners'-style sweetener or equivalent amount of powdered or

- amount of powdered sweetener
- ◄ ½ teaspoon vanilla extract
- ◄ ¼ teaspoon fine sea salt
- ◄ 1 cup sliced fresh raspberries or strawberries

- ◄ 2½ tablespoons very cold unsalted butter, cut into pieces
- ◄ ¼ teaspoon fine sea salt

- liquid sweetener
- ◄ 1 tablespoon unsweetened, unflavored almond milk or heavy cream
- ◄ Fresh raspberries or strawberries, for garnish

1. Preheat the air fryer to 400ºF (204ºC). Grease a pie pan. 2. In a large mixing bowl, use a hand mixer to combine the cream cheese, egg, and sweetener until smooth. Stir in the vanilla and salt. Gently fold in the raspberries with a rubber spatula. Pour the mixture into the prepared pan and set aside. 3. Make the biscuits: Place the egg whites in a medium-sized mixing bowl or the bowl of a stand mixer. Using a hand mixer or stand mixer, whip the egg whites until very fluffy and stiff. 4. In a separate medium-sized bowl, combine the almond flour and baking powder. Cut in the butter and add the salt, stirring gently to keep the butter pieces intact. 5. Gently fold the almond flour mixture into the egg whites. Use a large spoon or

ice cream scooper to scoop out the dough and form it into a 2-inch-wide biscuit, making sure the butter stays in separate clumps. Place the biscuit on top of the raspberry mixture in the pan. Repeat with remaining dough to make 4 biscuits. 6. Place the pan in the air fryer and bake for 5 minutes, then lower the temperature to 325ºF (163ºC) and bake for another 17 to 20 minutes, until the biscuits are golden brown. 7. While the cobbler cooks, make the frosting: Place the cream cheese in a small bowl and stir to break it up. Add the sweetener and stir. Add the almond milk and stir until well combined. If you prefer a thinner frosting, add more almond milk. 8. Remove the cobbler from the air fryer and allow to cool slightly, then drizzle with the frosting. Garnish with fresh raspberries. 9. Store leftovers in an airtight container in the refrigerator for up to 3 days. Reheat the cobbler in a preheated 350ºF (177ºC) air fryer for 3 minutes, or until warmed through.

Per Serving:

calories: 535 | fat: 14g | protein: 13g | carbs: 14g | net carbs: 10g | fiber: 4g

Espresso Cheesecake with Raspberries

Prep time: 5 minutes | Cook time: 35 minutes | Serves 8

- ◄ 1 cup blanched almond flour
- ◄ ½ cup plus 2 tablespoons Swerve
- ◄ 3 tablespoons espresso powder, divided
- ◄ 2 tablespoons butter
- ◄ 1 egg
- ◄ ½ cup full-fat heavy cream
- ◄ 16 ounces (454 g) cream

- cheese
- ◄ 1 cup water
- ◄ 6 ounces (170 g) dark chocolate (at least 80% cacao)
- ◄ 8 ounces (227 g) full-fat heavy whipping cream
- ◄ 2 cups raspberries

1. In a small mixing bowl, combine the almond flour, 2 tablespoons of Swerve, 1 tablespoon of espresso powder and the butter. 2. Line the bottom of a springform pan with parchment paper. Press the almond flour dough flat on the bottom and about 1 inch on the sides. Set aside. 3. In a food processor, mix the egg, heavy cream, cream cheese, remaining Swerve and remaining espresso powder until smooth. 4. Pour the cream cheese mixture into the springform pan. Loosely cover with aluminum foil. 5. Put the water in the Instant Pot and place the trivet inside. 6. Close the lid. Select Manual button and set the timer for 35 minutes on High pressure. 7. When timer beeps, use a natural pressure release for 15 minutes, then release any remaining pressure. Open the lid. 8. Remove the springform pan and place it on a cooling rack for 2 to 3 hours or until it reaches room temperature. Refrigerate overnight. 9. Melt the chocolate and heavy whipping cream in the double boiler. Cool for 15 minutes and drizzle on top of the cheesecake, allowing the chocolate to drip down the sides. 10. Add the raspberries on top of the cheesecake before serving.

Per Serving:

calories: 585 | fat: 54g | protein: 12g | carbs: 15g | net carbs: 11g | fiber: 4g

Coconut Lemon Squares

Prep time: 5 minutes | Cook time: 40 minutes | Serves 5 to 6

- 3 eggs
- 2 tablespoons grass-fed butter, softened
- ½ cup full-fat coconut milk
- ½ teaspoon baking powder
- ½ teaspoon vanilla extract
- ½ cup Swerve, or more to taste
- ¼ cup lemon juice
- 1 cup blanched almond flour

1. In a large bowl, mix together the eggs, butter, coconut milk, baking powder, vanilla, Swerve, lemon juice, and flour. Stir thoroughly, until a perfectly even mixture is obtained. 2. Next, pour 1 cup filtered water into the Instant Pot, and insert the trivet. Transfer the mixture from the bowl into a well-greased, Instant Pot-friendly pan (or dish). 3. Using a sling if desired, place the dish onto the trivet, and cover loosely with aluminum foil. Close the lid, set the pressure release to Sealing, and select Manual. Set the Instant Pot to 40 minutes on High Pressure, and let cook. 4. Once cooked, let the pressure naturally disperse from the Instant Pot for about 10 minutes, then carefully switch the pressure release to Venting. 5. Open the Instant Pot, and remove the dish. Let cool, cut into 6 squares, serve, and enjoy!

Per Serving:

calories: 166 | fat: 15g | protein: 6g | carbs: 3g | net carbs: 2g | fiber: 1g

Pumpkin Cookie with Cream Cheese Frosting

Prep time: 10 minutes | Cook time: 7 minutes | Serves 6

- ½ cup blanched finely ground almond flour
- ½ cup powdered erythritol, divided
- 2 tablespoons butter, softened
- 1 large egg
- ½ teaspoon unflavored gelatin
- ½ teaspoon baking powder
- ½ teaspoon vanilla extract
- ½ teaspoon pumpkin pie spice
- 2 tablespoons pure pumpkin purée
- ½ teaspoon ground cinnamon, divided
- ¼ cup low-carb, sugar-free chocolate chips
- 3 ounces (85 g) full-fat cream cheese, softened

1. In a large bowl, mix almond flour and ¼ cup erythritol. Stir in butter, egg, and gelatin until combined. 2. Stir in baking powder, vanilla, pumpkin pie spice, pumpkin purée, and ¼ teaspoon cinnamon, then fold in chocolate chips. 3. Pour batter into a round baking pan. Place pan into the air fryer basket. 4. Adjust the temperature to 300ºF (149ºC) and bake for 7 minutes. 5. When fully cooked, the top will be golden brown and a toothpick inserted in center will come out clean. Let cool at least 20 minutes. 6. To make the frosting: mix cream cheese, remaining ¼ teaspoon cinnamon, and remaining ¼ cup erythritol in a large bowl. Using an electric mixer, beat until it becomes fluffy. Spread onto the cooled cookie. Garnish with additional cinnamon if desired.

Per Serving:

calories: 186 | fat: 16g | protein: 4g | carbs: 5g | net carbs: 4g | fiber: 2g

Almond Butter Cookie Balls

Prep time: 5 minutes | Cook time: 10 minutes | Makes 10 balls

- 1 cup almond butter
- 1 large egg
- 1 teaspoon vanilla extract
- ¼ cup low-carb protein powder
- ¼ cup powdered erythritol
- ¼ cup shredded unsweetened coconut
- ¼ cup low-carb, sugar-free chocolate chips
- ½ teaspoon ground cinnamon

1. In a large bowl, mix almond butter and egg. Add in vanilla, protein powder, and erythritol. 2. Fold in coconut, chocolate chips, and cinnamon. Roll into 1-inch balls. Place balls into a round baking pan and put into the air fryer basket. 3. Adjust the temperature to 320ºF (160ºC) and bake for 10 minutes. 4. Allow to cool completely. Store in an airtight container in the refrigerator up to 4 days.

Per Serving:

calories: 199 | fat: 16g | protein: 7g | carbs: 7g | net carbs: 3g | fiber: 4g

Chocolate Mousse

Prep time: 10 minutes | Cook time: 0 minutes | Serves 2

- 1½ tablespoons heavy (whipping) cream
- 4 tablespoons butter, at room temperature
- 1 tablespoon unsweetened cocoa powder
- 4 tablespoons cream cheese, at room temperature
- 1 tablespoon Swerve natural sweetener

1. In a medium chilled bowl, use a whisk or fork to whip the cream. Refrigerate to keep cold. 2. In a separate medium bowl, use a hand mixer to beat the butter, cocoa powder, cream cheese, and sweetener until thoroughly combined. 3. Take the whipped cream out of the refrigerator. Gently fold the whipped cream into the chocolate mixture with a rubber scraper. 4. Divide the pudding between two dessert bowls. 5. Cover and chill for 1 hour before serving.

Per Serving:

calories: 486 | fat: 50g | protein: 4g | carbs: 5g | net carbs: 4g | fiber: 1g

Espresso Cream

Prep time: 10 minutes | Cook time: 9 minutes | Serves 4

- 1 cup heavy cream
- ½ teaspoon espresso powder
- ½ teaspoon vanilla extract
- 2 teaspoons unsweetened cocoa powder
- ¼ cup low-carb chocolate chips
- ½ cup powdered erythritol
- 3 egg yolks
- 1 cup water

1. Press the Sauté button and add heavy cream, espresso powder, vanilla, and cocoa powder. Bring mixture to boil and add chocolate chips. Press the Cancel button. Stir quickly until chocolate chips are completely melted. 2. In medium bowl, whisk erythritol and egg yolks. Fold mixture into Instant Pot chocolate mix. Ladle into four (4-inch) ramekins. 3. Rinse inner pot and replace. Pour in 1 cup of water and place steam rack on bottom of pot. Cover ramekins with foil and carefully place on top of steam rack. Click lid closed. 4. Press the Manual button and adjust time for 9 minutes. Allow a full natural release. When the pressure indicator drops, carefully remove ramekins and allow to completely cool, then refrigerate. Serve chilled with whipped topping.

Per Serving:

calories: 320 | fat: 29g | protein: 3g | carbs: 10g | net carbs: 8g | fiber: 2g

Mint-Chocolate Chip Ice Cream

Prep time: 10 minutes | Cook time: 30 minutes | Serves 2

- ½ tablespoon butter
- 1 tablespoon Swerve natural sweetener
- 10 tablespoons heavy (whipping) cream, divided
- ¼ teaspoon peppermint extract
- 2 tablespoons sugar-free chocolate chips (I use Lily's)

1. Put a medium metal bowl and your hand-mixer beaters in the freezer to chill. 2. In a small, heavy saucepan over medium heat, melt the butter. Whisk in the sweetener and 5 tablespoons of cream. 3. Turn the heat up to medium-high and bring the mixture to a boil, stirring constantly. Turn the heat down to low and simmer, stirring occasionally, for about 30 minutes. You want the mixture to be thick, so it sticks to the back of a spoon. 4. Stir in the peppermint extract. 5. Pour the thickened mixture into a medium bowl and refrigerate to cool. 6. Remove the metal bowl and the mixer beaters from the freezer. Pour the remaining 5 tablespoons of cream into the bowl. With the electric beater, whip the cream until it is thick and fluffy and forms peaks. Don't overbeat, or the cream will turn to butter. Take the cream mixture out of the refrigerator. 7. Using a rubber scraper, gently fold the whipped cream into the cooled mixture. 8. Transfer the mixture to a small metal container that can go in the freezer (I use a mini loaf pan since I only make enough for two). 9. Mix in the chocolate chips, and cover the container with foil or plastic wrap. 10. Freeze the ice cream for 4 to 5 hours before serving, stirring it twice during that time.

Per Serving:

calories: 325 | fat: 33g | protein: 3g | carbs: 17g | net carbs: 4g | fiber: 4g

Iced Tea Lemonade Gummies

Prep time: 10 minutes | Cook time: 5 minutes | Serves 4

- ¾ cup (180 ml) boiling water
- 3 tea bags
- ¼ cup (40 g) unflavored gelatin
- ¾ cup (180 ml) fresh lemon

juice
- 2 tablespoons confectioners'-style erythritol or granulated xylitol

Special Equipment:
- Silicone mold(s) with 36 (½ ounce/15 ml) cavities

1. Set the silicone mold(s) on a rimmed baking sheet. 2. Place the boiling water in a heat-safe mug and steep the tea according to type, following the suggested steep time on the package. Once complete, remove the tea bags and wring out as much liquid from the bags as possible. Sprinkle the gelatin over the tea and set aside. 3. Pour the lemon juice into a small saucepan. Add the erythritol and bring to a light simmer over medium heat, about 5 minutes. 4. Once at a light simmer, remove the pan from the heat. Whisk the tea mixture until the gelatin dissolves, then pour it into the hot lemon juice mixture. Whisk to combine. 5. Pour the hot mixture into the mold(s) and transfer the baking sheet to the fridge to set for at least 1 hour. Once firm, remove the gummies from the mold(s) and enjoy!

Per Serving:

calories: 48 | fat: 0g | protein: 10g | carbs: 1g | net carbs: 1g | fiber: 0g

Coconut Muffins

Prep time: 5 minutes | Cook time: 25 minutes | Serves 5

- ½ cup coconut flour
- 2 tablespoons cocoa powder
- 3 tablespoons erythritol
- 1 teaspoon baking powder
- 2 tablespoons coconut oil
- 2 eggs, beaten
- ½ cup coconut shred

1. In the mixing bowl, mix all ingredients. 2. Then pour the mixture into the molds of the muffin and transfer in the air fryer basket. 3. Cook the muffins at 350ºF (177ºC) for 25 minutes.

Per Serving:

calories: 182 | fat: 14g | protein: 6g | carbs: 12g | net carbs: 5g | fiber: 7g

Berry-Pecan Mascarpone Bowl

Prep time: 5 minutes | Cook time: 0 minutes | Serves 2

◄ 1 cup chopped pecans
◄ 1 teaspoon Swerve natural sweetener or 1 drop liquid stevia
◄ ¼ cup mascarpone
◄ 30 Lily's dark-chocolate chips
◄ 6 strawberries, sliced

1. Divide the pecans between two dessert bowls. 2. In a small bowl, mix the sweetener into the mascarpone cheese. Top the nuts with a dollop of the sweetened mascarpone. 3. Sprinkle in the chocolate chips, top each dish with the strawberries, and serve.

Per Serving:

calories: 462 | fat: 47g | protein: 6g | carbs: 15g | net carbs: 6g | fiber: 7g

Vanilla-Almond Ice Pops

Prep time: 10 minutes | Cook time: 5 minutes | Makes 8 ice pops

◄ 2 cups almond milk
◄ 1 cup heavy (whipping) cream
◄ 1 vanilla bean, halved
lengthwise
◄ 1 cup shredded unsweetened coconut

1. Place a medium saucepan over medium heat and add the almond milk, heavy cream, and vanilla bean. 2. Bring the liquid to a simmer and reduce the heat to low. Continue to simmer for 5 minutes. 3. Remove the saucepan from the heat and let the liquid cool. 4. Take the vanilla bean out of the liquid and use a knife to scrape the seeds out of the bean into the liquid. 5. Stir in the coconut and divide the liquid between the ice pop molds. 6. Freeze until solid, about 4 hours, and enjoy.

Per Serving:

1 ice pop: calories: 166 | fat: 15g | protein: 3g | carbs: 4g | net carbs: 2g | fiber: 2g

Protein Powder Doughnut Holes

Prep time: 25 minutes | Cook time: 6 minutes | Makes 12 holes

◄ ½ cup blanched finely ground almond flour
◄ ½ cup low-carb vanilla protein powder
◄ ½ cup granular erythritol
◄ ½ teaspoon baking powder
◄ 1 large egg
◄ 5 tablespoons unsalted butter, melted
◄ ½ teaspoon vanilla extract

1. Mix all ingredients in a large bowl. Place into the freezer for 20 minutes. 2. Wet your hands with water and roll the dough into twelve balls. 3. Cut a piece of parchment to fit your air fryer basket. Working in batches as necessary, place doughnut holes into the air fryer basket on top of parchment. 4. Adjust the temperature to 380ºF (193ºC) and air fry for 6 minutes. 5. Flip doughnut holes halfway through the cooking time. 6. Let cool completely before serving.

Per Serving:

1 hole: calories: 89 | fat: 7g | protein: 5g | carbs: 2g | net carbs: 1g | fiber: 1g

Pistachio Coconut Fudge

Prep time: 10 minutes | Cook time: 0 minutes | Makes 16 pieces

◄ ½ cup coconut oil, melted
◄ 4 ounces cream cheese (½ cup), room temperature
◄ 1 teaspoon vanilla extract
◄ ¼ teaspoon plus 10 drops of
liquid stevia
◄ ½ cup shelled raw pistachios, roughly chopped, divided
◄ ½ cup unsweetened shredded coconut, divided

1. In a medium-sized bowl, beat the coconut oil and cream cheese with a hand mixer until smooth and creamy. Add the vanilla extract and stevia and mix until combined. 2. Fold in one-third of the pistachios and one-third of the coconut flakes using a rubber spatula. Pour the fudge mixture into a 5-inch square dish or pan and top with the remaining pistachios and shredded coconut. 3. Refrigerate for at least 2 hours prior to serving. To serve, cut into 16 pieces. 4. Store leftovers in a sealed container in the refrigerator for up to a week.

Per Serving:

calories: 123 | fat: 13g | protein: 1g | carbs: 2g | net carbs: 1g | fiber: 1g

Blueberry Fat Bombs

Prep time: 10 minutes | Cook time: 0 minutes | Makes 12 fat bombs

◄ ½ cup coconut oil, at room temperature
◄ ½ cup cream cheese, at room temperature
◄ ½ cup blueberries, mashed with a fork
◄ 6 drops liquid stevia
◄ Pinch ground nutmeg

1. Line a mini muffin tin with paper liners and set aside. 2. In a medium bowl, stir together the coconut oil and cream cheese until well blended. 3. Stir in the blueberries, stevia, and nutmeg until combined. 4. Divide the blueberry mixture into the muffin cups and place the tray in the freezer until set, about 3 hours. 5. Place the fat bombs in an airtight container and store in the freezer until you wish to eat them.

Per Serving:

calories: 115 | fat: 12g | protein: 1g | carbs: 1g | net carbs: 1g | fiber: 0g

Bacon Fudge

Prep time: 10 minutes | Cook time: 5 minutes | Serves 4

- ½ cup (70 g) bacon grease, melted
- ¼ cup (60 g) cacao butter
- ¼ cup (20 g) cacao powder
- 3 tablespoons confectioners'-style

- erythritol
- 1 teaspoon vanilla extract or powder
- ⅛ teaspoon finely ground gray sea salt

Special Equipment:
- Silicone mold with four 3-ounce (90-ml) cavities or
- a total volume capacity of 12 ounces (350 ml)

1. Place all the ingredients in a small bowl and whisk continuously until the erythritol has dissolved, about 5 minutes. 2. Pour the mixture into a silicone mold. Set the mold in the fridge to firm up for 1 hour. The fudge is best enjoyed after softening on the counter for about 30 minutes.

Per Serving:
calories: 196 | fat: 18g | protein: 4g | carbs: 4g | net carbs: 2g | fiber: 2g

Lemon Curd Pavlova

Prep time: 10 minutes | Cook time: 1 hour | Serves 4

Shell:
- 3 large egg whites
- ¼ teaspoon cream of tartar
- ¾ cup Swerve confectioners'-style sweetener or equivalent

- amount of powdered sweetener
- 1 teaspoon grated lemon zest
- 1 teaspoon lemon extract

Lemon Curd:
- 1 cup Swerve confectioners'-style sweetener or equivalent amount of liquid or powdered sweetener
- ½ cup lemon juice
- 4 large eggs

- ½ cup coconut oil
- For Garnish (optional):
- Blueberries
- Swerve confectioners'-style sweetener or equivalent amount of powdered sweetener

1. Preheat the air fryer to 275ºF (135ºC). Thoroughly grease a pie pan with butter or coconut oil. 2. Make the shell: In a small bowl, use a hand mixer to beat the egg whites and cream of tartar until soft peaks form. With the mixer on low, slowly sprinkle in the sweetener and mix until it's completely incorporated. 3. Add the lemon zest and lemon extract and continue to beat with the hand mixer until stiff peaks form. 4. Spoon the mixture into the greased pie pan, then smooth it across the bottom, up the sides, and onto the rim to form a shell. Bake for 1 hour, then turn off the air fryer and let the shell stand in the air fryer for 20 minutes. (The shell can be made up to 3 days ahead and stored in an airtight container in the refrigerator, if desired.) 5. While the shell bakes, make the lemon curd: In a medium-sized heavy-bottomed saucepan, whisk together the sweetener, lemon juice, and eggs. Add the coconut oil and place the pan on the stovetop over medium heat. Once the oil is melted, whisk constantly until the mixture thickens and thickly coats the back of a spoon, about 10 minutes. Do not allow the mixture to come to a boil. 6. Pour the lemon curd mixture through a fine-mesh strainer into a medium-sized bowl. Place the bowl inside a larger bowl filled with ice water and whisk occasionally until the curd is completely cool, about 15 minutes. 7. Place the lemon curd on top of the shell and garnish with blueberries and powdered sweetener, if desired. Store leftovers in the refrigerator for up to 4 days.

Per Serving:
calories: 524 | fat: 50g | protein: 7g | carbs: 12g | net carbs: 5g | fiber: 2g

Fudge Ice Pops

Prep time: 5 minutes | Cook time: 0 minutes | Serves 4

- ½ (13.5-ounce) can coconut cream, ¾ cup unsweetened full-fat coconut milk, or ¾ cup heavy (whipping) cream
- 2 teaspoons Swerve natural sweetener or 2 drops liquid

- stevia
- 2 tablespoons unsweetened cocoa powder
- 2 tablespoons sugar-free chocolate chips (I use Lily's)

1. In a food processor (or blender), mix together the coconut cream, sweetener, and unsweetened cocoa powder. 2. Pour into ice pop molds, and drop chocolate chips into each mold. 3. Freeze for at least 2 hours before serving.

Per Serving:
calories: 193 | fat: 20g | protein: 2g | carbs: 7g | net carbs: 5g | fiber: 2g

Vanilla Butter Curd

Prep time: 5 minutes | Cook time: 6 hours | Serves 3

- 4 egg yolks, whisked
- 2 tablespoon butter
- 1 tablespoon erythritol

- ½ cup organic almond milk
- 1 teaspoon vanilla extract

1. Set the instant pot to Sauté mode and when the "Hot" is displayed, add butter. 2. Melt the butter but not boil it and add whisked egg yolks, almond milk, and vanilla extract. 3. Add erythritol. Whisk the mixture. 4. Cook the meal on Low for 6 hours.

Per Serving:
calories: 154 | fat: 14g | protein: 4g | carbs: 7g | net carbs: 7g | fiber: 0g

Vanilla Crème Brûlée

Prep time: 7 minutes | Cook time: 9 minutes | Serves 4

- ◄ 1 cup heavy cream (or full-fat coconut milk for dairy-free)
- ◄ 2 large egg yolks
- ◄ 2 tablespoons Swerve, or more to taste
- ◄ Seeds scraped from ½

- vanilla bean (about 8 inches long), or 1 teaspoon vanilla extract
- ◄ 1 cup cold water
- ◄ 4 teaspoons Swerve, for topping

1. Heat the cream in a pan over medium-high heat until hot, about 2 minutes. 2. Place the egg yolks, Swerve, and vanilla seeds in a blender and blend until smooth. 3. While the blender is running, slowly pour in the hot cream. Taste and adjust the sweetness to your liking. 4. Scoop the mixture into four ramekins with a spatula. Cover the ramekins with aluminum foil. 5. Add the water to the Instant Pot and insert a trivet. Place the ramekins on the trivet. 6. Lock the lid. Select the Manual mode and set the cooking time for 7 minutes at High Pressure. 7. When the timer beeps, perform a quick pressure release. Carefully remove the lid. 8. Keep the ramekins covered with the foil and place in the refrigerator for about 2 hours until completely chilled. 9. Sprinkle 1 teaspoon of Swerve on top of each crème brûlée. Use the oven broiler to melt the sweetener. 10. Allow the topping to cool in the fridge for 5 minutes before serving.
Per Serving:
calories: 138 | fat: 13g | protein: 2g | carbs: 2g | net carbs: 2g | fiber: 0g

Hazelnut Butter Cookies

Prep time: 30 minutes | Cook time: 20 minutes | Serves 10

- ◄ 4 tablespoons liquid monk fruit
- ◄ ½ cup hazelnuts, ground
- ◄ 1 stick butter, room temperature
- ◄ 2 cups almond flour

- ◄ 1 cup coconut flour
- ◄ 2 ounces (57 g) granulated Swerve
- ◄ 2 teaspoons ground cinnamon

1. Firstly, cream liquid monk fruit with butter until the mixture becomes fluffy. Sift in both types of flour. 2. Now, stir in the hazelnuts. Now, knead the mixture to form a dough; place in the refrigerator for about 35 minutes. 3. To finish, shape the prepared dough into the bite-sized balls; arrange them on a baking dish; flatten the balls using the back of a spoon. 4. Mix granulated Swerve with ground cinnamon. Press your cookies in the cinnamon mixture until they are completely covered. 5. Bake the cookies for 20 minutes at 310ºF (154ºC). 6. Leave them to cool for about 10 minutes before transferring them to a wire rack. Bon appétit!

Per Serving:
calories: 244 | fat: 24g | protein: 5g | carbs: 6g | net carbs: 2g | fiber: 4g

Chia and Blackberry Pudding

Prep time: 5 minutes | Cook time: 0 minutes | Serves 2

- ◄ 1 cup full-fat natural yogurt
- ◄ 2 teaspoons swerve
- ◄ 2 tablespoons chia seeds

- ◄ 1 cup fresh blackberries
- ◄ 1 tablespoon lemon zest
- ◄ Mint leaves, to serve

1. Mix together the yogurt and the swerve. Stir in the chia seeds. Reserve 4 blackberries for garnish and mash the remaining ones with a fork until pureed. Stir in the yogurt mixture Chill in the fridge for 30 minutes. When cooled, divide the mixture between 2 glasses. Top each with a couple of blackberries, mint leaves, lemon zest and serve.
Per Serving:
calories: 190 | fat: 8g | protein: 8g | carbs: 23g | net carbs: 9g | fiber: 14g

Almond Butter Keto Fat Bombs

Prep time: 3 minutes | Cook time: 3 minutes | Serves 6

- ◄ ¼ cup coconut oil
- ◄ ¼ cup no-sugar-added almond butter

- ◄ 2 tablespoons cacao powder
- ◄ ¼ cup powdered erythritol

1. Press the Sauté button and add coconut oil to Instant Pot. Let coconut oil melt completely and press the Cancel button. Stir in remaining ingredients. Mixture will be liquid. 2. Pour into 6 silicone molds and place into freezer for 30 minutes until set. Store in fridge.
Per Serving:
calories: 142 | fat: 14g | protein: 3g | carbs: 9g | net carbs: 7g | fiber: 2g

Almond Butter Fat Bombs

Prep time: 5 minutes | Cook time: 0 minutes | Serves 4

- ◄ ½ cup almond butter
- ◄ ½ cup coconut oil
- ◄ 4 tablespoons unsweetened

- cocoa powder
- ◄ ½ cup erythritol

1. Melt butter and coconut oil in the microwave for 45 seconds, stirring twice until properly melted and mixed. Mix in cocoa powder and erythritol until completely combined. Pour into muffin molds and refrigerate for 3 hours to harden.
Per Serving:
calories: 247 | fat: 23g | protein: 6g | carbs: 4g | net carbs: 2g | fiber: 2g

Creamy Banana Fat Bombs

Prep time: 10 minutes | Cook time: 0 minutes | Makes 12 fat bombs

◀ 1¼ cups cream cheese, at room temperature
◀ ¾ cup heavy (whipping) cream
◀ 1 tablespoon pure banana extract
◀ 6 drops liquid stevia

1. Line a baking sheet with parchment paper and set aside. 2. In a medium bowl, beat together the cream cheese, heavy cream, banana extract, and stevia until smooth and very thick, about 5 minutes. 3. Gently spoon the mixture onto the baking sheet in mounds, leaving some space between each mound, and place the baking sheet in the refrigerator until firm, about 1 hour. 4. Store the fat bombs in an airtight container in the refrigerator for up to 1 week.

Per Serving:

calories: 134 | fat: 12g | protein: 3g | carbs: 1g | net carbs: 1g | fiber: 0g

Mini Peanut Butter Tarts

Prep time: 25 minutes | Cook time: 12 to 15 minutes | Serves 8

◀ 1 cup pecans
◀ 1 cup finely ground blanched almond flour
◀ 2 tablespoons unsalted butter, at room temperature
◀ ½ cup plus 2 tablespoons Swerve, divided
◀ ½ cup heavy (whipping) cream
◀ 2 tablespoons mascarpone cheese
◀ 4 ounces (113 g) cream

cheese
◀ ½ cup sugar-free peanut butter
◀ 1 teaspoon pure vanilla extract
◀ ⅛ teaspoon sea salt
◀ ½ cup stevia-sweetened chocolate chips
◀ 1 tablespoon coconut oil
◀ ¼ cup chopped peanuts or pecans

1. Place the pecans in the bowl of a food processor; process until they are finely ground. 2. Transfer the ground pecans to a medium bowl and stir in the almond flour. Add the butter and 2 tablespoons of Swerve, and stir until the mixture becomes wet and crumbly. 3. Divide the mixture among 8 silicone muffin cups, pressing the crust firmly with your fingers into the bottom and part way up the sides of each cup. 4. Arrange the muffin cups in the air fryer basket, working in batches if necessary. Set the air fryer to 300ºF (149ºC) and bake for 12 to 15 minutes, until the crusts begin to brown. Remove the cups from the air fryer and set them aside to cool. 5. In the bowl of a stand mixer, combine the heavy cream and mascarpone cheese. Beat until peaks form. Transfer to a large bowl. 6. In the same stand mixer bowl, combine the cream cheese, peanut butter, remaining ½ cup of Swerve, vanilla, and salt. Beat at medium-high speed until smooth. 7. Reduce the speed to low and add the heavy cream mixture back a spoonful at a time, beating after each addition. 8. Spoon the peanut butter mixture over the crusts, and freeze the tarts for 30 minutes. 9. Place the chocolate chips and coconut oil in the top of a double boiler over high heat. Stir until melted, then remove from the heat. 10. Drizzle the melted chocolate over the peanut butter tarts. Top with the chopped nuts and freeze the tarts for another 15 minutes, until set. 11. Store the peanut butter tarts in an airtight container in the refrigerator for up to 1 week or in the freezer for up to 1 month.

Per Serving:

calories: 610 | fat: 56g | protein: 16g | carbs: 19g | net carbs: 5g | fiber: 14g

Pine Nut Mousse

Prep time: 5 minutes | Cook time: 35 minutes | Serves 8

◀ 1 tablespoon butter
◀ 1¼ cups pine nuts
◀ 1¼ cups full-fat heavy cream
◀ 2 large eggs
◀ 1 teaspoon vanilla extract
◀ 1 cup Swerve, reserve 1 tablespoon
◀ 1 cup water
◀ 1 cup full-fat heavy whipping cream

1. Butter the bottom and the side of a pie pan and set aside. 2. In a food processor, blend the pine nuts and heavy cream. Add the eggs, vanilla extract and Swerve and pulse a few times to incorporate. 3. Pour the batter into the pan and loosely cover with aluminum foil. Pour the water in the Instant Pot and place the trivet inside. Place the pan on top of the trivet. 4. Close the lid. Select Manual mode and set the timer for 35 minutes on High pressure. 5. In a small mixing bowl, whisk the heavy whipping cream and 1 tablespoon of Swerve until a soft peak forms. 6. When timer beeps, use a natural pressure release for 15 minutes, then release any remaining pressure and open the lid. 7. Serve immediately with whipped cream on top.

Per Serving:

calories: 184 | fat: 19g | protein: 3g | carbs: 2g | net carbs: 2g | fiber: 0g

Chapter 10 Stews and Soups

Salsa Verde Chicken Soup

Prep time: 5 minutes | Cook time: 10 minutes | Serves 4

- ½ cup salsa verde
- 2 cups cooked and shredded chicken
- 2 cups chicken broth
- 1 cup shredded cheddar cheese
- 4 ounces cream cheese
- ½ teaspoon chili powder
- ½ teaspoon ground cumin
- ½ teaspoon fresh cilantro, chopped
- Salt and black pepper, to taste

1. Combine the cream cheese, salsa verde, and broth, in a food processor; pulse until smooth. Transfer the mixture to a pot and place over medium heat. Cook until hot, but do not bring to a boil. Add chicken, chili powder, and cumin and cook for about 3-5 minutes, or until it is heated through. 2. Stir in cheddar cheese and season with salt and pepper to taste. If it is very thick, add a few tablespoons of water and boil for 1-3 more minutes. Serve hot in bowls sprinkled with fresh cilantro.

Per Serving:

calories: 346 | fat: 23g | protein: 25g | carbs: 4g | net carbs: 3g | fiber: 1g

Beef Reuben Soup

Prep time: 10 minutes | Cook time: 20 minutes | Serves 6

- 1 onion, diced
- 6 cups beef stock
- 1 teaspoon caraway seeds
- 2 celery stalks, diced
- 2 garlic cloves, minced
- 2 cups heavy cream
- 1 cup sauerkraut, shredded
- 1 pound corned beef, chopped
- 3 tablespoons butter
- 1½ cups swiss cheese, shredded
- Salt and black pepper, to taste

1. Melt the butter in a large pot. Add onion and celery, and fry for 3 minutes until tender. Add garlic and cook for another minute. 2. Pour the beef stock over and stir in sauerkraut, salt, caraway seeds, and add a pinch of black pepper. Bring to a boil. Reduce the heat to low, and add the corned beef. Cook for about 15 minutes, adjust the seasoning. Stir in heavy cream and cheese and cook for 1 minute.

Per Serving:

calories: 595| fat: 37g | protein: 36g | carbs: 32g | net carbs: 29g | fiber: 3g

Chili-Infused Lamb Soup

Prep time: 5 minutes | Cook time: 25 minutes | Serves 6

- 1 tablespoon coconut oil
- ¾ pound ground lamb
- 2 cups shredded cabbage
- ½ onion, chopped
- 2 teaspoons minced garlic
- 4 cups chicken broth
- 2 cups coconut milk
- 1½ tablespoons red chili paste or as much as you want
- Zest and juice of 1 lime
- 1 cup shredded kale

1. Cook the lamb. In a medium stockpot over medium-high heat, warm the coconut oil. Add the lamb and cook it, stirring it often, until it has browned, about 6 minutes. 2. Cook the vegetables. Add the cabbage, onion, and garlic and sauté until they've softened, about 5 minutes. 3. Simmer the soup. Stir in the chicken broth, coconut milk, red chili paste, lime zest, and lime juice. Bring it to a boil, then reduce the heat to low and simmer until the cabbage is tender, about 10 minutes. 4. Add the kale. Stir in the kale and simmer the soup for 3 more minutes. 5. Serve. Spoon the soup into six bowls and serve.

Per Serving:

calories: 380 | fat: 32g | protein: 17g | carbs: 7g | net carbs: 6g | fiber: 1g

Slow Cooker Taco Bell Soup

Prep time: 20 minutes | Cook time: 2 hours 20 minutes | Serves 8

- 2 pounds lean ground beef
- 1 medium onion, peeled and chopped
- 2 cloves garlic, peeled and minced
- 6 cups beef broth
- 2 cups water
- 8 ounces full-fat cream cheese, cubed
- ½ cup finely chopped cilantro
- 2 (4-ounce) cans diced green chilies, drained
- 2 tablespoons taco seasoning

1 In a medium skillet over medium heat, brown ground beef 10–15 minutes while stirring. Drain fat. Add onion and garlic. Sauté 5 minutes. 2 Add meat mixture to slow cooker along with rest of ingredients. 3 Cover with lid and cook 2 hours on high or 4 hours on low. 4 Let cool 10 minutes and then serve.

Per Serving:

calories: 307| fat: 16g | protein: 26g | carbs: 6g | net carbs: 4g | fiber: 2g

Cauliflower & Blue Cheese Soup

Prep time: 15 minutes | Cook time: 20 minutes | Serves 5

- 2 tablespoons extra-virgin avocado oil
- 1 small red onion, diced
- 1 medium celery stalk, sliced
- 1 medium cauliflower, cut into small florets
- 2 cups vegetable or chicken stock
- ¼ cup goat's cream or heavy whipping cream
- Salt and black pepper, to taste
- 1 cup crumbled goat's or sheep's blue cheese, such as Roquefort
- 2 tablespoons chopped fresh chives
- 5 tablespoons extra-virgin olive oil

1. Heat a medium saucepan greased with the avocado oil over medium heat. Sweat the onion and celery for 3 to 5 minutes, until soft and fragrant. Add the cauliflower florets and cook for 5 minutes. Add the vegetable stock and bring to a boil. Cook for about 10 minutes, or until the cauliflower is tender. Remove from the heat and let cool for a few minutes. 2. Add the cream. Use an immersion blender, or pour into a blender, to process until smooth and creamy. Season with salt and pepper to taste. Divide the soup between serving bowls and top with the crumbled blue cheese, chives, and olive oil. To store, let cool and refrigerate in a sealed container for up to 5 days.

Per Serving:
calories: 367 | fat: 31g | protein: 12g | carbs: 11g | net carbs: 8g | fiber: 3g

Creamy Mushroom Soup

Prep time: 10 minutes | Cook time: 30 minutes | Serves 4

- 2 slices bacon, cut into ¼-inch dice
- 2 tablespoons minced shallots or onions
- 1 teaspoon minced garlic
- 1 pound (454 g) button mushrooms, cleaned and quartered or sliced
- 1 teaspoon dried thyme

For Garnish:
- Fresh thyme leaves
- MCT oil or extra-virgin

leaves
- 2 cups chicken bone broth, homemade or store-bought
- 1 teaspoon fine sea salt
- ½ teaspoon freshly ground black pepper
- 2 large eggs
- 2 tablespoons lemon juice

olive oil, for drizzling

1. Place the diced bacon in a stockpot and sauté over medium heat until crispy, about 3 minutes. Remove the bacon from the pan, but leave the drippings. Add the shallots and garlic to the pan with the drippings and sauté over medium heat for about 3 minutes, until softened and aromatic. 2. Add the mushrooms and dried thyme and sauté over medium heat until the mushrooms are golden brown, about 10 minutes. Add the broth, salt, and pepper and bring to boil. 3. Whisk the eggs and lemon juice in a medium bowl. While whisking, very slowly pour in ½ cup of the hot soup (if you add the hot soup too quickly, the eggs will curdle). Slowly whisk another cup of the hot soup into the egg mixture. 4. Pour the hot egg mixture into the pot while stirring. Add the cooked bacon, then reduce the heat and simmer for 10 minutes, stirring constantly. The soup will thicken slightly as it cooks. Remove from the heat. Garnish with fresh thyme and drizzle with MCT oil before serving. 5. This soup is best served fresh but can be stored in an airtight container in the fridge for up to 3 days. To reheat, place in a saucepan over medium-low heat until warmed, stirring constantly to keep the eggs from curdling.

Per Serving:
calories: 185 | fat: 13g | protein: 11g | carbs: 6g | net carbs: 4g | fiber: 2g

Parmesan Zucchini Soup

Prep time: 10 minutes | Cook time: 1 minute | Serves 2

- 1 zucchini, grated
- 1 teaspoon ground paprika
- ½ teaspoon cayenne pepper
- ½ cup coconut milk
- 1 cup beef broth
- 1 tablespoon dried cilantro
- 1 ounce (28 g) Parmesan, grated

1. Put the grated zucchini, paprika, cayenne pepper, coconut milk, beef broth, and dried cilantro in the instant pot. 2. Close and seal the lid. 3. Cook the soup on Manual (High Pressure) for 1 minute. Make a quick pressure release. 4. Ladle the soup in the serving bowls and top with Parmesan.

Per Serving:
calories: 223 | fat: 18g | protein: 10g | carbs: 8g | net carbs: 5g | fiber: 3g

Beef and Cauliflower Soup

Prep time: 10 minutes | Cook time: 14 minutes | Serves 4

- 1 cup ground beef
- ½ cup cauliflower, shredded
- 1 teaspoon unsweetened tomato purée
- ¼ cup coconut milk
- 1 teaspoon minced garlic
- 1 teaspoon dried oregano
- ½ teaspoon salt
- 4 cups water

1. Put all ingredients in the Instant Pot and stir well. 2. Close the lid. Select Manual mode and set cooking time for 14 minutes on High Pressure. 3. When timer beeps, make a quick pressure release and open the lid. 4. Blend with an immersion blender until smooth. 5. Serve warm.

Per Serving:
calories: 106 | fat: 8g | protein: 7g | carbs: 2g | net carbs: 1g | fiber: 1g

Chicken Cauliflower Rice Soup

Prep time: 5 minutes | Cook time: 20 minutes | Serves 4

- ◄ 4 tablespoons butter
- ◄ ¼ cup diced onion
- ◄ 2 stalks celery, chopped
- ◄ ½ cup fresh spinach
- ◄ ½ teaspoon salt
- ◄ ¼ teaspoon pepper
- ◄ ¼ teaspoon dried thyme
- ◄ ¼ teaspoon dried parsley
- ◄ 1 bay leaf
- ◄ 2 cups chicken broth
- ◄ 2 cups diced cooked chicken
- ◄ ¾ cup uncooked cauliflower rice
- ◄ ½ teaspoon xanthan gum (optional)

1. Press the Sauté button and add butter to Instant Pot. Add onions and sauté until translucent. Place celery and spinach into Instant Pot and sauté for 2 to 3 minutes until spinach is wilted. Press the Cancel button. 2. Sprinkle seasoning into Instant Pot and add bay leaf, broth, and cooked chicken. Click lid closed. Press the Soup button and adjust time for 10 minutes. 3. When timer beeps, quick-release the pressure and stir in cauliflower rice. Leave Instant Pot on Keep Warm setting to finish cooking cauliflower rice additional 10 minutes. Serve warm. 4. For a thicker soup, stir in xanthan gum.

Per Serving:

calories: 228 | fat: 14g | protein: 22g | carbs: 3g | net carbs: 2g | fiber: 1g

Garlic Beef Soup

Prep time: 12 minutes | Cook time: 42 minutes | Serves 8

- ◄ 10 strips bacon, chopped
- ◄ 1 medium white onion, chopped
- ◄ Cloves squeezed from 3 heads roasted garlic, or 6 cloves garlic, minced
- ◄ 1 to 2 jalapeño peppers, seeded and chopped (optional)

For Garnish:
- ◄ 1 avocado, peeled, pitted, and diced
- ◄ 2 radishes, very thinly sliced
- ◄ 2 pounds (907 g) boneless beef chuck roast, cut into 4 equal-sized pieces
- ◄ 5 cups beef broth
- ◄ 1 cup chopped fresh cilantro, plus more for garnish
- ◄ 2 teaspoons fine sea salt
- ◄ 1 teaspoon ground black pepper
- ◄ 2 tablespoons chopped fresh chives

1. Place the bacon in the Instant Pot and press Sauté. Cook, stirring occasionally, for 4 minutes, or until the bacon is crisp. Remove the bacon with a slotted spoon, leaving the drippings in the pot. Set the bacon on a paper towel-lined plate to drain. 2. Add the onion, garlic, and jalapeños, if using, to the Instant Pot and sauté for 3 minutes, or until the onion is soft. Press Cancel to stop the Sauté. 3. Add the beef, broth, cilantro, salt, and pepper. Stir to combine. 4. Seal the lid, press Manual, and set the timer for 35 minutes. Once finished, let the pressure release naturally. 5. Remove the lid and shred the beef with two forks. Taste the liquid and add more salt,

if needed. 6. Ladle the soup into bowls. Garnish with the reserved bacon, avocado, radishes, chives, and more cilantro.

Per Serving:

calories: 456 | fat: 36g | protein: 25g | carbs: 6g | net carbs: 4g | fiber: 2g

Pancetta and Jalapeño Soup

Prep time: 10 minutes | Cook time: 10 minutes | Serves 4

- ◄ 3 ounces (85 g) pancetta, chopped
- ◄ 1 teaspoon coconut oil
- ◄ 2 jalapeño peppers, sliced
- ◄ ½ teaspoon garlic powder
- ◄ ½ teaspoon smoked paprika
- ◄ ½ cup heavy cream
- ◄ 2 cups water
- ◄ ½ cup Monterey Jack cheese, shredded

1. Toss the pancetta in the Instant Pot, then add the coconut oil and cook for 4 minutes on Sauté mode. Stir constantly. 2. Add the sliced jalapeños, garlic powder, and smoked paprika. Sauté for 1 more minute. 3. Pour in the heavy cream and water. Add the Monterey Jack cheese and stir to mix well. 4. Close the lid and select Manual mode and set cooking time on High Pressure. 5. When timer beeps, make a quick pressure release. Open the lid. 6. Serve warm.

Per Serving:

calories: 234 | fat: 20g | protein: 12g | carbs: 2g | net carbs: 1g | fiber: 0g

Chicken Zucchini Soup

Prep time: 8 minutes | Cook time: 14 minutes | Serves 6

- ◄ ¼ cup coconut oil or unsalted butter
- ◄ 1 cup chopped celery
- ◄ ¼ cup chopped onions
- ◄ 2 cloves garlic, minced
- ◄ 1 pound (454 g) boneless, skinless chicken breasts, cut into 1-inch cubes
- ◄ 6 cups chicken broth
- ◄ 1 tablespoon dried parsley
- ◄ 1 teaspoon fine sea salt
- ◄ ½ teaspoon dried marjoram
- ◄ ½ teaspoon ground black pepper
- ◄ 1 bay leaf
- ◄ 2 cups zucchini noodles

1. Place the coconut oil in the Instant Pot and press Sauté. Once melted, add the celery, onions, and garlic and cook, stirring occasionally, for 4 minutes, or until the onions are soft. Press Cancel to stop the Sauté. 2. Add the cubed chicken, broth, parsley, salt, marjoram, pepper, and bay leaf. Seal the lid, press Manual, and set the timer for 10 minutes. Once finished, let the pressure release naturally. 3. Remove the lid and stir well. Place the noodles in bowls, using ⅓ cup per bowl. Ladle the soup over the noodles and serve immediately; if it sits too long, the noodles will get too soft.

Per Serving:

calories: 253 | fat: 15g | protein: 21g | carbs: 11g | net carbs: 10g | fiber: 1g

Chicken Enchilada Soup

Prep time: 10 minutes | Cook time: 40 minutes | Serves 6

- 2 (6-ounce / 170-g) boneless, skinless chicken breasts
- ½ tablespoon chili powder
- ½ teaspoon salt
- ½ teaspoon garlic powder
- ¼ teaspoon pepper
- ½ cup red enchilada sauce
- ½ medium onion, diced
- 1 (4-ounce / 113-g) can green chilies
- 2 cups chicken broth
- ⅛ cup pickled jalapeños
- 4 ounces (113 g) cream cheese
- 1 cup uncooked cauliflower rice
- 1 avocado, diced
- 1 cup shredded mild Cheddar cheese
- ½ cup sour cream

1. Sprinkle seasoning over chicken breasts and set aside. Pour enchilada sauce into Instant Pot and place chicken on top. 2. Add onion, chilies, broth, and jalapeños to the pot, then place cream cheese on top of chicken breasts. Click lid closed. Adjust time for 25 minutes. When timer beeps, quick-release the pressure and shred chicken with forks. 3. Mix soup together and add cauliflower rice, with pot on Keep Warm setting. Replace lid and let pot sit for 15 minutes, still on Keep Warm. This will cook cauliflower rice. Serve with avocado, Cheddar, and sour cream.

Per Serving:

calories: 318 | fat: 19g | protein: 21g | carbs: 10g | net carbs: 7g | fiber: 3g

Spicy Sausage and Chicken Stew

Prep time: 10 minutes | Cook time: 25 minutes | Serves 10

- 1 tablespoon coconut oil
- 2 pounds (907 g) bulk Italian sausage
- 2 boneless, skinless chicken thighs, cut into ½-inch pieces
- ½ cup chopped onions
- 1 (28 ounces / 794 g) can whole peeled tomatoes, drained
- 1 cup sugar-free tomato sauce
- 1 (4½ ounces / 128 g) can green chilies
- 3 tablespoons minced garlic
- 2 tablespoons smoked paprika
- 1 tablespoon ground cumin
- 1 tablespoon dried oregano leaves
- 2 teaspoons fine sea salt
- 1 teaspoon cayenne pepper
- 1 cup chicken broth
- 1 ounce (28 g) unsweetened baking chocolate, chopped
- ¼ cup lime juice
- Chopped fresh cilantro leaves, for garnish
- Red pepper flakes, for garnish

1. Place the coconut oil in the Instant Pot and press Sauté. Once melted, add the sausage, chicken, and onions and cook, stirring to break up the sausage, until the sausage is starting to cook through and the onions are soft, about 5 minutes. 2. Meanwhile, make the tomato purée: Place the tomatoes, tomato sauce, and chilies in a food processor and process until smooth. 3. Add the garlic, paprika, cumin, oregano, salt, and cayenne pepper to the Instant Pot and stir to combine. Then add the tomato purée, broth, and chocolate and stir well. Press Cancel to stop the Sauté. 4. Seal the lid, press Manual, and set the timer for 20 minutes. Once finished, let the pressure release naturally. 5. Just before serving, stir in the lime juice. Ladle the stew into bowls and garnish with cilantro and red pepper flakes.

Per Serving:

calories: 341 | fat: 23g | protein: 21g | carbs: 10g | net carbs: 8g | fiber: 2g

Power Green Soup

Prep time: 10 minutes | Cook time: 15 minutes | Serves 6

- 1 broccoli head, chopped
- 1 cup spinach
- 1 onion, chopped
- 2 garlic cloves, minced
- ½ cup watercress
- 5 cups veggie stock
- 1 cup coconut milk
- 1 tablespoon ghee
- 1 bay leaf
- Salt and black pepper, to taste

1. Melt the ghee in a large pot over medium heat. Add onion and garlic, and cook for 3 minutes. Add broccoli and cook for an additional 5 minutes. Pour the stock over and add the bay leaf. Close the lid, bring to a boil, and reduce the heat. Simmer for about 3 minutes. 2. At the end, add spinach and watercress, and cook for 3 more minutes. Stir in the coconut cream, salt and black pepper. Discard the bay leaf, and blend the soup with a hand blender.

Per Serving:

calories: 392 | fat: 38g | protein: 5g | carbs: 7g | net carbs: 6g | fiber: 1g

Lamb and Broccoli Soup

Prep time: 10 minutes | Cook time: 25 minutes | Serves 4

- 7 ounces (198 g) lamb fillet, chopped
- 1 tablespoon avocado oil
- ½ cup broccoli, roughly chopped
- ¼ daikon, chopped
- 2 bell peppers, chopped
- ¼ teaspoon ground cumin
- 5 cups beef broth

1. Sauté the lamb fillet with avocado oil in the Instant Pot for 5 minutes. 2. Add the broccoli, daikon, bell peppers, ground cumin, and beef broth. 3. Close the lid. Select Manual mode and set cooking time for 20 minutes on High Pressure. 4. When timer beeps, use a natural pressure release for 10 minutes, then release any remaining pressure. Open the lid. 5. Serve warm.

Per Serving:

calories: 169 | fat: 6g | protein: 21g | carbs: 7g | net carbs: 6g | fiber: 1g

Garlicky Chicken Soup

Prep time: 5 minutes | Cook time: 20 minutes | Serves 6

- 10 roasted garlic cloves
- ½ medium onion, diced
- 4 tablespoons butter
- 4 cups chicken broth
- ½ teaspoon salt
- ¼ teaspoon pepper
- 1 teaspoon thyme
- 1 pound (454 g) boneless, skinless chicken thighs, cubed
- ½ cup heavy cream
- 2 ounces (57 g) cream cheese

1. In small bowl, mash roasted garlic into paste. Press the Sauté button and add garlic, onion, and butter to Instant Pot. Sauté for 2 to 3 minutes until onion begins to soften. Press the Cancel button. 2. Add Chicken Broth, salt, pepper, thyme, and chicken to Instant Pot. Click lid closed. Press the Manual button and adjust time for 20 minutes. 3. When timer beeps, quick-release the pressure. Stir in heavy cream and cream cheese until smooth. Serve warm.

Per Serving:

calories: 291 | fat: 21g | protein: 17g | carbs: 4g | net carbs: 3g | fiber: 1g

Sausage Zoodle Soup

Prep time: 10 minutes | Cook time: 25 minutes | Serves 8

- 1 tablespoon olive oil
- 4 cloves garlic, minced
- 1 pound (454 g) pork sausage (no sugar added)
- ½ tablespoon Italian seasoning
- 3 cups regular beef broth
- 3 cups beef bone broth
- 2 medium zucchini (6 ounces / 170 g each), spiralized

1. In a large soup pot, heat the oil over medium heat. Add the garlic and cook for about 1 minute, until fragrant. 2. Add the sausage, increase the heat to medium-high, and cook for about 10 minutes, stirring occasionally and breaking apart into small pieces, until browned. 3. Add the seasoning, regular broth, and bone broth, and simmer for 10 minutes. 4. Add the zucchini. Bring to a simmer again, then simmer for about 2 minutes, until the zucchini is soft. (Don't overcook or the zoodles will be mushy.)

Per Serving:

calories: 216 | fat: 17g | protein: 12g | carbs: 2g | net carbs: 2g | fiber: 0g

OG Zuppa Toscana Soup

Prep time: 20 minutes | Cook time: 51 minutes | Serves 8

- 1 pound loose Italian sausage
- 1 tablespoon unsalted butter
- 1½ cups chopped onion
- 3 cloves garlic, peeled and minced
- 8 cups water
- 2 (1 teaspoon) chicken bouillon cubes
- ½ pound no-sugar-added bacon, cooked and crumbled
- 4 cups chopped cauliflower, chopped into bite-sized chunks
- 4 cups chopped kale
- 1½ cups heavy whipping cream

1. In a medium-sized skillet over medium heat, cook sausage 10–15 minutes while stirring until brown. Drain fat. 2. In a large soup pot over medium heat, melt butter and then add onion. Sauté 3–5 minutes until soft and clear. Add garlic and cook 1 more minute. Add water and bouillon cubes. 3. Add crumbled bacon, cauliflower, and cooked sausage to pot. 4. When water reaches boil, reduce heat to low, cover pot, and simmer 15–20 minutes, stirring regularly until cauliflower reaches desired softness. 5. Add kale and cream. Cook, stirring regularly, for 10 minutes. 6. Let cool 10 minutes and then serve.

Per Serving:

calories: 488| fat: 39g | protein: 21g | carbs: 10g | net carbs: 8g | fiber: 2g

Chicken and Mushroom Soup

Prep time: 5 minutes | Cook time: 15 minutes | Serves 4

- 1 onion, cut into thin slices
- 3 garlic cloves, minced
- 2 cups chopped mushrooms
- 1 yellow summer squash, chopped
- 1 pound (454 g) boneless, skinless chicken breast, cut into large chunks
- 2½ cups chicken broth
- 1 teaspoon salt
- 1 teaspoon freshly ground black pepper
- 1 teaspoon Italian seasoning or poultry seasoning
- 1 cup heavy (whipping) cream

1. Put the onion, garlic, mushrooms, squash, chicken, chicken broth, salt, pepper, and Italian seasoning in the inner cooking pot of the Instant Pot. 2. Lock the lid into place. Select Manual and adjust the pressure to High. Cook for 15 minutes. When the cooking is complete, let the pressure release naturally for 10 minutes, then quick-release any remaining pressure. Unlock the lid. 3. Using tongs, transfer the chicken pieces to a bowl and set aside. 4. Tilt the pot slightly. Using an immersion blender, roughly purée the vegetables, leaving a few intact for texture and visual appeal. 5. Shred the chicken and stir it back in to the soup. 6. Add the cream and stir well. Serve.

Per Serving:

calories: 427 | fat: 28g | protein: 31g | carbs: 13g | net carbs: 11g | fiber: 2g

Coconut Red Curry Soup

Prep time: 10 minutes | Cook time: 20 minutes | Serves 4

- ◄ ¼ cup (55 g) coconut oil, or ¼ cup (60 ml) avocado oil
- ◄ 2 cloves garlic, minced
- ◄ 1 (2-in/5-cm) piece fresh ginger root, peeled and minced
- ◄ 1 pound (455 g) boneless, skinless chicken thighs, cut

For Serving:
- ◄ 2 medium zucchinis, spiral sliced
- ◄ 3 green onions, sliced

- into small cubes
- ◄ 2 cups (475 ml) chicken bone broth
- ◄ 1 cup (240 ml) full-fat coconut milk
- ◄ ⅓ cup (80 g) red curry paste
- ◄ 1 teaspoon finely ground sea salt

- ◄ ¼ cup (15 g) fresh cilantro leaves, chopped

1. Heat the oil in a large saucepan over medium-low heat. Add the garlic and ginger and cook until fragrant, about 2 minutes. 2. Add the chicken thighs, broth, coconut milk, curry paste, and salt. Stir to combine, cover, and bring to a light simmer over medium-high heat. Once simmering, reduce the heat and continue to simmer for 15 minutes, until the flavors meld. 3. Divide the spiral-sliced zucchinis among 4 bowls and top with the curry soup. Sprinkle with the green onions and cilantro before serving.

Per Serving:

calories: 567 | fat: 40g | protein: 40g | carbs: 11g | net carbs: 10g | fiber: 1g

Bacon Broccoli Soup

Prep time: 12 minutes | Cook time: 12 minutes | Serves 6

- ◄ 2 large heads broccoli
- ◄ 2 strips bacon, chopped
- ◄ 2 tablespoons unsalted butter
- ◄ ¼ cup diced onions
- ◄ Cloves squeezed from 1 head roasted garlic, or 2 cloves garlic, minced
- ◄ 3 cups chicken broth or beef broth

- ◄ 6 ounces (170 g) extra-sharp Cheddar cheese, shredded (about 1½ cups)
- ◄ 2 ounces (57 g) cream cheese, softened
- ◄ ½ teaspoon fine sea salt
- ◄ ¼ teaspoon ground black pepper
- ◄ Pinch of ground nutmeg

1. Cut the broccoli florets off the stems, leaving as much of the stems intact as possible. Reserve the florets for another recipe. Trim the bottom end of each stem so that it is flat. Using a spiral slicer, cut the stems into "noodles." 2. Place the bacon in the Instant Pot and press Sauté. Cook, stirring occasionally, for 4 minutes, or until crisp. Remove the bacon with a slotted spoon and set aside on a paper towel-lined plate to drain, leaving the drippings in the pot. 3.

Add the butter and onions to the Instant Pot and cook for 4 minutes, or until the onions are soft. Add the garlic (and, if using raw garlic, sauté for another minute). Add the broth, Cheddar cheese, cream cheese, salt, pepper, and nutmeg and sauté until the cheeses are melted, about 3 minutes. Press Cancel to stop the Sauté. 4. Use a stick blender to purée the soup until smooth. Alternatively, you can pour the soup into a regular blender or food processor and purée until smooth, then return it to the Instant Pot. If using a regular blender, you may need to blend the soup in two batches; if you overfill the blender jar, the soup will not purée properly. 5. Add the broccoli noodles to the puréed soup in the Instant Pot. Seal the lid, press Manual, and set the timer for 1 minute. Once finished, let the pressure release naturally. 6. Remove the lid and stir well. Ladle the soup into bowls and sprinkle some of the bacon on top of each serving.

Per Serving:

calories: 258 | fat: 19g | protein: 13g | carbs: 9g | net carbs: 8g | fiber: 1g

New England Clam Chowder

Prep time: 10 minutes | Cook time: 30 minutes | Serves 8

- ◄ ¼ pound uncured bacon, chopped
- ◄ 2 tablespoons grass-fed butter
- ◄ ½ onion, finely chopped
- ◄ 1 celery stalk, chopped
- ◄ 2 teaspoons minced garlic
- ◄ 2 tablespoons arrowroot
- ◄ 4 cups fish or chicken stock
- ◄ 1 teaspoon chopped fresh thyme

- ◄ 2 bay leaves
- ◄ 3 (6½-ounce) cans clams, drained
- ◄ 1½ cups heavy (whipping) cream
- ◄ Sea salt, for seasoning
- ◄ Freshly ground black pepper, for seasoning
- ◄ 2 tablespoons chopped fresh parsley

1. Cook the bacon. In a medium stockpot over medium-high heat, fry the bacon until it's crispy. Transfer the bacon with a slotted spoon to a plate and set it aside. 2. Sauté the vegetables. Melt the butter in the stockpot, add the onion, celery, and garlic and sauté them until they've softened, about 3 minutes. Whisk in the arrowroot and cook for 1 minute. Add the stock, thyme, and bay leaves and bring the soup to just before it boils. Then reduce the heat to medium-low and simmer until the soup thickens, about 10 minutes. 3. Finish the soup. Stir in the clams and cream and simmer the soup until it's heated through, about 5 minutes. Find and throw out the bay leaves. 4. Serve. Season the chowder with salt and pepper. Ladle it into bowls, garnish with the parsley, and crumbles of the bacon, then serve.

Per Serving:

calories: 384 | fat: 28g | protein: 23g | carbs: 6g | net carbs: 6g | fiber: 2g

Chicken Soup

Prep time: 15 minutes | Cook time: 45 minutes | Serves 4

- 3 tablespoons olive oil
- 1 (14 ounces / 397 g) bag frozen peppers and onions
- 1 pound (454 g) chicken thigh meat, diced
- 1 tablespoon dried thyme
- ½ tablespoon garlic powder
- 1 teaspoon salt
- 1 teaspoon freshly ground
- black pepper
- 1 (32 ounces / 907 g) container chicken or vegetable broth, or bone broth
- ½ pound (227 g) spinach
- 1 teaspoon dried basil (optional)

1. Heat the oil in a large pot over medium heat. 2. Add the peppers and onions and cook until no longer frozen, 8 to 10 minutes. 3. Add the chicken and cook, stirring occasionally. 4. Stir in the thyme, garlic powder, salt, and pepper. Add the broth and cook for about 25 minutes. 5. Add the spinach and cook for another 5 minutes. 6. Serve the soup in bowls, sprinkled with the basil (if using).

Per Serving:
calories: 323 | fat: 19g | protein: 28g | carbs: 10g | net carbs: 7g | fiber: 3g

Broccoli Brie Soup

Prep time: 5 minutes | Cook time: 14 minutes | Serves 6

- 1 tablespoon coconut oil or unsalted butter
- 1 cup finely diced onions
- 1 head broccoli, cut into small florets
- 2½ cups chicken broth or vegetable broth
- 8 ounces (227 g) Brie cheese, cut off rind and cut
- into chunks
- 1 cup unsweetened almond milk or heavy cream, plus more for drizzling
- Fine sea salt and ground black pepper, to taste
- Extra-virgin olive oil, for drizzling
- Coarse sea salt, for garnish

1. Place the coconut oil in the Instant Pot and press Sauté. Once hot, add the onions and sauté for 4 minutes, or until soft. Press Cancel to stop the Sauté. 2. Add the broccoli and broth. Seal the lid, press Manual, and set the timer for 10 minutes. Once finished, let the pressure release naturally. 3. Remove the lid and add the Brie and almond milk to the pot. Transfer the soup to a food processor or blender and process until smooth, or purée the soup right in the pot with a stick blender. 4. Season with salt and pepper to taste.

Ladle the soup into bowls and drizzle with almond milk and olive oil. Garnish with coarse sea salt and freshly ground pepper.

Per Serving:
calories: 210 | fat: 16g | protein: 9g | carbs: 7g | net carbs: 6g | fiber: 1g

Green Minestrone Soup

Prep time: 10 minutes | Cook time: 20 minutes | Serves 4

- 2 tablespoons ghee
- 2 tablespoons onion-garlic puree
- 2 heads broccoli, cut in florets
- 2 stalks celery, chopped
- 5 cups vegetable broth
- 1 cup baby spinach
- Salt and black pepper to taste
- 2 tablespoons Gruyere cheese, grated

1. Melt the ghee in a saucepan over medium heat and sauté the onion-garlic puree for 3 minutes until softened. Mix in the broccoli and celery, and cook for 4 minutes until slightly tender. Pour in the broth, bring to a boil, then reduce the heat to medium-low and simmer covered for about 5 minutes. 2. Drop in the spinach to wilt, adjust the seasonings, and cook for 4 minutes. Ladle soup into serving bowls. Serve with a sprinkle of grated Gruyere cheese.

Per Serving:
calories: 123 | fat: 9g | protein: 5g | carbs: 8g | net carbs: 6g | fiber: 2g

Miso Magic

Prep time: 5 minutes | Cook time: 10 minutes | serves 8

- 8 cups water
- 6 to 7 tablespoons miso paste
- 3 sheets dried seaweed
- 2 cups thinly sliced shiitake
- mushrooms
- 1 cup drained and cubed sprouted tofu
- 1 cup chopped scallions
- 1 teaspoon sesame oil

1. In a large stockpot over medium heat, add the miso paste and seaweed to the water and bring to a low boil. 2. Toss in the mushrooms, tofu, scallions, and sesame oil. 3. Allow to simmer for about 5 minutes and serve.

Per Serving:
calories: 80 | fat: 2g | protein: 4g | carbs: 12g | net carbs: 10g | fiber: 2g

Blue Cheese Mushroom Soup

Prep time: 15 minutes | Cook time: 20 minutes | Serves 4

◄ 2 cups chopped white mushrooms
◄ 3 tablespoons cream cheese
◄ 4 ounces (113 g) scallions, diced
◄ 4 cups chicken broth

◄ 1 teaspoon olive oil
◄ ½ teaspoon ground cumin
◄ 1 teaspoon salt
◄ 2 ounces (57 g) blue cheese, crumbled

1. Combine the mushrooms, cream cheese, scallions, chicken broth, olive oil, and ground cumin in the Instant Pot. 2. Seal the lid. Select Manual mode and set cooking time for 20 minutes on High Pressure. 3. When timer beeps, use a quick pressure release and open the lid. 4. Add the salt and blend the soup with an immersion blender. 5. Ladle the soup in the bowls and top with blue cheese. Serve warm.

Per Serving:

calories: 142 | fat: 9g | protein: 10g | carbs: 5g | net carbs: 4g | fiber: 1g

No-Guilt Vegetable Soup

Prep time: 20 minutes | Cook time: 35 minutes | Serves 12

◄ 2 tablespoons vegetable oil
◄ 1 cup diced celery
◄ 1 small carrot, peeled and diced
◄ 1 medium head cauliflower, chopped into bite-sized florets
◄ 1 small eggplant, diced
◄ 2 cups finely cut broccoli florets
◄ 2 (64-ounce) cans chicken bone broth
◄ 1 cup cut green beans (cut into 1" sections)

◄ 2 medium zucchini, diced
◄ 1½ teaspoons dried basil
◄ ¼ teaspoon dried thyme leaves
◄ 1 teaspoon black pepper
◄ ¼ teaspoon dried sage
◄ ¼ teaspoon garlic salt
◄ 4 ounces full-fat cream cheese

1. In a large soup pot over medium heat, add oil and then sauté celery, carrot, cauliflower, eggplant, and broccoli until lightly softened (about 3–5 minutes), stirring regularly. 2. Add bone broth and remaining vegetables and spices. 3. Cover pot and bring to boil. Reduce heat and simmer 30 minutes until vegetables reach desired level of softness. Stir every 5 minutes. 4. Stir in cream cheese until fully blended. 5. Let cool 10 minutes and then serve.

Per Serving:

calories: 95| fat: 7g | protein: 3g | carbs: 6g | net carbs: 4g | fiber: 2g

Beef and Eggplant Tagine

Prep time: 15 minutes | Cook time: 25 minutes | Serves 6

◄ 1 pound (454 g) beef fillet, chopped
◄ 1 eggplant, chopped
◄ 6 ounces (170 g) scallions, chopped
◄ 4 cups beef broth

◄ 1 teaspoon ground allspices
◄ 1 teaspoon erythritol
◄ 1 teaspoon coconut oil

1. Put all ingredients in the Instant Pot. Stir to mix well. 2. Close the lid. Select Manual mode and set cooking time for 25 minutes on High Pressure. 3. When timer beeps, use a natural pressure release for 15 minutes, then release any remaining pressure. Open the lid. 4. Serve warm.

Per Serving:

calories: 158 | fat: 5g | protein: 21g | carbs: 8g | net carbs: 5g | fiber: 4g

Appendix 1: Measurement Conversion Chart

MEASUREMENT CONVERSION CHART

VOLUME EQUIVALENTS(DRY)

US STANDARD	METRIC (APPROXIMATE)
1/8 teaspoon	0.5 mL
1/4 teaspoon	1 mL
1/2 teaspoon	2 mL
3/4 teaspoon	4 mL
1 teaspoon	5 mL
1 tablespoon	15 mL
1/4 cup	59 mL
1/2 cup	118 mL
3/4 cup	177 mL
1 cup	235 mL
2 cups	475 mL
3 cups	700 mL
4 cups	1 L

WEIGHT EQUIVALENTS

US STANDARD	METRIC (APPROXIMATE)
1 ounce	28 g
2 ounces	57 g
5 ounces	142 g
10 ounces	284 g
15 ounces	425 g
16 ounces (1 pound)	455 g
1.5 pounds	680 g
2 pounds	907 g

VOLUME EQUIVALENTS(LIQUID)

US STANDARD	US STANDARD (OUNCES)	METRIC (APPROXIMATE)
2 tablespoons	1 fl.oz.	30 mL
1/4 cup	2 fl.oz.	60 mL
1/2 cup	4 fl.oz.	120 mL
1 cup	8 fl.oz.	240 mL
1 1/2 cup	12 fl.oz.	355 mL
2 cups or 1 pint	16 fl.oz.	475 mL
4 cups or 1 quart	32 fl.oz.	1 L
1 gallon	128 fl.oz.	4 L

TEMPERATURES EQUIVALENTS

FAHRENHEIT(F)	CELSIUS(C) (APPROXIMATE)
225 °F	107 °C
250 °F	120 °C
275 °F	135 °C
300 °F	150 °C
325 °F	160 °C
350 °F	180 °C
375 °F	190 °C
400 °F	205 °C
425 °F	220 °C
450 °F	235 °C
475 °F	245 °C
500 °F	260 °C

The Dirty Dozen and Clean Fifteen

The Environmental Working Group (EWG) is a nonprofit, nonpartisan organization dedicated to protecting human health and the environment Its mission is to empower people to live healthier lives in a healthier environment. This organization publishes an annual list of the twelve kinds of produce, in sequence, that have the highest amount of pesticide residue-the Dirty Dozen-as well as a list of the fifteen kinds ofproduce that have the least amount of pesticide residue-the Clean Fifteen.

THE DIRTY DOZEN

- The 2016 Dirty Dozen includes the following produce. These are considered among the year's most important produce to buy organic:

Strawberries	Spinach
Apples	Tomatoes
Nectarines	Bell peppers
Peaches	Cherry tomatoes
Celery	Cucumbers
Grapes	Kale/collard greens
Cherries	Hot peppers

- *The Dirty Dozen list contains two additional itemskale/collard greens and hot peppers-because they tend to contain trace levels of highly hazardous pesticides.*

THE CLEAN FIFTEEN

- The least critical to buy organically are the Clean Fifteen list. The following are on the 2016 list:

Avocados	Papayas
Corn	Kiw
Pineapples	Eggplant
Cabbage	Honeydew
Sweet peas	Grapefruit
Onions	Cantaloupe
Asparagus	Cauliflower
Mangos	

- *Some of the sweet corn sold in the United States are made from genetically engineered (GE) seedstock. Buy organic varieties of these crops to avoid GE produce.*

Made in the USA
Las Vegas, NV
12 November 2023

80677620R00059